AF606951

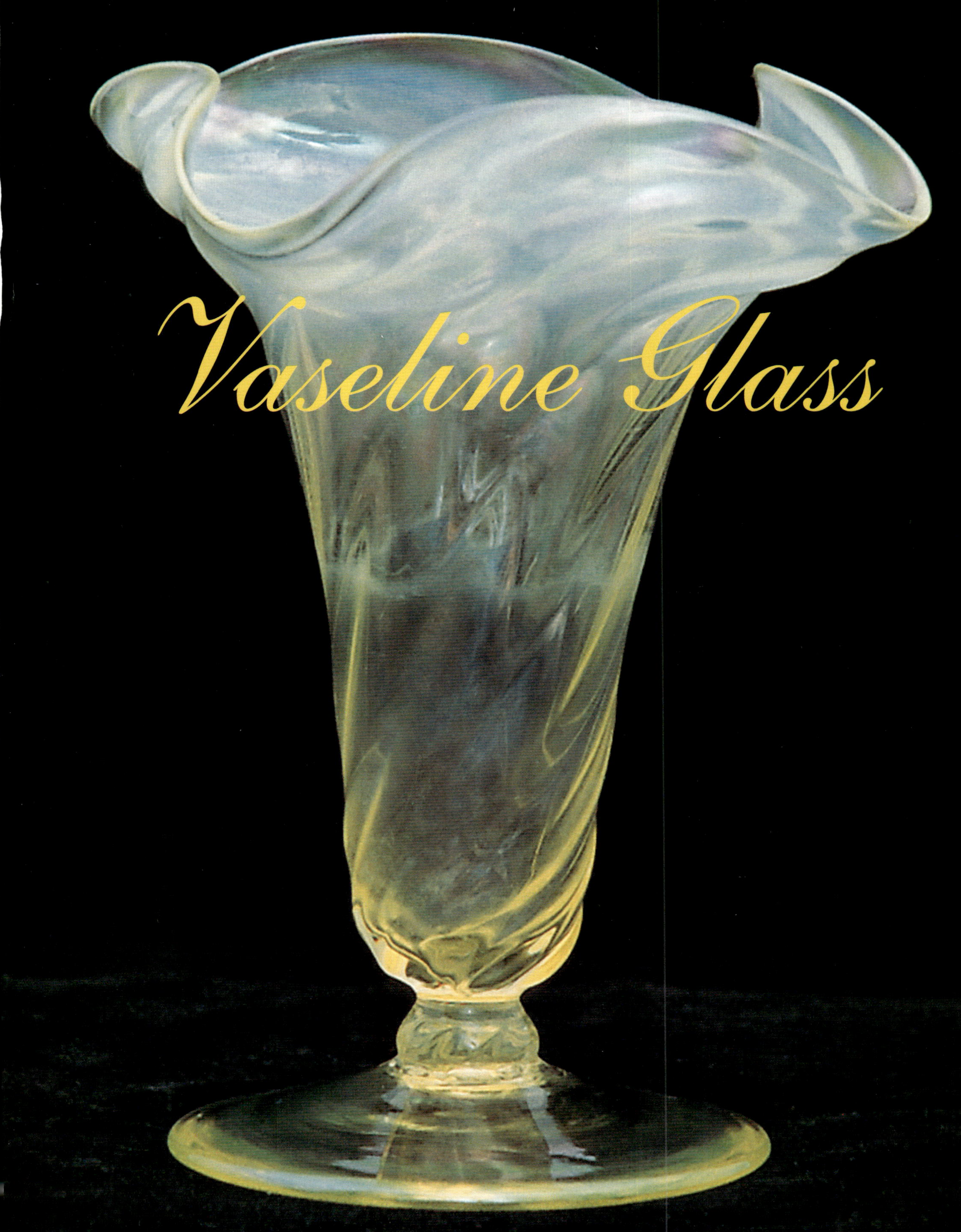

Vaseline Glass

The Big Book of *Vaseline Glass*

Barrie W. Skelcher

Schiffer Publishing Ltd®

4880 Lower Valley Road, Atglen, PA 19310 USA

Library of Congress Cataloging-in-Publication Data

Skelcher, Barrie W.
The big book of vaseline glass / Barrie W. Skelcher.
p. cm.
ISBN 0-7643-1474-2
1. Vaseline glass. 2. Vaseline glass--England. I. Title.
NK5439.V37 S58 2001
748.292--dc21
2001007271

Designed by Bonnie M. Hensley
Cover designed by Bruce M. Waters
Type set in Seagull HvBT/Korinna BT

ISBN: 0-7643-1474-2
Printed in China
1 2 3 4

Published by Schiffer Publishing Ltd.
4880 Lower Valley Road
Atglen, PA 19310
Phone: (610) 593-1777; Fax: (610) 593-2002
E-mail: Schifferbk@aol.com
Please visit our web site catalog at **www.schifferbooks.com**

In Europe, Schiffer books are distributed by Bushwood Books
6 Marksbury Avenue Kew Gardens
Surrey TW9 4JF England
Phone: 44 (0) 20-8392-8585; Fax: 44 (0) 20-8392-9876
E-mail: Bushwd@aol.com
Free postage in the UK. Europe: air mail at cost.

Contents

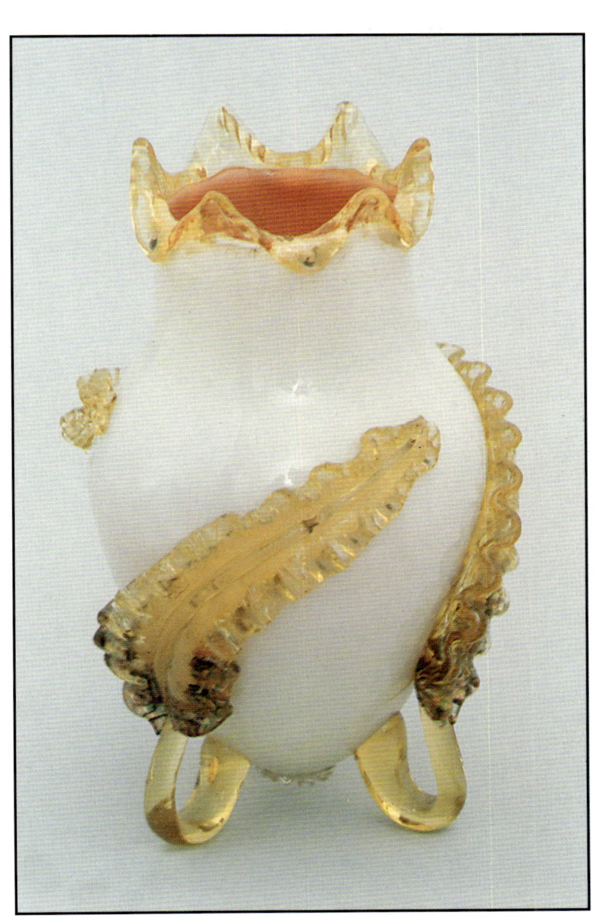

Acknowledgments

In the fifteen years or so I have been studying glass much of the knowledge I have gained has been by learning from others. Indirectly they have all contributed to this book and I would like to have mentioned them all by name. That however is just not possible. If I attempted to do so I would inevitably miss out some and then there are others whose names I do not even know! In the written text and the notes at the end of the chapters I have acknowledged the principle sources of my information. Not withstanding the foregoing there are some names of which I would make special mention.

First, my wife Shirley; she not only helped put our collection together and undertook some of the research, but also proof read and corrected my grammar in the drafting of this book.

Photographer Roger Bloxham for virtually all the pictures you find in this book.

The late Cyril Manley was the first of my contacts with the major collectors and he pointed me in the direction of Stan Eveson, a retired Technical Director of Thomas Webb & Sons, who is an authority on the products of that firm and has helped me understand some of the technical aspects of glass making. Sam Thompson, curator of the Royal Brierley museum, who has helped me identify some of the products of that firm. I would also acknowledge the help from many members of the UK Glass Association with whom I have discussed aspects of my collection, Charles Hajdamach, Roger Dodsworth, Dil Hier, Peter Helm, Tom Percival, Jenny Thompson, Eva Frumin, Eric Reynolds, Tom Dearden, Christine Golledge, Alex Werner, and John Westmoreland, also a retired Health Physicist, who checked my physics in the book.

My researches have also been assisted by Broadfield House Glass Museum, Sunderland Museum and Art Gallery, Stuart Crystal, Plowden & Thompson, Johnson and Matthey, Fenton Art Glass, City of Birmingham Museum, and the Public Records Office at Kew.

Finally there are all those dealers, auctioneers, and fair stallholders who have put up with my persistent checking of their wares with a geiger counter!

Preface

Why write a book about the use of uranium in glass? The short answer is that I have been collecting it for over a decade and this has, inevitably, been coupled with research trying to find out what every collector wishes to know: the answer to *how, when, where,* and *by whom.* Uranium glass added another question, *why.* Inevitably folk asked me to give talks and on more than one occasion I have been referred to as an "expert." (When this happens I shudder for my definition of the word is perhaps a little different. "X" is an unknown quantity and "spurt" an uncontrolled drip!). That aside I would be cautious about accepting such an accolade for I will be the first to admit there is a lot I do not know about glass. On the other hand there is a lot I have found out about the use of uranium in glass and others have suggested I write a book about it. But this does not tell why I chose to collect glass with uranium in it in the first place so there is a longer explanation.

Virtually all my working life has been spent in the nuclear industry. Contrary to what some folk may expect, I make no apology and am proud to have made some small contribution to this much-maligned technology. However this is not the place to discuss the pros and cons of whether we should have nuclear power stations but it was just such debating that led me to collect uranium glass. In the 1980s there were proposals to build another nuclear power station in Suffolk. While most of the local people probably thought it a good idea, others did not. The like of Greenpeace, Friends of the Earth, and their sympathizers lodged objections. There followed a lively public debate. One of the main issues was safety and with it the fear about the effects of radiation. Much was made of this aspect. The nuclear opponents presented the scenario that all radiation, no matter how small, was dangerous and should be avoided. It seemed odd to me that those who trumpeted this argument the loudest showed no concern for radiation from natural sources. As a health physicist it was my lot to join the public debate on the side of technology. My quoting cosmic radiation doses from jetting off on holidays or demonstrating the radioactivity on gas mantles was greeted with skepticism. I sought something else, something that had for many years been used in every day life, namely radioactive glass. Throughout a meeting I would sip water from my glass and then just as an opponent had passionately denounced the extreme dangers of radioactivity, I would put the Geiger counter against the vessel from which I had drunk.

After the issue had been decided, (yes the nuclear power station was built), I became curious. Just how widespread was uranium glass? Who had made it? What colors were involved? Indeed was uranium still being used? There was little published on the subject. If I wanted to know more I would have to research it myself. The more I found out about glass in general and "U" glass as I came to call it, the more fascinated I became. I was to discover that uranium was used in a range of colors, in items of almost every type. From decorative glassware to utilitarian items like candlesticks to food and drinking vessels, to jewelry, all had examples with uranium. In the course of this research I have collected more than 900 such items and resisted adding as many more through lack of storage space. From the late nineteenth century to the start of World War 2, if U glass was not prevalent in every household it was certainly no rarity. I would be surprised if there were not at least one item in every domestic dwelling.

One of the advantages of collecting glass is the relatively low cost involved. With few exceptions, most of which involve the fashionable glasshouses, prices seldom exceed three figures. A collection can be put together at very modest expense. Over the course of the last decade I have bought over a thousand items, I have also sold a number of them. Even so I am reluctant to value any particular piece. For the examples I have illustrated there is no official price catalogue; however I do know what I have paid. That does not necessarily represent their "value," if by value we mean the price that could repeatedly be obtained in an open market between willing buyer and willing seller. In some circumstances I am sure I have paid more than any other collector would have done simply because I needed the item for my research. On the other hand I know I have also bought well below the price that might have been obtained if other collectors were wanting to buy at the time. Because glass is not a popular antique, it is not uncommon for a dealer not to realize the significance of the piece he was selling. To me the importance of an item is what it tells me, its history, and whether I like it. These factors influence what I am prepared to pay; what value others may put on it is irrelevant. Notwithstanding the publisher persuades me that the reader would appreciate some idea of free market value. In deference to this, in Sections 2 &3, I have indicated, for each illustrated item a price range. This is simply my opinion of what I think a similar specimen, undamaged and in good condition, would sell today in an open market in England between a willing buyer and willing seller. *This should not be taken as a fair price guide and I do not accept any liability for what may result if any reader uses these values as such.* If you buy or sell, make your own mind up what you are prepared to pay or accept. Glass collecting is not an investment game.

Glass is brittle and has a tendency to deteriorate. Some collectors look for perfection in the items they accumulate. A piece that is damaged, perhaps with a chip or a crack, is shunned. Items that show advanced crizzling are treated as if they had the plague. In some circles this attitude has lead to a degree of aloofness. In contrast, my view is that if a glass item, perhaps for fifty or a hundred years, has survived at all it is an achievement. Any damage it has sustained in its struggle for continued existence is a mark of its history. As a consequence there are many items in my collection that are not perfect and some are included in the illustrations. I love them all!

To help you find your way around this book I will explain its layout philosophy. There are three Sections. The first deals with factors generic to glass and uranium, such as the techniques I have used for dating and attribution. Of general interest I have looked at the density of different glasses with a view to estimating their lead content. I also discuss the nature of radioactivity and the radiation from uranium glass. Section 2 illustrates and discusses items that I have been able to attribute with a degree of confidence. Section 3 illustrates pieces of unknown birthplace but which have curiosity, interest and/or serve to illustrate just how wide spread has been the use of uranium in glass.

The object of my study was to establish how commonplace was the use of uranium in glass production and my research into the history of certain glasshouses has been limited to this aim. For readers who would like to learn more about their history I refer them to other authors that I have listed. Generally the footnotes at the end of each chapter are only short references and should be read in conjunction with the bibliography at the end of the book.

Through out the script I have used terms that should be familiar to most British glass collectors, however, in case they may be misunderstood I will now explain. *Pontil* or *punty* is the iron rod that is attached, usually to the foot of an object, to enable the glass blower to work on it after the blowpipe has been removed. When the task is completed it is cracked off leaving a telltale mark. *Metal* is a term used in the industry for glass itself. In this context it does not refer to the more general meaning. *Glasshouse* is the firm or business where the glass item was made. An alternative would be glass works. It should not be confused with the building used to grow plants in artificial climates! *Crizzling* is a term used to describe a condition that sometimes occurs with age in a glass item. I use it in two contexts. One is when the metal develops very fine internal cracks that can ultimately lead to the vessel collapsing. The other is when the surface of the metal becomes sticky, not unlike a sweet left unwrapped. These conditions are brought about by the metal degrading and are probably due to faulty mixes, such as having an excess of alkali.

I have tried to reproduce colors as closely as possible. This is always difficult with the printed picture, especially difficult with glass and almost impossible to achieve with uranium glass. The additional problem with the latter is that shades change according to the illuminating light. This is largely due to the contribution made by ultraviolet component. The shades will differ in daylight to tungsten or electronic flash because the ultraviolet in the latter, if any, is much less. In taking the pictures for the following chapters electronic flash has been used and the colors shown, no matter how accurately reproduced by the film, will not be quite the same as they would be if viewed outside in daylight. Generally I have used light gray as a background as, in my view, this more closely resembles how the glass will be seen in every day use or viewing. However on occasions where I want to bring out particular characteristics, I have used black. This tends to over dramatize the object and makes dark objects difficult to see.

I have given dimensions in centimeters, and although shown to two decimal places they are only to the nearest quarter centimeter. This is probably well within the limits which a lot of items were made.

Although I have written in the first person, I would like to acknowledge the contribution my wife has made to our collection. Back in the early days Shirley found our first piece of uranium glass, which I subsequently used during the many public debates in which I was then engaged. Since then she has helped find and identify many of the pieces we now have.

Section 1
Background

Introduction
About Uranium and Glass

Most collectors of glass specialize in a particular field. Often it is the manufacturer, sometimes the type of article, the period or the color. Sometimes it is a combination of several of these factors such as "Queen's Burmese" made by Thomas Webb & Sons, or Victorian Finger bowls or Vaseline glass and so on. Such specialization narrows the field of that which the collector has to investigate. My interest in uranium glass is rather different and the only restriction this appears to impose is one of limiting the date range to a couple of hundred years. I set out to investigate the extent that uranium had been used in the glass industry and this meant that whenever I found a piece I wanted to know not so much about the item itself but rather who made it, when was it made, how much uranium it contains and why it was used. There is no easy way of answering these questions, items are not date stamped and seldom signed and unlike the food item on the supermarket shelf, they do not have notes indicating their contents! In this section I will discuss some of the properties of uranium and glass, describe measurements I have made, and explain the basis for my dating and attributions.

Chapter 1
The History of Uranium in Glass

The element, named after the planet Uranus, was reported by the German chemist Martin Heinrich Klaproth to a meeting of the Royal Prussian Academy of Science in 1789. In fact Klaproth had discovered the oxide of uranium and for a long time it was regarded as a "half metal." The element itself was not isolated until 1841 when the French Chemist, Eugene Peligot, prepared it by reducing uranium tetrachloride with an alkali metal. It was not until 1870 that it was realized Uranium was the heaviest naturally occurring metal. (Technically this is probably not true as a natural uranium nuclear reactor is believed to have operated at Oklo in Gabon millions of years ago and if that were the case then traces of plutonium would have been formed). Back in the 1800s the fact that the metal itself had not been extracted did not deter the use of the oxide for industrial purposes, the principle of which was probably for the coloring of glass. We should appreciate that technology, as we know it to day, was in its very early stages.

Klaproth had separated the oxide of uranium from pitchblende, a heavy black mineral that is essentially U_3O_8 but which also contained other elements such as iron, bismuth, lead and radium. At this time chemistry was just emerging from the alchemy era. For example some scientists still held to the Phlogiston Theory of combustion. It was Lavoisier, in the 1775-80 period, who showed that the process of combustion was not due to the loss of Phlogiston but rather the combination of the material with oxygen. In 1784 Cavendish's experiments showed that the product of burning hydrogen in oxygen was water. John Dalton's Atomic Theory, used to explain the combination of reacting substances in set proportions, was not published until early in the nineteenth century. Although Avogadro put forward his hypothesis in 1811 it was not until 1858 that Cannizzaro showed how it could be used to construct a list of atomic weights. In 1896, Becquerel discovered the natural radioactivity of uranium, (by which time it had been used in glass for well over fifty years), and 1913 before Hans Geiger invented the nuclear particle counter.

Against this background we must see the chemistry of glass, certainly until the latter part of the nineteenth century, as being very hit or miss and little understood. Surely there would only be the most vague appreciation that silica was really silicon dioxide and that this was the main constituent of quartz, flint and sand. That glass was a composition of sodium, potassium, calcium and or lead silicates. That these could "dissolve" other elements such as iron, gold, copper, uranium and so on to produce colors and that the acidity of the melt or the oxidation state of the element would determine the shade or color. The glass mixes had to be found by trial and error rather than chemical theory, and once found they would be closely guarded secrets. Analysis of a rival's product would have been exceedingly difficult and well beyond the capacity of the glasshouses of the day. In this scenario it seems likely that different manufacturers developed their products in parallel. The ordinary glass worker would not know the composition of the mixes, these would be securely held by the foreman or manager. Thus only the defection of such a key worker to a rival would lead to the compromise of formulae. It therefore seems likely that the use of uranium to color glass developed simultaneously at different places and that no one can justifiably claim credit for "inventing" the process.

When we study the old surviving recipe books we see that, unlike modern times, different and ill defined terms are used for the raw material. For example in the Whitefriars Batch Book of 1832[1] on the same page we see the terms "Saltpetre" and "Nitre" used in adjacent recipes when they were in fact the same chemical, i.e. potassium nitrate. Why use different names for the same item? Was it because they came from different suppliers? Yet again we see "lead" used in some recipes, "litharge," " red lead" and even "lead or litharge." Did they really add lead metal, or was lead used as a generic term, did they understand the difference between red lead and litharge? Litharge, (PbO), contains about 93% Pb, (lead), by wt. Red lead (Pb_3O_4), the commercial variety of which may contain up to 35% of PbO_2, could have as little as 90% Pb by wt.

The terms "uranium" and "uranium oxide" as used in these early recipes, also have ambiguity. It was common practice to refer to other compounds by "shorthand," thus "arsenic" almost certainly would mean arsenious oxide and "manganese," "manganese dioxide." In the light of this, and the difficulty in preparing uranium metal, we assume that recipes that simply use the word uranium really refer to its oxide, but which one?

Is it the U_3O_8 which predominates in pitchblende, UO_3 which occurs with two water molecules in becquerelite, or even "uranium yellow" which is a stage product of processing pitchblende and whose chemical name is sodium diuranate. This has the formula $Na_2U_2O_7$,$6H_2O$. The percentage uranium, by weight, in each of these is 85%, 83% (or 74% if the 2 H_2O is present), and 64% respectively. Thus in estimating the uranium content of the old mixes there is some degree of uncertainty. It seems likely that in the early days impure U_3O_8 was used but this was replaced by the diuranate, which was in common use in the United Kingdom until 1939. Several employees of the glass industry have told me that uranium supplies were withdrawn during the war.

The development of atomic weapons and then civil nuclear power by the Atomic Energy Authority produced a quantity of a type of uranium, which was not required by them. It was known as "depleted uranium" and was sold on the market in the form of UO_2 [2]. However by the 1950s the use of uranium in glass was in decline and is now almost extinct.

The chemistry of uranium is not simple, the element can act as a base forming salts such as uranyl nitrate, or as an acid producing salts such as sodium diuranate. It also has several different valency (oxidation) states. It will respond to the chemistry of the glass in which it is dissolved and show the appropriate characteristics of color and fluorescence. This is why in some glasses it gives a yellow color, in others green, why some respond to ultraviolet light more than others. Generally the U^{4+} ion gives a green coloration and the complex UO_2^{++} uranyl ion yellow. It is reported[3] that U^{3+} gives a claret color in aqueous solution but I have not discovered it in glass.

In the practical world of glass making, and collecting, the uranium containing items have colors other than the aforementioned green or yellow. In my own collection I have dark amber, light amber, pink, ivory. straw, lemon, strawberry, turquoise, blue as well as shades of green and yellow. In many cases these "corrupted uranium colors" are due to the presence of other elements. The literature also tells us of uranium red and uranium black but to-date I have not found any examples.

So how much uranium is there in glass? In searches I have found glass with estimated concentrations which vary up to just over 3% U by wt. Other authors have quoted much higher values although, as far as I am aware, have not actually located any such specimens. Eveson[4] mentioned that he had seen a Thomas Webb Ltd. formula for a very rich Topaz with a U content of 7.3%. Landa & Councell quote "up to 25 weight percent of sodium uranate to produce green- yellow glass"[5] In the chapter on *Greener and Jobling* I report a glass with 7% wt U but again I know of no existing example.

For the historian as well as the collector the inevitable question arises, "who was the first to use uranium to color glass? Who invented the process?" Some authors consider that credit should go to Josef Reidel who produced Annagrun and Annagelb, a green and yellow uranium glass and named after his wife, at his Bohemian glass works in the 1830s. Klein & Lloyd[6] suggests that the process then spread to France in 1835, by means of a delegation that visited Bohemia and took back samples for French factories to copy. Be that as it may, there is no doubt that in 1835 experiments were carried out at Whitefriars Glass Works, in London, to produce a yellow glass with uranium coloring and that by March 1836 the best batch had been worked into candlesticks, a pair of which was presented to the Queen[7] The Whitefriars stock book[8] for 1836 refers to "Topaz jugs," which suggests that the new uranium glass, developed the previous year, was now a production item. Further more, at the banquet given by the Corporation of London for the new and as then uncrowned Queen Victoria in November 1837, engraved finger bowls and hock glasses made by Whitefriars in Topaz Glass were used.

In 1834 William Vernon Harcourt, who was the founder of the British Association for the Advancement of Science, started experiments with glass, relating their optical properties with composition[9]. In this he may have been associated with Faraday who was involved in trying to improve optical glass for navigational instruments. Harcourt did not publish his work but it would appear that by 1861 his study had extended to at least 116 different melts using a total of 29 elements, one of which was uranium. Unfortunately there is no evidence to indicate whether this was in the 1830s or the latter part of the period. Neither is there any evidence to indicate whether any knowledge he gained from these experiments was passed on to glassmakers. However we do know that in the late 1820s Faraday was, while working for the Royal Institution, involved with the glass making firm of Pellatt and Green[10] so there are possible connections. In 1849 Apsley Pellatt wrote about the use of uranium to produce a yellow-green glass[11] and quotes a formula for "gold Topaz" which would have a uranium content of about 0.75% wt..

Predating all this is a glass beaker which Lesser describes and dates as 1825[12]. It has a cut in date of 1825 and a cut portrait of Friedrich Schiller who was a famous German poet and dramatist. Schiller died in 1805. Unfortunately Lesser does not indicate who may have made the glass or give any details such as size, uranium content or density.

An earlier reference to uranium in glass comes from C. S. Gilbert[13] who devoted 60 pages to "Mineralogy and Mining Concerns" in Cornwall. He mentions a number of elements used in glass manufacture and with reference to uranium states "*its oxides impart bright colors to glass, which are according to the proportions, brown, apple green, or emerald green.*" He does not say whether glassmakers were using uranium at that time but, in the context of these remarks, there might be a reasonable supposition that they were. On the other hand it is strange that he does not include the color yellow, also commonly associated with uranium salts and mentioned by Klaproth in his original paper. In the absence of more definite information this must raise some doubts over the suggestion that Cornish uranium was being used in glass manufacture as early as 1817.

There is other evidence of early British involvement with uranium coloring of glass, and for this we look at the history of the well known firm, still trading, of Johnson Matthey plc., of Hatton Garden, London. Percival Norton Johnson who set up on his own as an assayer of ores and metals in 1817 founded the Company. In 1835 the business was trading as P N Johnson and we know from Whitefriars notes that they were supplying "uranium oxide." Johnson's brother-in-law was Thomas Cock and it would appear that between 1800 and 1809, when he was working at the famous laboratory of William Allen at Plough Court in Lombard Street, he studied the extraction of uranium oxide from pitchblende and its application to the coloring of glass[14]. Of Cock's other interests the refining of platinum is predominant. He is known to have supplied platinum crucibles to Sir Humphry Davey so it is likely that he was also in contact with William Vernon Harcourt.

It is interesting to note that P.N. Johnson's source of pitchblende was Joachimsthal, (now in Czech Republic), and it was not until the 1850s that it became available from Cornwall[15]. William J Cock, a partner with Percival Johnson described in 1842 a process for making "Artificial Uranite." The first stage of the process involved uranium being precipitated from a nitric acid solution with ammonia. After washing it was ignited. This would have produced U_30_8.

The earliest claim for the use of uranium in glass goes back to Roman times. Uranium is a well-dispersed element and traces of it occur in many minerals. Sophisticated modern chemical analysis, assisted by neutron fission, will undoubtedly find the odd part per million in a whole range of glass[16] . Glass with a trace presence of uranium, probably through an accident of nature, is not my concern but evidence that may suggest the Romans deliberately used uranium is. In 1912, R.T. Gunther[17] reported on a glass mosaic he had found while excavating an Imperial Roman Villa on Cape Posilipo near Naples, which he believed, dated about 79 A.D. This mosaic was composed of different colored tesserae. In particular there were green, blue and yellow. Samples of the blue and green were given to J.J. Manley of Oxford University for analysis. The results are discussed by Caley[18] The analysis on each sample was carried out by different students. E.G. Laws of Magdalen College tackled the green and reported finding uranium in significant quantities. There is some uncertainty about the exact amount as he reported his results in terms of uranium oxide and did not specify which. He was working with small quantities and Caley estimates the amount of sample used in the uranium determination would have been about 70mg. and concludes the uranium content , as UO_2 , would be 1.5%. It seems that to confirm his finding. Laws made two glasses using the composition found by his analysis, but in one of these did not add the uranium. The uranium sample appeared to resemble the color to the original specimen, but the non-uranium sample much darker. It would thus appear that uranium was used in glass, (commercially ?), long before Klaproth's time, but there are doubts.

The amount of uranium in the glass, i.e. 1.4% U, is generally higher than I have found in the light green specimens that I have studied and I have only occasionally found in the dark greens. This does not mean that light green will always have a lower uranium content but rather that it is more likely. If the uranium, although it would not be known as such, was intentionally used by the glassmakers from where did they get it? As far as we know it was not a local material to that part of the world. It is hardly likely that some budding Roman alchemist, who had happened to have been tripping round the world studying geology, would have come rushing up to the glass makers clutching a bag of strange earth and suggest they stirred it into the mix they were preparing for the Villa contract! Further, if uranium was in use, why has it only been found in this one specimen? It is highly improbable that the formula used for the green melt in this particular project would not have been used elsewhere. So where are the other examples? The other components of this mix and the one for the blue tesserae, all use compounds which remained in continuous use through the ensuing centuries. Why then should uranium have been forgotten down the ages? I do not doubt that Laws thought he had found uranium but had he made an error? Until the measurement can be repeated we will not know for sure. If these tesserae were available to day it would be simple to confirm the presence of uranium but it seems difficult to find. In 1964 Brill et al[19]. studying the dating of glass by fission tracks, were sent a sample, which is believed to have come from Manley's laboratory. Their analysis confirmed the composition to be comparable with that of the mosaics and the uranium content was 1.56% as UO_3 , but their dating made it more like 50 rather than the expected 1900 years old. They could only conclude that they had been sent a piece of glass made by Laws rather than the original. Freestone,[20] of the British Museum Research Laboratory, quotes Geiger counter surveys in post war years, on mosaics in the Bay of Naples area as well as examples in German museums failing to find evidence of the use of uranium in their manufacture. He also points out that over the past few decades hundreds of colored samples of Roman glass have been analyzed and none have been found to contain uranium in quantities greater than that which might occur in the sand used in glassmaking.

So who was the first with uranium glass? My opinion, though others may disagree, is that it is unlikely that any one manufacturer "invented" uranium glass. Most likely that in the early 1800s experiments in coloring glass with uranium were taking place in different glass houses across the world. As they developed successful formula so they gradually brought their new colors into production. There is an interesting note in *Pottery Gazette*, (Sept 1891), that tells us "fifty years ago, it [uranium] was first used in glass and we think then it was new, or in all events a scarce mineral, and our older readers will remember the rage "canary colour" had at that period in hock glasses, toilet bottles, &c. Amongst the early makers of this colour in glass were Hawkes and Bacchus & Green, who priced it at 3s. 6p per lb. It was then only made in transparent glass, now we find it in semi-opaque and ivory body, but like everything in fancy glass it has its day and is seen no more." (This last comment is difficult to accept, as Davidsons was then producing their Primrose Pearline in copious quantities.) The *fifty years ago* dates back to the beginning of the 1840s, only a few years after Whitefriars had produced their finger bowls for the Queen. An old notebook at Royal Brierley Crystal museum (originally Stevens & Williams) suggests that they started using uranium sometime between 1843 and 1853. Eveson tells me that *the earliest mention of uranium in Thos. Webb's formula was in the 1880s,* but I consider it likely they were using it long before that date. A recipe book from Coalbourne Hill Glass Works, (Stourbridge), dating to the 1860-1877 period not only contains formula for uranium mixes but also gives us an idea of the cost of uranium compared with other materials. In an "opaque yellow" batch which contained about 0.7% "uranium" the uranium costs £1-11s-3p out of a total of £2-13s-1p, that is nearly 60% of the total material cost! Summarizing all this I consider that while early experiments with uranium in glass took place in the in the first quarter of the 19th century, commercial exploitation grew from the mid to late 1830s. The cost of uranium was probably a major factor in restraining its development until discoveries of deposits in the USA in the 1880s.

From the items I have collected it would appear that uranium glass was popular before the end of the century and continued to be so into the depression years before the Second World War. It may be my imagination but it does seem that the emphasis changed from the yellow topaz and Vaseline to green and amber in the 1910/20 interval. (An exception to this must be the yellow primrose of Walsh Walsh and Stevens & Williams which was made in substantial quantities in the 1920s). We can only guess at the reason for this apparent change of fashion, perhaps the association of yellow with cowardice and the Great (1914-18) War were just not compatible.

As Europe prepared to tear itself apart in another conflict the demand for uranium for military purposes must have grown. It was already known that it could increase the elasticity and hardness of steels. But the greatest demand probably came with the Manhatten Project, (the US drive to build the atomic bomb), in 1942. As already mentioned British Government requisitioned stocks of uranium, presumably for the UK weapons program. Some writers believe that the use of uranium to color glass died with the war. This is certainly *not* the case but increasing concerns over toxicity of radioactive material lead to tighter controls and safety precautions, which discouraged its use despite the fact that depleted[21] uranium became readily available. A few glass producers still use it to day, particularly in the USA but its use for glass coloring in Great Britain is probably extinct. Thos. Webb used uranium as late as 1970s, In the USA the Fenton Art Glass Company were using it until at least only a few years ago.

Now comes the inevitable question, why use uranium? There are two principle answers namely because of the color it gives to glass and because of its fluorescence. It's oily Vaseline, greenish yellow is almost unique. In the right setting it is extremely attractive. It must surely be our loss that it is seldom made to day. With modern chemistry, imitations can come close but nothing that I have yet seen can match the appeal of the genuine article. Perhaps only a poet or a photographer can describe the beauty of this glass, I am not a poet so I must leave it to the pictures in the accompanying pages. Then there is the opaque yellow so ably exploited by Walsh Walsh and Stevens & Williams with their 1920s' Primrose. Non-uranic imitations come close but do not quite match the quality of color. It is much more difficult to argue the same case for the greens. Most of these shades can be produced by other elements and frequently it is hard to tell the difference without the aid of a Geiger counter or a fluorescent lamp.

Why make green from uranium when iron offers a cheaper and equivalent alternative? Why add uranium to the off whites and grays? The answer to this must surely be because, unlike any other alternative, the uranium glass will fluoresce. "So what?" you may ask, "folk don't flood their homes with ultraviolet light just to watch their uranium glass change color." This is true but, in certain conditions, nature does! In the electromagnetic wave spectrum ultraviolet light comes after violet and before x-rays. This means that when the suns rays are refracted, i.e. bent, as happens when they pass through droplets of rain, the red component is bent least and the violet most, hence the colors of the rainbow. A similar effect occurs when the sun is setting, its rays are bent as they strike the earth's atmosphere. At first the sky goes red then blue and finally darkness. The reverse happens with the sunrise. In the blue stage, the twilight before dark, there is a much higher fraction of ultra violet with respect to visible light than under normal conditions. This is sufficient to make the fluorescence of the uranium glass apparent. I always think the effect is particularly noticeable at the large outdoor antique fairs. In the multi-day events the dealers leave their tables uncovered until darkness finally forces them to close. Now try this, in the twilight stand back and scan the scene. The fluorescing uranium glass will stand out from the dull shapes of other objects and catch the eye. A similar effect can be observed in the home. Place the uranium glass in a west-facing window and resist the temptation to turn on the lights. As the daylight gives way to darkness the uranium glass will glow and even change its shade of color. In the modern home this effect goes unnoticed, but not so in Victorian or Edwardian times. Even as late as the start of WW2 many homes did not have electricity and lighting up was delayed until the last possible moment. Supporting this idea are the words of Apsley Pellatt who, in 1849 wrote of the "chameleon-like effect..., which is lost in candle light."

So we have two good reasons for using uranium, and one for it being largely discontinued in the floodlight era of today. But why do we find it in other glass, why in some greens which do not fluoresce. Why in pinks and dark blues? There is no sure answer to these questions but some possibilities spring to mind. The first is that the uranium is present by accident and probably found its way into the mix by way of cullet. Perhaps when preparing a melt some odd pieces of uranium glass scrap was thrown into the cullet just to make up the weight. This may well have happened on odd occasions but I doubt it is the real answer. As we have seen uranium was an expensive commodity so why waste it in a non-uranium melt? The only alternative explanation that I can offer is that it was used by habit or tradition. In the 19th and early 20th centuries the composition of glass mixes were closely guarded secrets held in supervisors' notebooks. They were developed on an empirical, hit or miss, basis. If a particular melt were not satisfactory then they would try adding a bit of this or a bit less of that. Having developed some good quality metal using uranium they may well have been reluctant to dispense with the element altogether in other mixes in case things went wrong. An early version of today's saying, "If it ain't bust don't fix it"!

There were some specialist uses for uranium glass. I have come across one but not been able to find an example. Pottery Gazette, 1st July 1893 tells us, "Window-glass colored with oxide of uranium is coming into use for glazing photographers' "dark rooms." Such glass appears to possess the power to a remarkable degree of preventing those rays of light from passing through it which, by reason of their great actinic power, would affect the sensitive plate and films, and interfere with or prevent the proper development of the photograph."

[1]Museum of London, Whitefriars Batch Book, 1832.
[2]Taylor J R private communication.
[3]Greenwood N N & Earnshaw, A - Chemistry of the Elements p 1468.
[4]Eveson S R - private communication.
[5]Landa E R & Councell T B - Leaching Uranium from Glass.
[6]Klein D & Lloyd W - The History of Glass, p174-5
[7]Museum of London, Whitefriars Batch Book 1832.
[8]Museum of London, Whitefriars Stock Book 1836
[9]Cable M & Smedly J W - Glass Technology, 1992 p92-97.
[10]James F - Bull. Hist. Chem. 11 (1991), p 36 - 40.
[11]Pellatt A - Curiosities of Glass Making, London 1849.
[12] Lesser R - Bref apercu de l'histoire non nucleaire de l'element uranium, RGN 1989.
[13]Gilbert C S - Historical Survey of Cornwall, 1817.
[14]McDonald D - Unpublished notes.
[15] McDonald D - Biography of Percival Norton Johnson. p143-144 & 186-187.
[16]Fleischer R I & Price P B - General Electric Research Laboratory Reports, 4897 & 4-RL-3634M
[17]Gunther A - Mural Glass Mosaic from the Imperial Roman Villa Near Naples.
[18]Caley E R - Analyses of Ancient Glasses. Corning Museum.
[19]Brill R H, Fleischer R L, Burford Price P and Walker R M - Fission Track Dating of Man Made Glass.
[20]Freestone I - Nuclear Europe Worldscan, 1-2/ 1998
[21]Depleted uranium is a bye product of the "enrichment process" used to prepare uranium for military weapons and some civil reactor fuel. It is rich in isotope 238 and is of course chemically identical to natural uranium.

Chapter 2
A Brief Note About the Nature of Radioactivity

An appreciation of the nature of radiation and radioactivity helps to understand some of the methods of analysis and detection, which I have used. Those readers who have a technical background, or those who don't want to be bothered, feel free to skip this chapter.

Radiation is simply the transmission of energy across space. Radiant heat, light, sound, radar are all examples of radiation and each has its own characteristics. In the present case we are concerned about radiation that originated from the atom itself. It is often known as ionizing radiation because when it passes through matter it causes the atoms and molecules to become electrically charged, these are ions. It is this property that is used for detecting and measuring this type of radiation.

Now we could think of an atom as being something like a very small version of the solar system. There is a central nucleus around which particles called electrons rotate in specific orbits. This center consists of a heavy mass, in fact it accounts for virtually the entire mass of the atom. Unlike the sun, which is one body, the nucleus consists of a mixture of two types of particles, called neutrons and protons. The textbooks usually show them as looking like billiard balls and that concept will do for our purpose. The neutrons have a mass of one unit, and no electric charge. The protons also have a mass of one unit but carry a single positive charge. It is only the electric charge that distinguishes between these two. If a proton captures an electron, which has a single charge of negative electricity and very little mass, then it becomes a neutron. Likewise if a neutron were to throw out an electron it becomes a proton.

The number of orbiting electrons is equal to the number of protons in the nucleus, consequently the atom has no overall electric charge. They don't just buzz round anywhere but have to be in one of a set of (permitted) orbits, well that's how we used to think of it and while modern physics has a different concept, this notion will suffice for our present purpose. Generally when the atom is in a non-excited state the electrons fill the orbits closest to the nucleus. However if it becomes excited an electron may jump from one orbit to another further away from the nucleus and in doing so it will absorb energy. When it subsequently falls back into a lower orbit it gives out a pulse of energy. Rather crudely we might think of it as being like a flash of lightning. This is often called a quantum, (or photon), and is in the form of radiation. Thus radiation as we experience it is not continuous, as it may seem, but a series of pulses, often so numerous that they appear to be continuous.

We might think of it as analogous to when a pebble is dropped into a pond. It sends a ripple of waves to the edge. If a succession of pebbles were dropped one wave would follow another and to an observer on the shore it would appear that the waves were continuous. In this case the energy of the falling stone is transferred by a wave to wall of the pond. This is how we regard the pulse or quantum of radiation given out when an electron falls into a lower orbit. The actual wavelength, that is the distance between crests, depends on the distance of the orbits from the nucleus and their separation. It is the wavelength that characterizes the radiation, thus the difference between visible light and radio waves is that the former has a much shorter wavelength than the latter. The radiation given out when an electron falls back into one of the outer orbits is in the visible light region, but that given out when the inner orbits are involved is in the x-ray region that is of even shorter wavelength. If the outer electrons are excited by radiation, such as ultraviolet, (black), light they jump to a higher orbit. Then they drop back into lower orbit and in doing so give out quanta of visible light. This effect is called fluorescence.

The protons and neutrons in the nucleus do not revolve in orbits but they are arranged in an energy dependant pattern. An analogy would be to think of a pyramid of cannon balls stacked on top of each other. If they were then disturbed, the pyramid would collapse and all the balls fall to the same level. In doing so energy would be liberated. But before and after the collapse the number of balls would be the same. All that has changed is the energy level of the system. So it is with the neutrons and protons, they can rearrange themselves and when they do energy is liberated in the form of radiation. As with the planetary electrons, it is in discrete packets or quanta. The wavelength of these is shorter than x-rays and is known as gamma rays.

A property of these is that their wavelength is a characteristic of the particular atom from which they came. This provides a means of identifying the source of gamma radiation and is known as gamma spectrometry, (See chapter on measuring radioactivity).

Now it is not always waves of energy that are given off with nuclear changes. Sometimes particles are ejected from the atom. (From a physics point of view these particles can have wave properties but that does not concern us here). As previously mentioned a neutron can spit out an electron and so become a proton. When it does this the electron moves with very high velocity and we call it a beta particle or beta ray. Another thing that can happen is that two neutrons and two protons pair up and quit the nest together. They form an alpha particle, which is in effect the same as a helium atom but without it's two electrons.

These processes are known as radioactive decay. Generally speaking an atom is only radioactive once in its life. When it has given off its gamma ray it becomes stable. On the other hand if it emits a beta or alpha particle it changes into an atom of a different element that in turn may or may not be radioactive.

Perhaps there is one other phenomenon that should be mentioned in passing although it is barely relevant to our study. If a spare neutron hits a uranium atom, and the conditions are right, which often they are not, it may first get captured then a very short time later cause the atom to split into approximately equal parts. This is called nuclear fission and produces a lot of energy, more neutrons and radiation! The two "half atoms" are not half atoms but newly formed elements. They are not unique but very similar to elements that already exist except that, in most cases, they are radioactive. Because this process produces a lot of energy, when fission takes place in glass, it leaves a "track" and this is the basis of glass dating by fission track counting.

As far as our study of radioactive glass is concerned we are interested in three of these types of radiation, namely alpha, beta, and gamma rays.

The alpha rays, because they are large particles and carry a double positive charge, have very little penetrating power. They are stopped by a thin sheet of paper, the outer layers of our skin and travel only a centimeter or two in air. Beta rays, being small particles but carrying a single negative charge are more penetrating, will pass through paper and may travel half a meter in air. Gamma rays, having negligible mass and no charge are even more penetrating and require several inches of lead to stop them.

In the context of this book we will be concerned with three radioactive elements. The predominant one is uranium the others are potassium and thorium. It is necessary to understand their different radioactivity.

Uranium, as found in nature, is composed of two principal atoms, namely U235 and U238. They are chemically identical, and therefore called isotopes, but do have a different radiation character. Their decay chains are complex and involve the emissions of alpha, beta and gamma radiation. Approximately 93% of natural uranium is the U238 isotope and 0.7% the U235 isotope. In the development of the atomic bomb, processing plants were built to separate them, the U235 isotope being required for military purposes. The remainder, from which some but not all the U235 had been removed, is known as "depleted uranium." It became available for commercial use. The radioactivity of natural uranium and depleted uranium are much the same when seen by a Geiger counter. They can be distinguished only by advanced techniques of gamma spectrometry and mass spectrometry.

Thorium also has a complex decay chain and emits alpha, beta and gamma rays. Without the more advanced techniques it is not easy to distinguish its radioactivity from that of uranium. On the other hand potassium has only one natural radioactive isotope, which is K40. It emits only a beta and a gamma ray when it decays to become stable calcium. Furthermore the gamma ray has a precise energy that is easy to identify with gamma spectrometry.

This book is about uranium glass. I mention these other two elements because, as will be seen later in this script, they can also be present and can be confusing when the Geiger counter is in use.

Chapter 3

A Health Hazard From Radioactivity in Glass?

Mention the word "Radioactivity" and everyone, well almost everyone, recoils in horror. Inevitably I get asked about the uranium glass "is it dangerous and is there a health hazard? The short answer is "no" and "yes and no" which itself requires further explanation!

We are all familiar with one example of radiation hazard, it is called sunburn and is caused by ultraviolet rays present with daylight. As the only difference between ultraviolet and gamma rays is one of wavelength there are similarities with their impact on living material. With sunburn we observe both stochastic and non-stochastic effects.

The former are those that occur on a probability basis and can usually only be determined by statistical analysis. The most prominent of these is cancer and it is now well established that chronic exposure to direct sunlight gives rise to a risk of skin cancer with the passage of time. This does not mean that everyone who sunbathes will get skin cancer but rather that their probability of doing so is increased.

Sunburn, the blistering of the skin, is a non-stochastic effect, it occurs soon after excessive acute exposure. However for most folk there is a threshold and a limited amount of sun can be accepted without any apparent detriment to the skin. Further more it is not additive as the body makes a complete recovery between exposures.

The reason for these two different scenarios lies in the way the radiation reacts with living cells. It may kill the cell outright, cause reparable damage, or leave the cell crippled with non-reparable damage. In the first case the dead cell is usually replaced, in the second the cell recovers to its normal self. Here we see the non-stochastic effects. The sun burnt skin dies but within a few days is replaced and back to normal. The story with the crippled cell is different, the damage is in the DNA and it becomes a potential source of cancer. It would seem that this is a freak occurrence rather than the norm. Consequently there is only a chance that a cancer will develop and the more the exposure the greater that chance. The risk becomes cumulative with every exposure no matter how small. There is no threshold. (It is somewhat like crossing a road. The more you do it the greater the chance that sooner or later you will get hit by a passing vehicle). A good deal is not understood about the mechanism that ultimately leads to cancer, although those who have studied it have put forward theories. Why does the crippled cell not turn cancerous soon after it is formed? Why does it usually take years and sometimes decades to develop? Does the crippled cell need to be activated by a second radiation strike or by some chemical or biological process in the body? At present there are no confirmed answers and hence some uncertainty in our understanding of stochastic effects of radiation.

Nuclear radiation follows this pattern, however because gamma rays are more penetrating they affect the internal organs as well as the skin. Yet again if radioactive material is ingested, i.e. swallowed or breathed into the lungs, then it gets dissolved in body fluid and the less penetrating rays, such as alpha and beta particles that would normally be stopped by the skin, are also able to damage the cells of internal organs.

So far, by using sunburn as an analogy, I have dealt only with somatic effects, that is those which occur in the body which has been irradiated. If the radiation damage occurs in the reproductive organs a corrupt egg or sperm may lead to a genetic defect on the next or even succeeding generations. Thus exposure to penetrating or ingested radiation can lead to the risk of genetic damage. This is of course a stochastic risk.

I will mention that radiation exposure is measured as dose or dose rate. The unit in common use to day is the Sievert (Sv) and is a measure of the energy that has been deposited in the material receiving the radiation modified by a factor that reflects the potency of that type of radiation. Thus exposure to a Sv of any type of radiation should lead to equal biological risks. The Sievert is quite a large unit of dose, the milli-Sievert (mSv), which is a thousandth smaller, is in more common use.

With this background in mind let us consider the possible problems from our radioactive glass. There are four scenarios that could involve risks from the radiation and radioactivity of uranium, (and thorium) in glass, but only two of these apply to potassium in glass. The amount of thorium, which is present by an accident of nature, is usually small. The amount of potassium in some glasses is much larger, say up to 10%, however the radioactivity in natural potassium is low. From a health hazard point of view we can neglect both these sources and consider only uranium.

1. The decay of the uranium gives rise to other radioactive "daughter" products that include radon gas. Although radon is naturally occurring there is considerable evidence that it does cause lung cancer. It is thought to be the cause of lung cancer in uranium miners and the National Radiological Protection Board advises that precautions should be taken against high levels of radon in certain buildings such as those built on granite. However in the case of uranium glass, the radon produced by the uranium decay is encapsulated by the glass where it is formed and the amount of radon that escapes is expected to be minuscule. I have not made any measurements to verify this, nor am I aware of any that have been made by other workers. I have discussed the matter with other health physicists and their expectations are the same as mine. More over radon also has a short half-life so it decays before it can build up inside the glass. I would expect the risk from radon exposure to be so low that it can be neglected.

2. Uranium, and its daughters, emits alpha, beta, and gamma types of radiation. The Alpha and beta can be hazardous if ingested, the most likely route of which would be drinking from a uranium glass wine, tumbler, or goblet. However glass is highly resistant to leaching and consequently the uptake in a normal drink should be very small and personally I would consider it quite acceptable. In 1991 Graziano & Blum[1] reported on the leaching of lead from lead crystal decanters and drinking glasses. They showed that there was some lead uptake by wines and spirits and it may be that this and other warnings persuaded the English manufacturers to reduce the lead content of their "full lead crystal" to the more generally adopted 25%. Following this Landa & Councell[2] investigated the leaching of uranium from a number of glass containers. They concluded that the ingestion hazard from uranium associated with culinary use of Vaseline glass appears to be minimal.

3. When glass is placed next to our skin, i.e. when we handle it, drink from glassware, or wear jewelry, the main health consideration is from the radiation dose received by the skin from the beta radioactivity. I have made a few crude "snapshot" measurements of the radiation dose likely to be received. Extrapolating from these results I would expect that for glass with a U content of 3% (which is slightly greater than any I have found so far), the contact skin dose rate would be 0.06 mSv/hr. Perhaps the worst scenario would arise if such a glass were used to make a necklace that was worn next to the skin. For the sake of example, suppose the necklace was worn on average two days each week for 14 hours a day. The number of hours per year that the glass would be in skin contact would be 1,456, which would mean an annual skin dose of 87 mSv. This compares with the 500 mSv (averaged over 1 cm^2) limit for occupationally exposed persons and for other persons, 50 mSv[3]. Thus we see that in exceptional circumstances if high uranium glass were regularly worn next to the skin, there could be a very slight risk of developing a skin complaint. As an aside I would mention that the limits for radiation dose to the eyes are lower, some 150 mSv and 15 mSv per year respectively and the radiation from the natural potassium in spectacle lenses can contribute a few mSv.

4. The gamma radiation from uranium is not stopped by the glass or wood in cupboards or display places and will travel significant distances, say several meters. However the dose received, even from a full cabinet of uranium glass, is small and unlikely to produce any measurable health risk. Snow[4] describes an experiment to measure the dose rate from shelves full of an assortment of uranium glass. It was estimated that in a year the extra radiation dose would only be 0.5 mSv, which compares with 2 - 4 mSv that could be expected from natural background radiation.

So we conclude that the dose of radiation to the uranium glass collector/handler will be very small but does that mean there is no risk at all? This is where the "yes and no" answer comes in. The establishment view among radiation protection experts "holds that any level of ionizing radiation poses a stochastic risk" even down to the low levels as I have just discussed. Having said that it is fair to add this is not a unanimous opinion of all scientists involved in radiation protection. There is a minority that subscribes to the view that very low levels of radiation, such as might be experienced in scenarios 1,2 & 4 above, can have a net beneficial effect.

Briefly this uncertainty arises as follows. The basic data for assessing risk from radiation exposure comes from studies of the survivors of Hiroshima and Nagasaki, together with occasional accidents and incidents, and radiation exposure for medical purposes. All these involve radiation that has been received in high doses or at high dose rates. There is little scientific evidence to say that the same pro rata effects will apply for low doses at low dose rates. Further more studies of people living in areas of higher natural background radiation usually show them to be healthier and have a lower cancer rate than the average. Even the workers in the nuclear industries, (I used to be one), statistically are healthier and have lower cancer rates than that expected for the general population. These findings might not be attributable to the effects of radiation, perhaps the folk in the high background areas live a healthier life or have pollution free air. As for the nuclear industry employees this might be explained by "the healthy worker effect." Employees in a modern progressive industry are likely to be healthier than the average person because they are a selected rather than a random sample and usually undergo medical examinations before being offered an appointment. There are objections to these assumptions and some scientists offer an alternative explanation. They suggest that radiation at very low doses and dose rates could have a homeopathic effect and increase the body's resistance to cancer. The scientific argument goes on and while the "all radiation carries a risk" argument prevails if for no other reason that it is considered to be the safer of the options from the point of radiation protection, my view is that the jury is still out.

Perhaps the only reasonable conclusion to draw from this uncertainty is that if low dose, low dose rate radiation does have any effect at all, it is so small that it can not be distinguished from all the other factors which affect our health. On that basis I do not worry about the radiation dose from collecting uranium glass!

[1]Graziano J H & Blum C - Lead Exposure from Lead Crystal. 1991

[2]Landa E R & Councell T B - Leaching of Uranium from Glass and Ceramic Foodware and Decorative Items. 1992.

[3]Ionising Radiations Regulations, 1999.

[4]Snow Dr P J D. - Letter to Glass Cone, (Glass Association U K), No 41, Spring 1996

Chapter 4
Measuring Radioactivity and Estimating Uranium Concentrations

Part of my studies, in particular the assessment of the concentration of uranium in the glass, involved the measurement of radioactivity. To appreciate the significance of the results that I report it is advantageous to have an understanding of the principles involved. As previously stated the source of the radioactivity in glass is from uranium, potassium, and thorium, the latter is present by an accident of nature, the former as a deliberate attempt to color the metal and potassium because its used as the alkali in certain glasses mixtures. Of the types of radiation already mentioned I was particularly interested in two, namely beta particles and gamma rays. I have mainly used a Geiger counter but on occasions had access to a gamma spectrometer.

As already explained radioactivity is the process of an atom giving off a pulse (quantum) of energy. By measuring the rate at which these are emitted, (known as counting) it is possible to evaluate the intensity of the radiation, (usually referred to as flux), and also estimate the amount of radioactive material present. The unit of radioactivity now in use is the "Becquerel," (Bq), and we would say that there was one Becquerel present in any particular mass when one atom was disintegrating every second. This might sound a lot, it is in fact quite small because there are a huge number of atoms present even in a grain of sand. The curious thing about radioactive decay, that is the disintegration of atoms, is the rate at which it takes place. The same percentage decays in each equal period of time. The time for half of those present to decay is called its "half life." Thus if a particular isotope had a half life of one year then no matter how much was present originally, after one year it would be down to a half, after two years a quarter, after three years an eighth and so on.

To return to the problem of how to measure these disintegrations. There are a number of ways of doing this but for beta radiation one of the most convenient is the Geiger Counter although it can measure both beta and gamma radiation. It works on the simple principle that when these rays pass through a gas they cause it to "ionize," which makes the gas a conductor to electricity.

A Geiger counter consists of a small chamber with two electrodes, one of which may be the chamber wall. An electric potential is then applied across theses electrodes at such a level that an electrical discharge will just not take place. Then, when a beta particle or gamma ray passes through the chamber and ionizes the gas, a small electrical discharge occurs and a pulse of electric current flows. This is subsequently measured on some suitable meter. It is like a very minute electric storm but without visible lightning. The potential has to be carefully set, if it is too low there will be no pulse discharge, if it too high the system breaks down and the discharges cascade. The size and shape of the chamber varies according to the type of radiation that it is designed to measure. I was only interested in measuring beta rays that come from a small surface area of glass. I therefore choose a detector with a thin end window. The instrument is shown in photo 1. Geiger counters of this type tend to be expensive, costing several hundred pounds. I was lucky enough to get this one at reduced cost as it was a prototype by a local manufacturer. It also turned out to have a suitable sensitivity range.

The Geiger counter, as its name implies, counts the number of pulses it detects in a given time and its read-

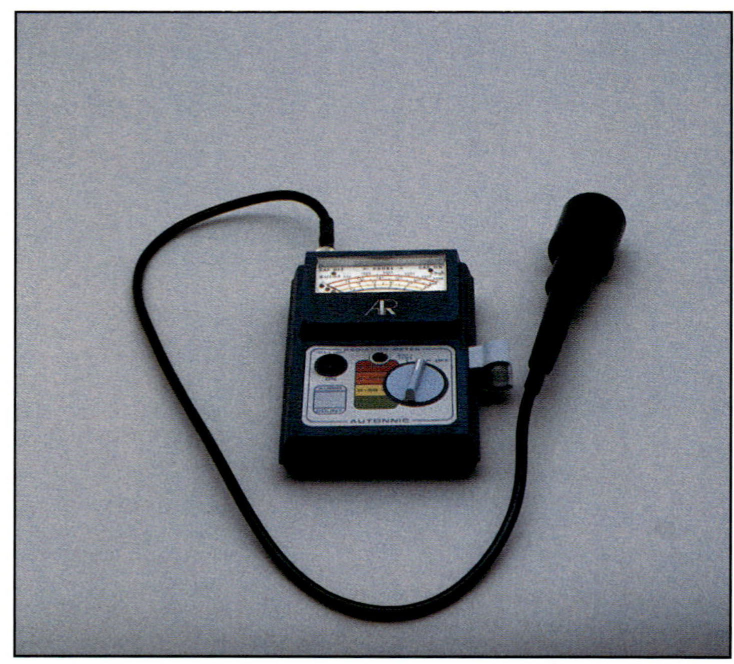

Photo 1. The Geiger counter used by the Author for the measurements quoted in this book. Size, excluding the detector and lead, 15 cm x 10 cm.

ings are often expressed in "counts per second" abbreviated to "cps." The familiar click of the Geiger counter is the electronic way in which each measured pulse is presented, the instrument often has a rate meter as well to display the counts per second for the observer. When monitoring for radioactivity it is often convenient to listen for the crackle then refer to the meter only when the crackle rate becomes significant. The instrument indicates what passes through it rather than what is present in the source, thus it does not provide an absolute measurement and needs to be calibrated. The reading is noted when it is presented to a known amount of radioactive material. In deciding how to calibrate it, it is necessary to take account of the nature of the source of radioactivity it will be measuring. Ideally this should be a point source and have radiation that closely resembles that expected from the samples (which should also be in the form of a point source). This is obviously is not the case when estimating the uranium, (or potassium) in a glass vase, plate, jug, etc.

To overcome this difficulty I make use of what is known as the "infinite depth" method, which is well suited for measuring beta radioactivity. The principle of which can be explained as follows. Suppose a very thin layer of radioactive material was placed under the end window of our Geiger. The instrument would show a certain reading. If another identical layer was then placed on top of the first we might expect the reading to double because the amount of radioactivity under the window had doubled. In fact this would not quite happen. Some of the radiation in the lower layer would be absorbed by the material in the upper layer through which it had to pass, before it reached the detector. It would be acting as shielding. If the layers were very thin, then the loss from the lower layer would be very small, but if building layer upon layer continued the "sandwich" would become so thick that most of the radiation from the lower layers was absorbed before it could reach the detector. The stage would eventually be reached when no matter how many more layers we added it would make no noticeable difference to the reading on the meter. From the detectors point of view the radiation depth has become infinite. Nevertheless, the reading the instrument gave would reflect the concentration of radioactivity in the layers. Thus if a calibration source at infinite depth is then compared with a sample at infinite depth, the radioactivity in the sample can be calculated. This is a standard procedure[1]

Because it is fairly dense, (SG usually between 2.4 and 3.4) beta rays have a short range in glass and a millimeter would approximate to infinite depth. Except in cases of very thin glass, or where the uranium glass has been flashed, presenting a beta sensitive Geiger to a piece of glassware is, defacto, measuring the radiation at "infinite depth."

The specific radioactivity, (i.e. radioactivity per unit mass) in the glass Rg = (Rs x Cg) / Cs. where Rs is the specific radioactivity of the standard and Cg and Cs are the Geiger counter readings from the glass and standard respectively.

With readily obtainable material I have used two methods of calibration. The first is to calibrate against an infinite depth of a potassium salt, the other against glass where the uranium concentration is known. Potassium sulphate can be bought from most garden centers and, providing it is reasonably pure, may be used as a standard. Alternatively potassium chloride may be used. (For potassium chloride the specific beta radioactivity is 14.4 Bq/g, and for Potassium sulphate is 12.4 Bq/g).

As it turned out, on my instrument, a reading of 1 cps was indicated against an infinite depth of potassium sulphate, which means Cs = 1. Thus the specific radioactivity in a sample (Rg), becomes the Geiger reading x 12.4. (It is worth noting that potassium sulphate is approximately 45% potassium so that a reading of 1 on my Geiger from a piece of clear crystal would indicate 45% potassium in the glass. Most potassium glasses have only up to about 10% potassium, and consequently if the Geiger counter were presented to one of these it would only indicate about 0.2 cps, a level that is too low for this instrument to measure with any reliability. A more sensitive counter would have to be used to determine the potassium in glass and then there would have to be the proviso that there was no uranium or thorium present).

To use the Geiger to estimate the weight of uranium present it is necessary to know the specific beta radioactivity of uranium. This is not quite straightforward as it may seem. When uranium is mined it is contaminated with radioactive daughter elements. These are the products of radioactive decay over many thousand years. Generally speaking they will be removed in the chemical extraction process and I assume this to be the case. In the early days of using uranium, as I have already pointed out, chemistry was much less sophisticated than it is today and it is conceivable that some traces of daughter products may remain. If this did happen then it would mean that I have over estimated the uranium concentrations. I have taken the radioactivity of natural uranium to be 24,800 Bq/g. Thus 1 cps on the Geiger counter would be equivalent to 12.4/24800 grams of uranium per gram of sample that equates to 0.05% . Although this may be taken as a good indicative figure it is probably *too low* because the energy of the beta radiation from potassium is significantly higher than that from natural uranium, a factor that affects the calibration of the instrument. In my particular case this method has another problem, namely that the reading from the sulphate of potash was at the lower end of the instrument's range where there is likely to be a greater margin of error. (Because the radioactive emissions are not equally time spaced, but come in a random distribution, the more pulses that are measured the greater is the accuracy of the measurement.)

Thus for measuring uranium in glass a better method of calibration is to use a glass with a known uranium content as a standard. Without access to an analytical laboratory this method also presents difficulties as with commercial glass, even when the recipe is known, there must be some doubts over its exact composition. For example I have measured the radioactivity in 12 examples of Webb's "Sunshine Amber" and found an average count rate of 19.4 cps but with a range of 18 to 22 cps. For my calibration sources I have used four types of uranium glass, where the recipes are known. These are (1) a sample supplied by Plowden & Thompson of 1960s boro-silicate glass with quoted uranium content, (2) examples of Webb's 1930s "Sunshine Amber" and "Bristol Green" recipes published by Eveson[2] and Jobling's Jade recipe published by Baker & Crowe[3] From these results I conclude that 1 cps on my counter indicates a uranium content of 0.062% (results range from 0.07% to 0.054%) with a range of about +/- 15%. This conclusion is quite consistent with what would be expected from the calibration against potassium. *All the uranium concentrations quoted in the following text have been estimated by this Geiger counter method.*

I have used the 0.062% factor for all my estimates of uranium concentration. If it is in error it will show a consistent bias. The closeness of the readings for different examples of identical glass items are probably well within the variations that might be expected between batches of glass and confirms that this is a reasonable method of estimating uranium concentration without resort to chemical analysis which would be cumbersome and involve destructive testing.

On some items the layer of uranium is too thin to approximate to infinite depth. In others the shape or size is such that I cannot present the full face of the Geiger to the glass. In such cases I have quoted the uranium measurement in cps to give some indication of the level of radioactivity present.

However a word of caution, all that clicks is not necessarily uranium. Ralph Sheets[4], has pointed out that some glass may contain thorium, a natural contaminant of some sands. His particular concern was where ceria/titania had been used, instead of uranium, to produce the yellow. The cerium being obtained from monazite sands, would have associated thorium. Thorium is also radioactive and would cause the Geiger to click away much the same as uranium. If in doubt the first test should be with uv light. The fluorescence of uranium is characteristic and if the lack of such fluorescence cannot be explained by the presence of quenching elements, further investigation is required. This inevitably means gamma spectrometry. I have only found one item and that was in near clear glass, which had significant radioactivity due to thorium (see Photo 257 Section 2, American Glass).

Another method of detecting (and measuring) uranium in glass is by gamma spectrometry. This is a technique that analyses the gamma rays originating from the nucleus of the uranium atom. They have energies that are characteristic of the atom from which they originate. In the case of some nuclides such as potassium 40, the gamma rays of only one energy, (1.46 MeV) are emitted and this makes identification relatively simple. The same cannot be said of natural uranium because of the daughter elements that may be associated with it. Here the gamma spectrum is complex.

The gamma spectrometer is an expensive and sophisticated piece of equipment, the operation of which requires specialized knowledge. It is not generally available to the glass collector consequently it has only been used in glass analysis to a limited extent. The process requires the sample to be is placed on a detector which measures the energy of the incident gamma ray. It then plots, or tabulates, the measured energy against the number of pulses having that energy. The early spectrometers generally in use until the 1970s, used a sodium iodide crystal. Unfortunately these do not have very good energy resolution, that is, they cannot distinguish between energies that were close together, and they also have high background noise at the lower energies that made analysis of low energy spectra difficult. Although sodium iodide crystals are still used for some work, germanium lithium drifted (geli) crystals are now available. While these have disadvantages they give much better energy resolution and have lower background noise. This makes identification of the originating isotope more precise.

Although gamma spectrometry is valuable for identifying the isotopes present, it requires the sample to be in a defined geometry for accurate quantitative analysis. Only the gamma rays are analyzed and unlike the beta measurements, there is little self-absorption, however not all of the rays coming from the sample will strike the detector, many will miss and be absorbed by the surrounding shielding. The proportion striking the detector has to be known, for a quantitative estimate of the amount of isotope present to be made. If the geometry is defined, say a standard volume container sitting on the detector, then this factor can be calculated or measured by calibration. Glass objects, such as wines, vases, tumblers, dishes do not conform to this requirement and the analysis will need to estimate the factor. This inevitably leads to uncertainty in the result. Murray and Haggith[5] minimized this problem by using two large sodium iodide crystals either side of the specimen. Unfortunately their specimens were not positively identified so they could only conjecture over the accuracy of their results compared with the theoretical values from known mix recipes.

I have had a number of glass samples examined by gamma spectrometry using geli detectors, not for quantitative determination of uranium concentration, but for radio nuclide identification. In contrast to the four peaks that Murray & Haggith recorded with their sodium iodide crystals, I have been able to utilize thirty-four peaks in the samples that have been analyzed. The results tend to be indicative rather than conclusive and will be referred to in the script when individual items are described. I had thought that a distinction between pre 1930s, pre WW2 and post WW2 uranium glass might be possible by this technique. The idea hinged on the assumption that early uranium glass would have been made using uranium oxide which, according to the way it had been processed, would be contaminated with daughter products. Although I have not been able to determine when a change took place, by the 1930s sodium or potassium diuranate was used in the mixes instead of oxide. The diuranates, having been chemically processed, would probably be less contaminated than the cruder oxides. Commercial supplies post-WW2 are usually from depleted uranium[6]. That is uranium that has been processed to extract some of the 235 isotope. The ore would not only have been chemically processed but also through a gaseous diffusion or ultra centrifuge plant. This I would expect to remove even more contaminants. Examination of my limited number of results does not appear to bear this out. I suspect that fallout from weapons and the use of different sources of raw material in the mixes may account for the lack of consistency in the presence of the more rare isotopes.

Another approach to seek to confirm the presence of depleted uranium would be to look for the radiations associated with the respective isotopes. In natural uranium there is 0.71% U 235, but in depleted uranium, that figure falls to about 0.3%[7]. In analyzing the gamma spectrum results I have used peak at 143 KeV as datum and assessed other peaks with respect to this. The 143 KeV comes from the 235 isotopes. In one example, where I anticipated depleted uranium would have been used, the 92 KeV peak was found to be double/triple that of the other samples which could not have been made from depleted uranium. As this peak comes from a short-lived daughter of uranium 238, such a result is consistent with indicating the presence of depleted uranium. It was interesting to note that the same was not observed on a piece of 1970s Fenton but then perhaps not all post war commercial uranium supplies come from the stocks of depleted Uranium?

I also have results on six examples of Davidson's Primrose Pearline. Again using the 143 KeV peak as datum, these all appear to have certain common peaks, which are not all found in other pieces of non-pearline uranium glass. I would consider this indicative rather than conclusive but clearly there is scope for anyone who has access to a gamma spectrometer and a lot of time to develop this approach!

Potassium has one radioisotope, namely K 40, and this emits gamma rays with a single energy of 1.46 KeV. Gamma spectrometry can therefore be used to ascertain whether potash has been in the recipe.

Natural Thorium has a complex spectrum that is mainly associated with its daughters and it too can be assayed by advanced spectrometry.

No matter how accurate our measurements, whether by gamma spectrometry or by the beta Geiger, there will be variations in the measured uranium concentrations between items apparently made by the same formulae. This is likely to be less with the more modern, (mid 20th century) mixes than with older ones. For this there are three reasons. The first is the quality of the uranium oxide used. In the early days the quality control on the uranium product was not as good as to day. The second is the accuracy with which the uranium was measured, here the low level mixes would be particularly vulnerable. It could well be that in batches of 100 lb. total, which according to the old note books would appear not uncommon, the amount of uranium oxide might only be a lb. or less. An error of + or - an oz or two in adding this to the melt could cause a variation of 25% in uranium concentrations. The third is the extent to which a homogeneous mix was obtained. The melt is not stirred but has to rely on thermal mixing. Thus when interpreting uranium concentrations for the purpose of attribution or comparison, allowance must be made for variations greater than the accuracy of the method of measurement. The higher the concentration the less significant these considerations become. Thus a level of 0.05% - 0.1% u by wt could well be from the same nominal formula, but such a percentage variation at (say) 5 times that level would certainly indicate different melt formulae.

[1]UK Atomic Energy Authority Report, PG 403 (W).
[2]Eveson S R - Sixty Years in Crystal Glass Industry.
[3]Baker J & Crowe K - Guide to Jobling Glass
[4]Sheets R - Southwest Missouri State University, Private Communication.
[5]Murray S & Haggith J - Estimation of Uranium in Colored Glass 1973.
[6]Natural uranium is mainly comprised of two isotopes, namely 235, & 238. Originally for weapons purposes and later for use in certain commercial nuclear power stations, the uranium was *enriched* with the 235 isotopes. This requires removing it from natural uranium leaving behind *depleted* uranium.
[7]Verbal information from British Nuclear Fuels Plc, Feb. 1991.

Chapter 5
Fluorescence

As mentioned elsewhere, when the electrons in the outer orbits are excited then subsequently lose this excitation energy they may emit photons of visible light. One stimulant that can be used to cause the initial excitation is ultraviolet (uv) light. It is particularly effective with uranium that fluoresces a ghostly yellow/green.

The ultraviolet spectrum extends from about 400 nm[1] that is near to the visible spectrum and sometimes referred to as being in the "near" region, to 150 nm, which is sometimes referred as being in the "far" region, which is adjacent to the x-ray spectrum . For practical purposes, i.e. buying a uv lamp, this range is divided into three categories with wavelengths of 365 nm (long-wave), 300 nm (midrange), and 250 nm (short-wave).

Uranium fluoresces strongly with uv in the near range, which is also known as black light. It responds less to the far range. Near range uv lamps are readily available at reasonable prices. The small torch-like "code marker lights" used for checking the "invisible marking" often put on goods for security reasons, operate in the near range although they may be contaminated with visible violet light. They are easy to carry around, will cause uranium to fluoresce and are modestly priced at £10 - £20. Black light is also used for stage lighting effects and a 150w black light bulb used for this purpose, will cost around £35. These have very little violet contamination. I have used such a bulb to examine glass and also illuminate specimens for photographic purposes.

Ultraviolet radiation can be a health hazard, especially in the medium and far regions. Exposures to wavelengths shorter than 310 nm cause "sunburn" and eventually skin cancer. It can also damage the eyes. The longer wave radiation presents less hazard but I still treat it with respect and keep my exposure to a minimum.

While black light will nearly always indicate the presence of uranium it does not give any quantitative measurement of how much is in the metal. The intensity of the fluorescence should not be taken as an indication of uranium concentration. The response of the uranium to the uv light depends on the chemistry of the mix and some that contain more uranium fluoresce less strongly than others that have less.

Before reading any further take a look at the Photos (2) & (3). The first shows 7 items in photographic flash light, which for our purposes approximates to daylight. Photo (3) shows the same pieces in exactly the same position but in uv (black) light. Now, reading left to right, jot down their ranking order with respect to what you think are their uranium concentrations.

Having done all that turn to the end of this paragraph[2]. You will see the uranium concentrations as I have estimated them, the figures are %U by wt. This should illustrate how difficult it is to estimate uranium from the strength of the fluorescence. The piece with the highest uranium concentration shows hardly any at all! Also not everything that fluoresces ghostly green is uranium. I would also mention that clear colorless soda glass also has a faint green fluorescence in uv light which may be due to the manganese decolorize. Indeed I have heard of this being used as a method to distinguish between soda and lead glass.

[1]nm = nano meter or a thousand-millionth of a meter, and here refers to the wavelength of the radiation.
[2]Top row: 0, 0.14, 0.5, 0.5, 0.5 Lower row: 1.6, 2.7, 0.17

Opposite page;
Top: Photo 2. Glass under white light.

Bottom: Photo 3. Glass under ultraviolet light.

Chapter 6
Density of Glass

The density of glass, that is its weight per unit volume, is a function of its composition and this in turn can give some indication of its likely origin. It is not a fingerprint and any particular value is not unique to a particular mix formula or glasshouse. However I have observed that glass manufacturers are very conservative with their products and appear to have kept the same basic mixes over many years. Consequently the density of their metal stays within the bounds of the consistency of their mixes. We may therefore speculate that during such and such a period, a particular manufacturer will produce glass within a certain density range. It is unlikely to be greatly affected by the additions of different elements to produce color. For example, Pellatt[1] gives a formula for Flint Glass and the additions to achieve different colors, for Soft White Enamel add 24 lb. of arsenic to 6 cwt of batch, for Azure Blue add 6 lb. of copper to 6 cwt of batch, and so on. Such small additions would not significantly affect the density, consequently all the glass of a producer using these formula for its batch would have the same density.

Because all glasshouses are using the same basic materials, the compositions of their metals will not differ greatly and so it is likely that their densities will be close. As we shall see, in a number of cases, they do not match exactly. As glass density is very sensitive to lead content it can be a good indicator of the percentage lead present. If density cannot indicate who made the glass, it can certainly indicate who probably did not and so narrow down the field of attribution.

For most items density is easy to measure. The simplest method is to weigh the object in air, then while it is suspended in water. This requires some ingenuity in modifying a suitable balance. The density is calculated as (weight in air) divided by (weight in air - weight in water). Strictly speaking this gives the Specific Gravity, which is the density of a material with respect to the density of pure water at 4 degrees centigrade. In terms of grams per cc that is unity consequently for our purposes density and specific gravity are numerically the same.

In these measurements the water temperature is not very critical and I have found that ordinary tap water, probably with its dissolved solids, has a density close enough to 1 g / cc at 60 degrees for my purposes. Consequently, for convenience, all my measurements have been made in this way. There is no point in working to a greater degree of accuracy than is justified by the vagrancy of the manufacturers mix. The balance used for the weighing should be of good quality although the accuracy of a chemical analytical balance is not necessary. As most samples are likely to be between 100 g and 1000 g, a balance reliable to 0.1 g is sufficient to give a result to two decimal places. For lighter pieces a better balance would advisable.

The density of the glass is a function of its composition. Some elements have a lesser effect than others and those present in the larger proportions are likely to affect the density more than those present in trace quantities. The relative proportions of calcium, sodium and potassium do measurably affect the density to a small extent but this is masked by the presence of other elements such as lead or barium. It is not therefore possible to determine whether a glass has a sodium or potassium base solely on density measurement. In practice the elements that have the greatest impact on density are lead, barium and boron. The former two increase density, the latter reduces it. Barium, in the past has not been in common use thus glass with higher density usually has a significant lead content. The boro-silicate glasses, as used in "Pyrex" and other heat resistant glass, will have a lower density than the normal soda glass. However a low density is not always caused by boron, sometimes it can be the result of air in the trapped in the melt or, as in the case of Leerdam "Graniver," from the use of very coarse sand, (Section 2 Photo 264)

The effect of composition on density is discussed fully by Tooley and Morey. For typical glasses Tooley[2] quotes Boro-silicate Glass density 2.23 g/cc, Container Glass density 2.46 g/cc and Heavy Lead Glass density 3.2 g/cc. Morey[3] provides a graph showing how the density of sodium and potassium glasses vary with lead content. Elville[4] also discusses the value of density measurement and gives a graph showing the variation of density with lead content and quotes approximately 0.02 increase in density for every 1% of lead. The problem with using all this data is that these glasses only approximate to the metal used in production. Each glasshouse would use slightly different mixes. Thus without knowing the exact composition of a glass it is not possible to estimate its precise lead content. To obtain *an approximate* appreciation of density significance in terms of lead content I have amalgamated the aforementioned graphs and in the light of a few measurements I have made on samples of known lead content, constructed the Graph shown in fig.(1). I emphasize that this should be regarded as indicative rather than absolute. To test this graph I have used it to estimate the densities of three known compositions and compared these with their measured density. For Webb's Queen' s is often the Glasshouse's normal clear glass with a few extras added in small quantities. Thus the density of their colored glass is similar to that of their clear glass. With this in mind, in order to obtain a "benchmark" for the metal produced by different glass houses, a large number of clearly identifiable clear glass items have been measured for density. The results are shown in figs (2) to (8) and Table (1). When considering these scatter diagrams it should be appreciated that any error is likely to be in the

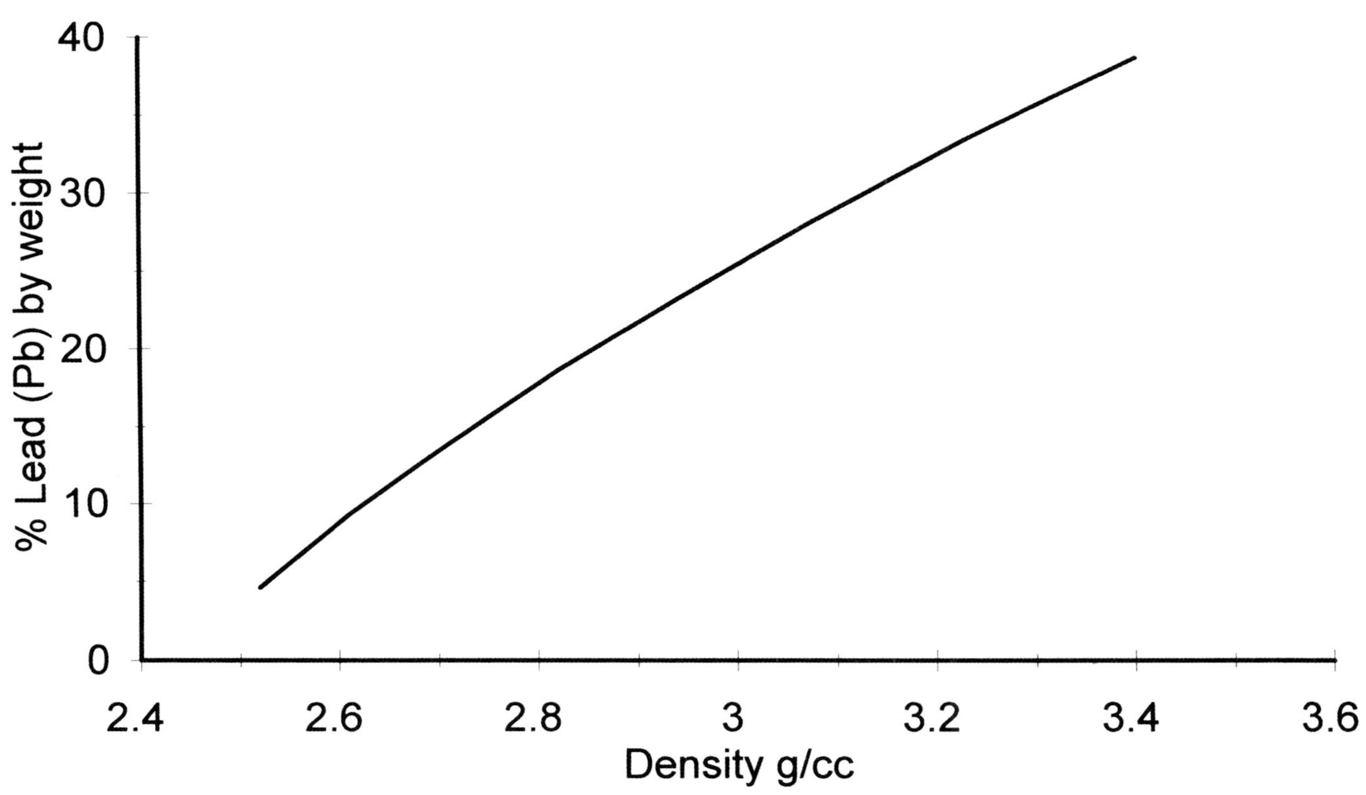

Fig. 1. Variation of density of glass with its lead content.

Burmese the expected density was 2.72 g/cc where as the average of 5 measurements was 2.76 g/cc. For nineteenth century Webb's crystal, estimated density was 3.18 g/cc while the average of three measurements gave 3.18 g/cc. Finally for a glass item labeled "24% lead crystal" I estimated its density should be 2.96 g/cc compared with the measured of 2.91 g/cc. The closeness of these graph-estimated values with the measured densities validates the graph.

Many of the formulae I have seen in old notebooks and other sources confirm my suspicion that colored glass dating. In most cases this is taken as the date of registration of design, (See Section 1, "Making Attributions" and "Dating Glass"). This really means it is the earliest date at which the item could be made. Many moulds were kept in use for years, or decades so the actual date of manufacture could be some considerable time after the registration date. In most cases, because glasshouses did not change their basic mixes, this is of little consequence. I have only used examples where I have a high degree of confidence in the attribution but it must also be borne in mind that moulds were sold and sometimes used by other producers.

I have only produced scatter diagrams where I have at least 10 reliable measurements. I have evaluated the average and also the standard deviation. For lesser numbers I have produced a Table (1), clearly these values are less reliable for drawing conclusions. I will now discuss the significance of these results.

George Davidson & Co.'s Glass

More than forty samples covering the period 1880 to 1930 have been examined. It will be seen that there appears to be no correlation with date, a strong indication that the firm probably kept the same basic mixes for more than 50 years. The densities are closely packed between 2.43 g/cc and 2.5 g/cc. The average is 2.47 g/c. and standard deviation 0.018. On the assumption that this is a normal distribution I would expect that more than 95% of Davidson's clear glass would have a density in the range 2.43 g/cc to 2.51 g/cc. In Section 2, I discuss the densities of Davidson's uranium glass and conclude that a 1% addition of uranium increases the density by about 0.07 g/cc.

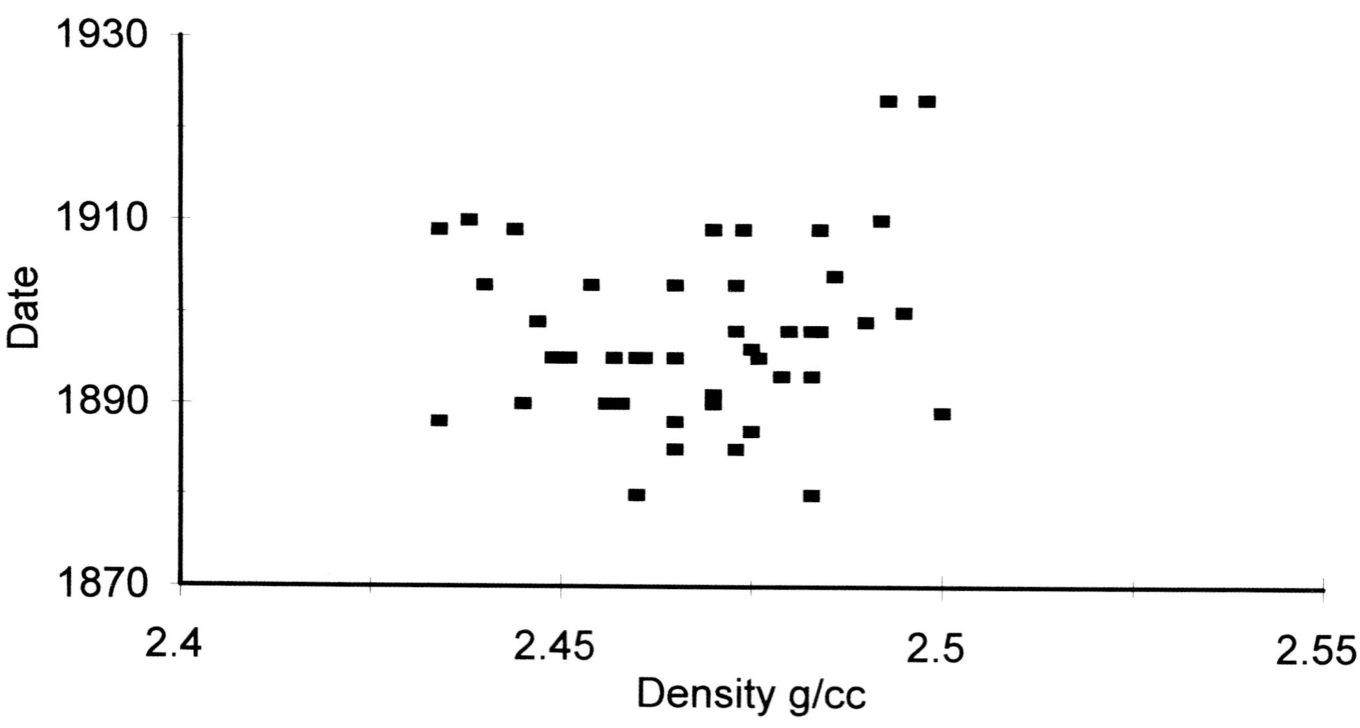

Fig. 2. Density measurements on examples of Davidson's clear glass.

Greener & Co.'s Glass.

Nearly thirty samples have been examined. It is immediately apparent that two have a much higher density than the others. These are very early pieces in the days when the firm was Angus & Greener. Thereafter a trend can be discerned to lower densities that suggest that over the period from the mid 1860s to the turn of the century there was a tendency to use cheaper, lower lead, metal in their products. This leads to a much wider scatter in density of their products over the half century. If we neglect the two early points the others have densities between 2.43 g/cc and 2.65 g/cc, their average being 2.52g/cc. The standard deviation being 0.067, which means the use of density to support a Greener attribution, is not going to be very likely.

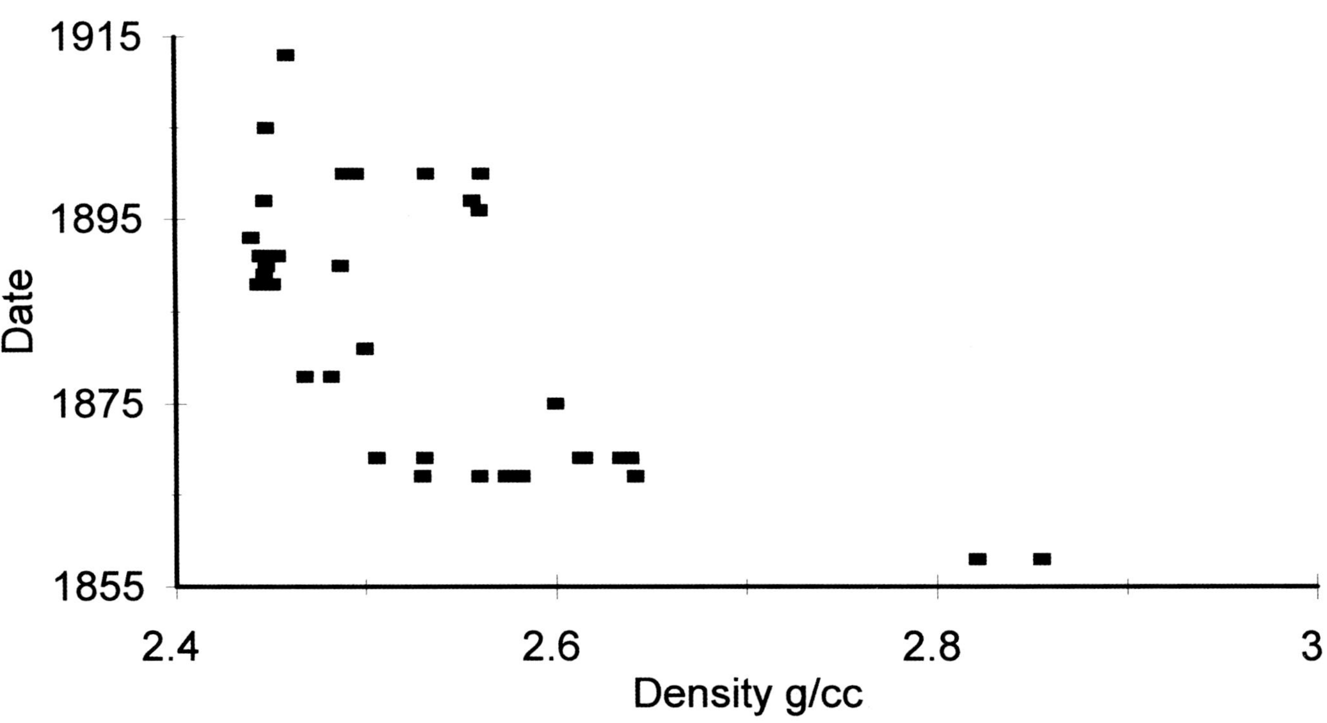

Fig. 3. Density measurements on examples of Greener's clear glass.

Jobling's Glass

After 1882 the company was taken over by James Jobling but continued to trade under the Greener name until early twentieth century. The graph, which does not include *Pryex* glass, for twelve items, indicates densities between 2.43 g/cc and 2.52 g/cc. The average is 2.476 g/cc with a standard deviation of 0.0266. Thus for a normal distribution 95% of all Jobling's glass should have a density of between 2.42 g/cc & 2.53 g/cc. which is the lower end of the Greener range thus suggesting that after the change of ownership there were changes in their basic mix. probably about the turn of the century.

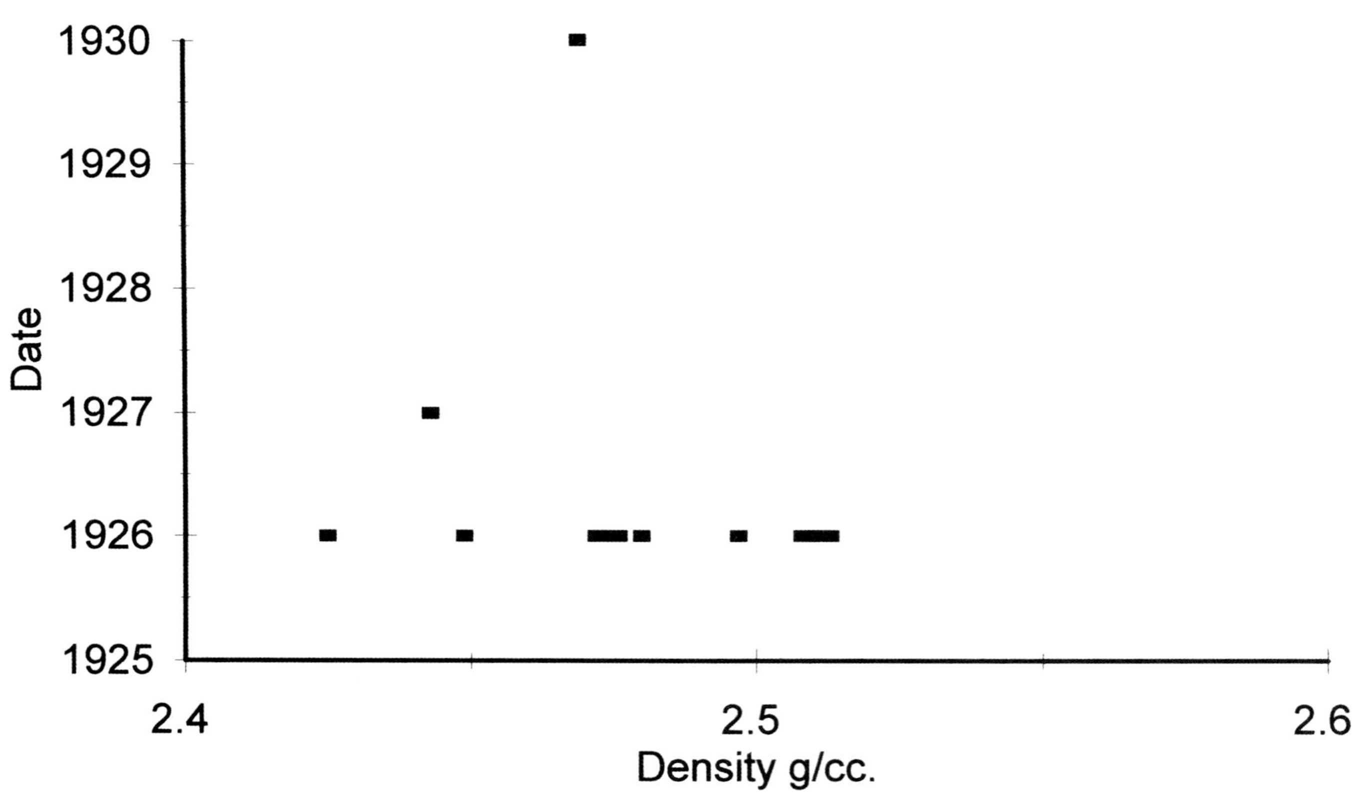

Fig. 4. Density measurements on examples of Jobling's clear glass

Molineaux, Webb & Co.'s Glass

The results of the measurements on ten items can be regarded as being in three groups. When interpreting these results I bear in mind the fact that there must be flexibility in designating the date. The piece with a density 2.55 g/cc and dated by Registration Number as 1888 could well have been made later than that date but not earlier. The graph suggests that the very early metal was probably heavily leaded at about 23% Pb wt. From about 1870 until after 1900 the lead content was reduced to about 17% Pb wt. The piece with density 2.55 g/cc could indicate that the Company changed its metal or, as seems more likely, (see Section 2, Molineaux, Webb & Co.), that it was made by Sowerby from an old mould.

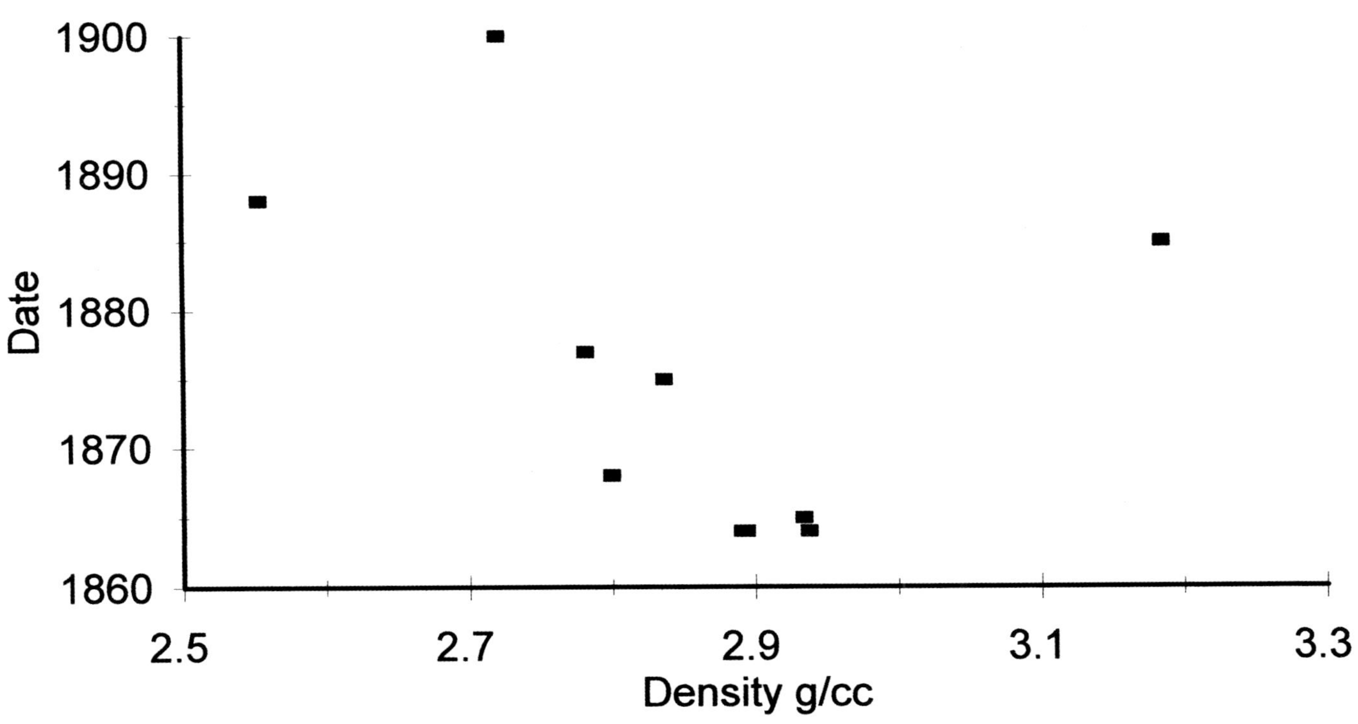

Fig. 5. Density measurements on examples of Molineaux, Webb's clear glass.

Edward Moore's Glass

Seventeen results all lie within 2.42 g/cc and 2.46 g/cc. The average is 2.444 g/cc and standard deviation 0.008. On the basis of a normal distribution I would expect 95% of Moore's products to have a density of between 2.43 g/cc & 2.46 g/cc. The fact that one result lies just outside this range is about what might be expected. They are all within the higher (99%) confidence limit of three standard deviations, i.e. 2.42 g/cc to 2.47 g/cc. .There appears to be no significant change with relation to date over the period 1865 to 1890. Against this Slack[5] reports that after a fire destroyed the factory in 1892 the quality of their metal improved to that of Manchester glass. However as we see Manchester glasshouses generally used significant quantities of lead in their mixes. The scatter diagram shows no evidence of this but some of the pieces shown in Section 2 that are colored with uranium do have densities indicating that there might be a small amount of lead in the metal.

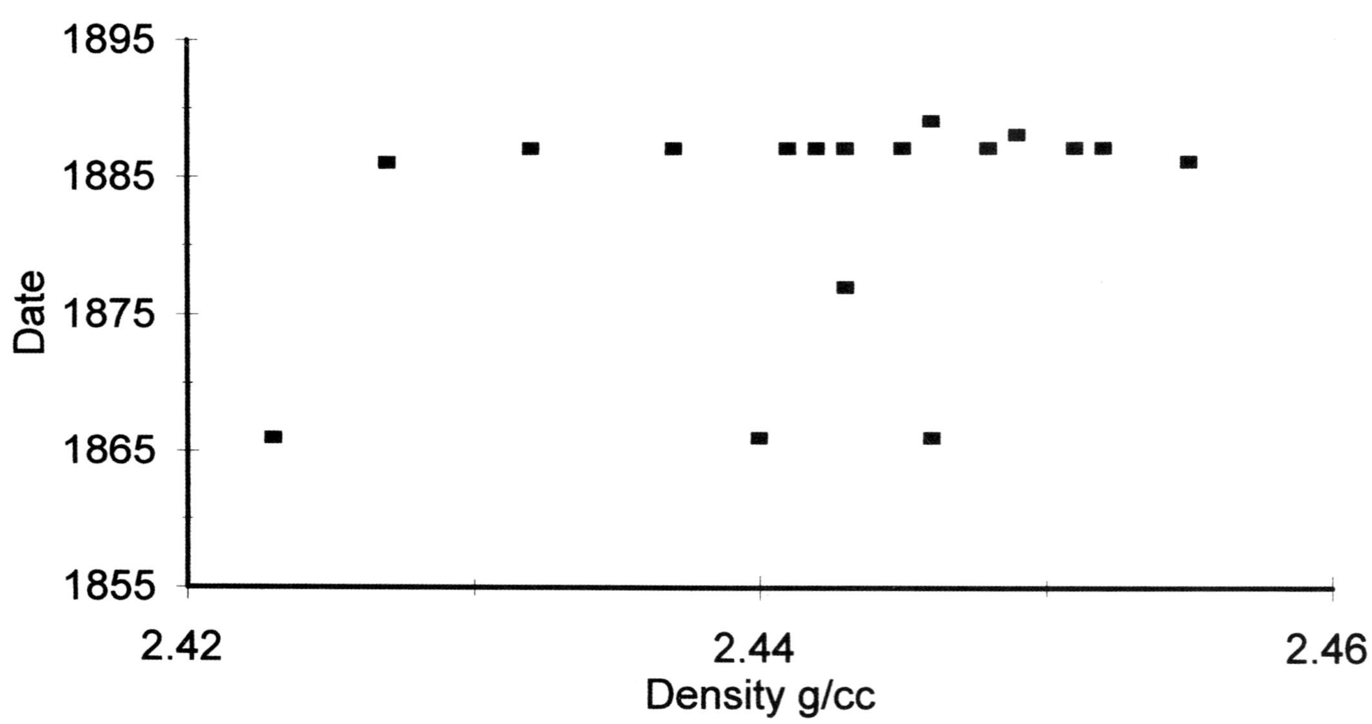

Fig. 6. Density measurements on examples of Ed. Moore's clear glass.

Percival, Vickers & Co.'s Glass

Fourteen specimens have been measured and are shown in the scatter diagram. The two with density greater than 3 g/cc appear to be outside the general group. Both these are from the earlier years but they do not show design registration marks and were identified from trade catalogues. Two possibilities come to mind, were they made by another glasshouse or did Percival Vickers use a heavier leaded metal in the early days? Looking at the other results they all lie between 2.63 g/cc and 2.93 g/cc with an average of 2.79 g/cc. The standard deviation being 0.076. The overall conclusion I draw from this is that this firm generally favored a leaded glass mix that fluctuated somewhat erratically around 16% wt Pb.

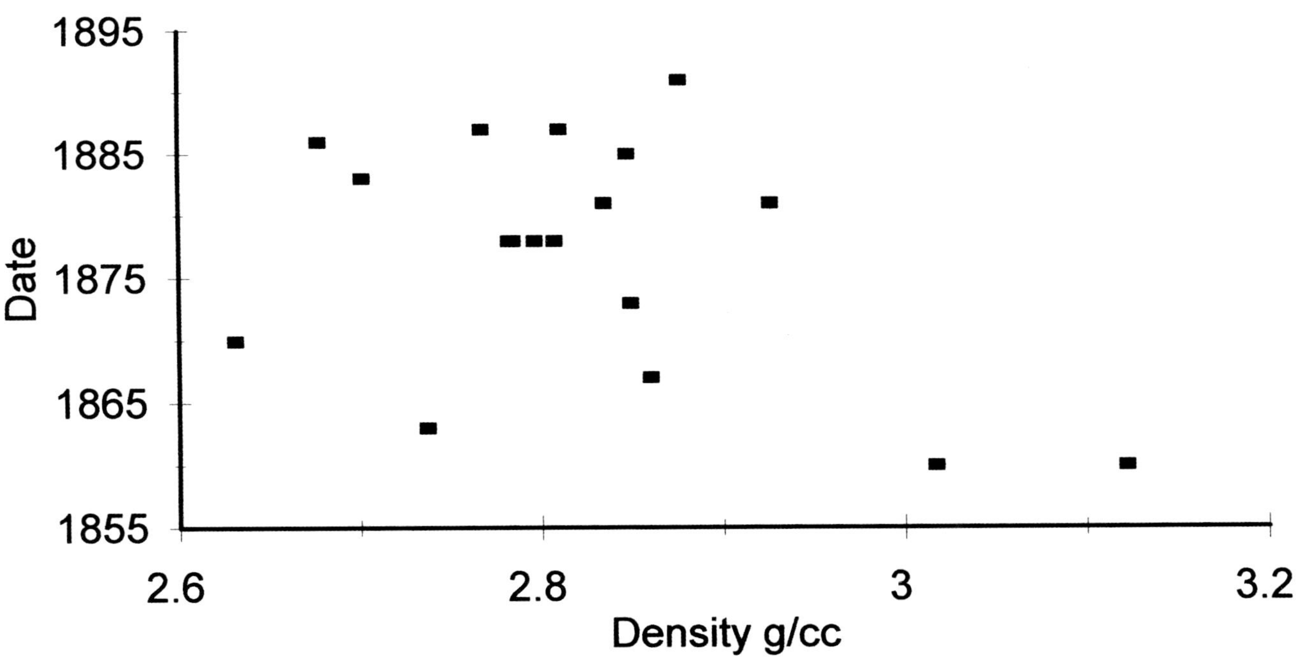

Fig. 7. Density measurements on examples of Percival, Vicker's clear glass.

Sowerby of Gateshead Glass

Some forty pieces of Sowerby glass, produced over nearly eighty years, have had their density determined. The scatter diagram, fig (8)), shows little scatter. There are no obvious misfits, the average density is 2.496 g/cc with a standard deviation of 0.033. Thus I would expect 95% of all Sowerby clear glass to have densities within the range 2.43 g/cc to 2.56 g/cc. 99% should lie within 2.34 g/cc and 2.6 g/cc. There appears to be no bias with respect to date.

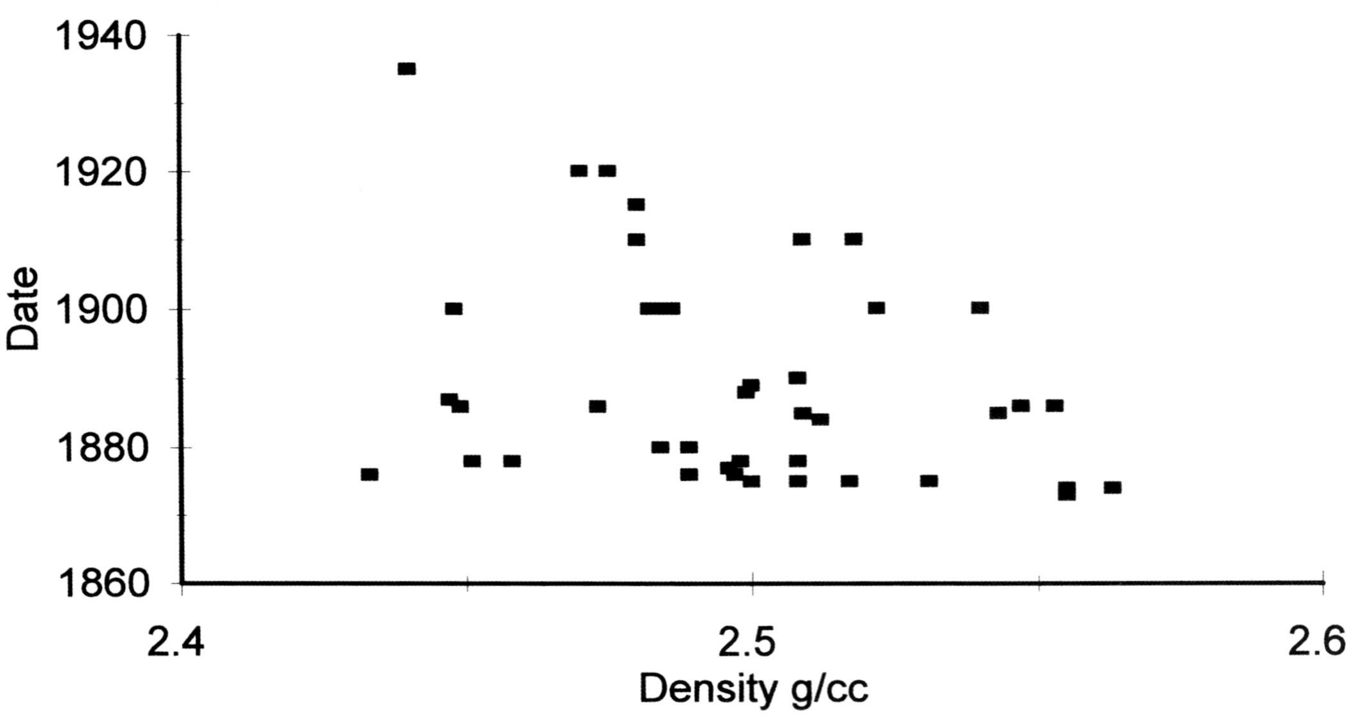

Fig. 8. Density measurements on examples of Sowerby's clear glass.

Table 1. Density of Clear Glass from Other Manufacturers.

Glasshouse	*Location of Glasshouse*	*No in Sample*	*Ave. Den.g/cc*	*Range*	*Dates*
Edward Bolton	Lancashire	2	2.45	2.4 - 2.5	1885
John Derbyshire	Lancashire	5	2.62	2.5 - 2.7	1875 - 1900
Ker Webb	Lancashire	1	2.56		1886
Robinson & Bolton	Lancashire	3	2.9	2.88 - 2.91	1865
Whittingham & Percival	Lancashire	1	2.75		1876
Jules Lang	London	7	2.49	2.47 - 2.54	1896 - 1929
Stevens & Williams	Stourbridge	2	3.01	2.89 - 3.12	1876 -1887
Stuart Crystal	Stourbridge	2	3.05	3.05	1880
Stuart Crystal	Stourbridge	1	3.12		1935
Thos Webb	Stourbridge	6	3.18	3.16 - 3.2	1886 - 1935
Jobling, Pyrex (clear)	Tyneside	6	2.25	2.2 - 2.3	1930 - 40s
Jobling, Pyrex (white)	Tyneside	4	2.53	2.52 - 2.55	1950 - 1980
Matthew Turnbull	Tyneside	2	2.52	2.52 - 2.52	1893
Thos. Gray	Tyneside	2	2.47	2.47 - 2.47	1875
W H Heppel (white opaque)	Tyneside	1	2.47		1881
Bagley	Yorkshire	4	2.47	2.45 - 2.48	1930 - 1950

In Table 1, there are listed a number of other glasshouses, the density of whose products I have measured. However I considered the numbers involved were insufficient to merit being produced as scatter diagrams. They should be regarded as indicative only. Indeed where there are only one or two pieces the density is no more than a snapshot and it must still be borne in mind that the item may not have been made by the glasshouse to which it is attributed, someone else may have taken over the mould! Never the less there are some points of interest.

Three out of the five Lancashire glass houses are using leaded glass in the 10% - 20% range. To these can be added Molineaux Webb and Percival Vickers leading to the general conclusion that Lancashire can generally be associated with this intermediate level of lead in their metals. In contrast the Tyneside and Yorkshire producers appear to have settled for glass with virtually no lead, while Stourbridge shows its commitment to full, or nearly full, leaded crystal. Perhaps too much significance should not be attached to the Thos. Gray and Heppell pieces as these could have been made by Davidson from acquired moulds, these they are reported to have bought in 1884.

Taking all the results together including the less reliable values quoted in table (1), we see that not only are there fine differences between some glasshouses but that geographical areas appeared to have metal characteristic of that area. Thus glass made in the Tyneside area, i.e. Davidson, Greener, Edward Moore, Sowerby, Matthew Turnbull, etc. use very low or even lead free glass. That in the Lancashire area, i.e. Percival Vickers, Molineaux Webb, John Derbyshire favor a modest lead content of around 15% while the Stourbridge Stuart, Thomas Webb and Stevens & Williams the full 33% lead. Furthermore within Tyneside we see that there is virtually no overlap between Greener and Edward Moore. I have shown Jules Lang as being London as that was where his business was based. In fact Lang made virtually no glass but had his products made by others so the density measurement is of limited value.

In the foregoing discussion I have assumed densities were influenced by lead. This may not always have been the case. Barium also increases the density of glass and barium glass is a good metal to press mould. It could be some of these "leaded" glasses were in fact barium glass. The only way to test this would be by chemistry and at the time of writing I have not found reference to any such work. From the point of my investigation, which was mainly concerned with uranium, it matters little whether the density value was due to lead or barium.

[1]Pellatt A - Curiosities of Glassmaking p33-4.

[2]Tooley F - The Handbook of Glass Manufacture, p919 - 922.

[3]Morey G - The Properties of Glass

[4]Elville E M - English Table Glass, p 257- 259

[5]Slack R - English Pressed Glass, p113/4

Chapter 7
Making Attributions

One of the most difficult aspects of glass collecting, and also one of the most interesting, is deciding who made each of the items in the collection. It otherwise known as making an attribution. It has been said that there are only two things in this life which are certain, namely that we will all die and we all have to pay taxes. That is arguable for there is still uncertainty, when we die and how much we have to pay. I mention this because no matter how sure we may feel that we know who made a piece and when they did it there is still an element of uncertainty. With the most confident there is always an element of doubt, when there is apparent uncertainty the scope for "getting it wrong" is far greater. It has oft been quoted that asking ten experts for an opinion on a piece of glass, will produce ten different answers! When experts proclaim "this was made by so and so" I am uneasy, when they add the qualification "probably" I am mystified. Just how sure are they? It seems to me that we should have some appreciation of the degree of uncertainty that exists in such statements.

Probably the surest way of making a correct attribution is to actually see the article being produced. This is sometimes possible with contemporary glass but is no use for items from the past. Very occasionally some one will say "I, (my aunt, mother, friend, late husband, next-door neighbor etc.) was visiting the factory and actually saw this being made. An attribution on this basis is only as reliable as the witness. Sometimes memory plays tricks leading to genuine mistakes. If you do witness a piece of your collection being made, write down the details for posterity! When I bought the swan, (Photo 289) from a local junk/second hand shop the proprietor insisted it had been made in Malta. He said it had been sold to him by an old lady who claimed she had seen it being made when she visited a glass factory, while on holiday, in Malta. I have no reason to doubt the sincerity of this statement but.... Had the old lady got confused, or perhaps the dealer, who was more concerned with pots, pans, old televisions and so on, made a mistake? These are very real possibilities. Subsequently I made enquiries in Malta but the opinion was that it had not been made on the Island. What started as a confident attribution is now in serious doubt!

Running a very close second in the certainty league is the item that is blessed with a trademark or signature. Unfortunately these are in a minority. Glass may be marked in one of several ways and the marks are sometimes difficult to see. In the case of pressed glass the mark may be raised and detectable by touch. On other glass, until the early part of the twentieth century, the marks were usually etched, or engraved. While some firms, such as Thos. Webb, continued this practice up to and even after WW2, others adopted the adhesive label. Needles to say the majority of these have not withstood the rigors of time. Having found a trademark, the next problem is to identify and date it. For this help is at hand and several books give illustrations of the marks of the Glasshouses about which they have written. However the most comprehensive list of trademarks and signatures available at the time of writing is probably that in the book by Anne Pullin[1]

Even the presence of a mark is no guarantee of authenticity, and with items that may attract a high price, forgeries are by no means unknown. However, on the run of the mill glassware, they are unlikely. With regard to items with stick on labels it possible for them to be transposed. This is not common but I have seen it occur by accident on a piece in an auction. In some circumstances the absence of a mark can represent an attempt to deceive. On more than one occasion I saw a piece of "Fenton Burmese" with its tell tale *FENTON* mark ground off. The artful dealer was waiting for some inexperienced collector to snap it up as a bargain thinking it to be Webb's. Such pitfalls are few and far between but they are possibilities and create a small degree of uncertainty.

Next in my hierarchy of confidence comes the " it was ordered direct from the factory, or it was supplied by..." When this is backed by documentation it is indeed powerful, but not foolproof, evidence. Perhaps the invoice for the "vase" was really for a different one and confusion has arisen over the passing years. Perhaps the supplier was not the actual manufacturer, it is not unknown for work to be subcontracted, or for one producer to sell another's product. If the items are in an established collection or a museum, the likelihood of error is very small. The same does not apply for more casual pieces. In the early nineteen sixties, long before I was interested in collecting glass, I was working in Caithness. At that time the Caithness Glass factory was being established and glass workers were being trained. Local shops offered their first production. I bought, not for collections, but for use in the home. It was good quality at very reasonable cost. Thirty-five years later there are only some pieces I remember with certainty, well certain enough to take an oath on, on others there is a doubt.

Another sure way, (or is it?) of identifying the origin of a hitherto, anonymous piece of glass is from the factory' s pattern books. There are snags to this approach. Firstly you need to have a good idea of where to start looking. That means having some idea of where and when it was made before you can make a start. That may well be the easiest part of the task. You may discover that the pattern book in which your item is illustrated has been lost. There are a number of glass houses such as Stevens & Williams, (now Royal Brierley) and Stuart Crystal who still have their old pattern books and will, by arrangement, allow them to be inspected. But what of those who have been liquidated? Some have been saved by museums and again, by arrangement, may be open for inspection. Unfortunately a large number of pattern books have been lost without trace. Where the books do exist the number of illustrations to view can be enormous. For example in the case of Stevens & Williams the 70,000 is exceeded before the end of WW2. Even if you can narrow the date to say within 20 years, which in the case of glass is by no means easy, such as from 1890 to 1910, there could be something like 20,000 pattern book numbers to view in each of the glasshouses you are searching! For the poor collector with a number of items to attribute, limited time, and having to work from his own photographs, the task of identification from pattern books is daunting. The best solution that I have to this problem is to skim through the books, picking out styles and designs that tend to repeat. These, with permission of the pattern book owner, I photograph for my own future reference. I usually consider that my failure to find an item in a pattern book does not necessarily mean it was not made by that firm. It could be that I had missed it in my search!

Even when an item is identified in a pattern book there is a possibility that near identical pieces were made by other firms. One fluted wine glass, a plain vase, or plate can look much the same as another. The old pattern books contain sketches that do not have the precision of a photograph or modern engineer's drawing. There is likely to be uncertainty as to whether your piece is exactly the same as that in the book. Only where the design is complex and clear, or where there is other corroborative evidence, can identification from a pattern book be taken with confidence.

In the United Kingdom The Design Acts of 1842 gave copyright protection to ornamental designs including manufactured goods. They were divided into 13 classes, glass being Class 3. The designs had to be registered by way of the deposit of a representation, (which could be a sample, drawing or photograph), and details of the proprietor. These, up to 1950, are held in separate registers at the Public Record Office, Chancery Lane, Kew, and are open to public inspection. The registered article was required to be marked. From 1842 to 1883 the mark was in the form of a diamond, now colloquially known as a *lozenge, (see* photo 4*),* after that it was a straight number preceded by the letters Rd.

Photo 4. A "lozenge" design registration mark molded on the glass.

These marks are not always easy to find and are most common on pressed items even so only a minority carry them. Here it is often better to feel with fingertips, rather than look, for the mark or number. Design registrations are much less common on blown glass but are occasionally found etched or engraved. These need to be identified by visual inspection. Having found a mark or number it may not be necessary to rush off to Kew to identify it. Slack[2] lists the glass registration numbers, together with the identity of who made the registration as well as the date it was made up to 1900. Thompson[3] gives similar information but up to 1908. The Glass Association[4] has complemented these for the period 1908 to 1945. Unfortunately for us collectors the majority of designs were not registered, perhaps because it offered only limited protection. Sometimes the wrong registration mark is used and sometimes the item is registered in a non-glass category in which case the aforementioned publications will be of little help.

The 1842 acts gave protection to glass designs for three years. The Patents, Designs and Trade Marks Act of 1883 amalgamated the previous categories and a single numerical system was adopted. This act gave protection for up to 5 years. The Patents and Designs Act of 1907 allowed the protection to be extended for a further five years and even another five years after that at the Comptroller's discretion.

Finding a registration mark only indicates who registered (i.e. holds the copyright) of the design. It does not always indicate who actually made the article. For example Rd 755481 ,(Section 3, Photo 278), was registered by the Dubarry Perfume Company but it is almost certain they did not make the bottle, likewise Rd 756950 (Section 3, Photos 275 & 276), was registered by Lillicrap but again they are unlikely to have made the glass hone themselves.

There is also the possibility that the mark itself is in error, I have a tumbler clearly marked Rd. 96945, which turns out to be incorrect. It should have read 99943. It would appear that the second figure was molded the reverse way round! This error came to light because the marked number did not correspond to a glass registration and I suspected the design was that of Davidson. In other circumstances a similar error could have been significantly misleading.

When in doubt, or when more information is required, it is possible to view and get copied the original submissions. At one time it was possible to order a copy of a known registration by post but that facility has now been discontinued. However there are private researchers who, for a modest fee, will obtain the information. Details of these may be obtained on the Internet via the Public Record Office Webb site, at the time of writing this is <http;//www.pro.gov.uk>. If that does not work, try searching for "PRO Kew."

With pressed glass there is always the possibility that moulds were sold by the original firm to another, possibly when the original closed. For example it is believed that when Molineaux & Webb closed in 1932 their moulds were sold to Chance of Birmingham and Sowerby's of Gateshead. The question remains did these firms produce from them? If not why buy them?. When in 1914 Percival Vickers factory was sold to iron and steel merchants, did they destroy all the moulds or were some sold off? We just do not know. The same questions can be asked of virtually all the Pressed glass firms of yesteryear. When identifying a molded item, it is no guarantee that the originator of the mould actually made the item in question.

Occasionally items carry an Rd mark that is engraved rather that pressed. One such example is the lampshade in Section 2 (Photo 113) It is highly unlikely that this is faked, as the item does not have any great value and the dealer who sold it did not even know it was there!

An important source of design information comes from trade catalogues and advertising. A number of the former are in the possession of museums and private individuals and it is sometimes possible to have access to them or even make photocopies. Adverts also appear in such journals as Pottery and Glass Trades Gazette, which are available at some libraries and museums. Again when an item is identified in this way there is still an element of uncertainty. Did the advertiser actually manufacture the item, or did they subcontract it out and simply put their name on it. This is very much the modern trend but probably also happened in the past. Only recently I saw British crystal on sale but closer inspection revealed that the items had been made in Poland! What will the collector, fifty years hence, make of this? The mind boggles.

Where an item has unusual design characteristics and these are discernible in the catalogue/advert, then there is a high probability that the item was the one illustrated, but on plain articles, such as a stem wine glass, almost identical items could have been made by a number of other glasshouses.

Sometimes a clue to the origin of a piece may be found in some particular characteristic of the design or workmanship that was probably unique to a particular glasshouse. Unfortunately only a few of these have been identified. The *daisy*, which is used to cover the pontil of the vase Photo 116 in Section 2, is one such example. This method of attribution is riddled with myth, usually propagated by dealers who ought to know better. Over the years I have been told "it must be Webb because it is threaded," "the iridescent effect confirms that it is Walsh" , "you can tell it is Clutha glass because of the air bubbles trapped in the metal," "only Webb's used a butterfly decoration" ... the list is almost endless so beware!

Sometimes a production method will support or quash an attribution, but again this technique has to be used with discretion. For example Pellatt[5] tells us "that in Bohemia and Germany, the workmen are said not to be sufficiently skilful to use the shears; but the edges of bowls are blown in the rough and cut smooth by the glass-cutter when cold." Manley[6] maintains that a Continental vase would have a flat ground top. This is supported by an article in Pottery Gazette, 2nd August 1880, p 501 on French glass making techniques. On this basis, at least up to the 1880s a blown vessel with a cut and ground flat top would be continental in origin. However there are examples of English manufacturers wares having a similar finish, such as Section 2 Photo 149 left and center. These I attribute to Walsh and date in the early 1880s. Such are not common and the occasional vase that I have examined that has a continental 7 inscribed on the underside, have all had hollow bases and a ground top.

Finally the nature of the metal frequently offers a clue to its origin. This not only applies to such specialties as Walsh's Pompeian but also properties like density, uranium content, (both of which are dealt with in more detail elsewhere), and reaction to ultraviolet light.

The foregoing says loud and clear that one can never be *absolutely certain* of a particular attribution, there is always a probability, albeit very small, that it is incorrect. It's a pity that this is seldom, if ever, admitted. Book after book, article after article, will quote the origin of piece after piece without reservation. Occasionally they are incorrect. Yet again where reservations are made and the word "probably" inserted, there is no indication of just what this means. Does it imply a 50/50, a 75/25 or a 99/1 chance of being correct? To me that there is little value in an attribution unless there is some indication of its reliability. A wrong attribution is like fitting the wrong piece in a jigsaw puzzle, it can throw out the whole subsequent picture!

My first reaction to this situation was to try and fit mathematical probabilities but this soon proved an absurd approach and instead I have to resort to "gut feelings" based on defined guidelines. These are described below and *are used throughout this book*. The confidence limits I have quoted, although numerical, are not mathematically based and represent my perception of how likely I am to be right in the attribution. To this end I have defined the implied confidence limits applied to specific words. When used in this context they are shown in italics.

An attribution made on the basis of strong prime evidence, in the absence of any contradicting factors, is not qualified and I assume a confidence level of greater than 99%, that is *an error level less than 1 in 100*. An example would be the Burtles and Tate Swan (Section 2, Photo 71) that is clearly marked with its Rd number.

Almost certainly is used when the attribution is made on weak primary evidence, backed by secondary evidence, or in the absence of primary evidence very strong secondary evidence. I assume a confidence level greater that 98%, i.e. *an error rate of less than 1 in 50*. An example is Section 2 Photo 30. It has "multi-diamond" pattern used extensively by Davidson, its color (primrose pearline), was a Davidson specialty, also its uranium, content and density lie within the range expected from this ware. Taken together these factors are strong secondary evidence.

Probably indicates a confidence level greater than 95%, i.e. *an error rate of less than 1 in 20*. It could have been reached on the basis of weak primary evidence and other substantiating factors, or moderately reliable secondary evidence. For example Section 2, Photo 71, the shell is identical in color, density and uranium content to the Burtles & Tate swan.

Could be indicates a much lower confidence level, which is greater than 80% or *an error rate of less than 1 in 5*. The knife rests, Section 2 Photo 79, look something like those illustrated in a Molineaux, Webb & Co. trade catalogue, but the shape is so undistinguished that too much weight cannot be placed upon this evidence. However the uranium content and density are also consistent with Molineaux, Webb & Co. metal, I would put them in the *could be* category.

Best guess is really what it means but I would expect a success rate of at least 50%, i.e. *an error rate less than 1 in 2*.

For the purpose of establishing "bench marks," that is features of factors that I conclude are typical of a particular glasshouse or metal, I only consider items where I have rated the confidence level at or above 98%, and then I would seek at least three examples. Where there is a small spread of data, such as is common in density and uranium measurements, I look for a minimum of 5 measurements and ideally seek 10.

[1]Pullin A - Glass Signatures, Trademarks, and Trade Names.
[2]Slack R. - English Pressed Glass.
[3]Thompson J - Identification of English Pressed Glass.
[4]The Glass Association. - Registration Numbers 1908 - 1945.
[5]Pellatt A - Curiosities of Glass Making, p82
[6]Manley C - Decorative Victorian Glass.

Chapter 8

When Was It Made?

Assigning a date to an item is probably more hazardous than attributing the original glasshouse. Again it is important to understand the uncertainties involved. In the following script I will describe and discuss the methods that I have used and explain their uncertainties.

The traditional method of dating antiques is by their style and design. Fashions come and go and these can indicate the period in which an article may have been made. It is by no means fool proof as reproduction, years later, is not uncommon. For example, in recent times "Pryce & Brise Antiques" of London have produced a leaflet that explains, "*As antique glass dealers for many years we are continually being asked to find early 19th. century champagne flutes for our customers ...At last we've solved the problem - we've had some original designs specially hand made ...*" This is not deception but genuine reproduction and it has, in one form or another, been going on throughout the period of our interest. In the January 1932 "Connoisseur" there is an advert from "Drood Society Ltd" for "*attractive replicas of Irish fourteenth century bubbly glass.*" Earlier in the same journal, December 1911, there is an advert from Osler of Birmingham for reproduction 18th century glass. The problem is widespread and has been more fully discussed elsewhere[1,2,3] Hajdamach devotes a chapter to "Fakes and Reproductions" and of special interest to me are quotes from a Hill Ouston catalogue of 1934 where illustrations identical to Photo 130, Photo 204, & Photo 101 appear to be included. However in these cases the presence of uranium in the metal makes them easily distinguishable them from their 18th century originals.

Notwithstanding, the period over which uranium was used may be grouped as "Victorian," "Art Nouveau," "Art Deco" and "Post War," covering the 1830-1910, 1910-19 30, 1930-1945 and after-1945 intervals. The demarcation in these is very hazy and, at the risk of bringing disagreement upon my head, would venture that the "Nouveau" period, as far as glass is concerned, is not easily discernible from the "Victorian" and "Deco" periods. In some cases, especially utilitarian ware, it is nonexistent. Glass lemon squeezers, similar to those that our grandparents may have used in the early part of this century are still sold to day!

A good indicator of age is wear, but again it is not fool proof and the tell tales have to be interpreted with great care. What I look for, and what I expect depends very much on the nature of the piece and how it would have been used. An article in every day use, such as a tumbler, jug, plate or dish will have been subject to constant handling, it will have been washed numerous times, and in the process rubbed against other items. In the case of dishes and plates food may well have stuck to them and had to be removed with pumice or steel wool. All this will leave scratch marks and a dulling of the surface at places other than the base. A heavy object, such as a candlestick would be expected to show a lot more wear on the base than (say) a wine glass that is much lighter. On the other hand an object which is largely ornamental, and which may have reasonably spent its life in a cupboard or display cabinet sheltered from the real world, would show little or no wear.

Another aspect of wear is the erosion of decoration, especially where gold work is involved. Again different circumstances and quality of product have to be taken into account.

While wear cannot date a piece it is frequently a good supportive indicator to either confirm or dismiss suspicions. Wear can be faked but it is difficult. A dealer once bragged to me that he had faked a piece of repro. by standing it on a stone sill and moving it several times a day for months on end! However this would have produced scratches only on the base. I would be highly suspicious of such an article that had no collateral wear elsewhere.

Yet another indicator of age is the nature of the metal. Old pressed glass is sometimes slightly discolored with a manganese mauve due to the excessive use of the element in attempting to decolorize the mix. On the other hand, as happened more often than not, when the optimum amount of decolorize was used the metal came out clear. So the absence of the mauve tint does not mean the piece is not old! Sometimes older glass has inclusions, grit or dust picked up in the furnace, or perhaps inadequately fused silica, these are known as seeds and are not usually found in glass produced in a modern furnace. (See photo 5)

Photo 5. A small impurity, probably from the furnace, lodged in the metal and known as a "seed".

Although it does not lead to dating there is a little aid to distinguishing between old and modern glass that is worth a mention. It is particularly useful where a reproduction is suspected. Items with attachments, such as flowers, leaves, or even "pump handles" have little crevices into which, over many years, specs of dark dust will penetrate. Some usually manage to escape even the most rigorous cleaning. I have heard it suggested that one way to seek these out is to fill the item with milk when they soon become apparent against the white background. The presence of ingrained dirt is not a foolproof method of distinguishing between old and reproductions, but it is a piece of evidence worth considering.

All the foregoing are, at best, just indicators and I have mainly used them to reinforce opinions formed from other data. In cases where the other data is not available I have only used them with caution and reluctance. My principle means of dating have been based upon design registration dates i.e. Rd Numbers; advert and trade catalogue dates; composition of the metal; and production techniques.

Design registration is discussed in this Section under Making Attributions. As every registration is dated we have a means of dating the article, or do we? Unfortunately there is no guarantee. All this date tells us is when the design was registered, it does not indicate when it went into production. Clearly if the piece actually carries the registration number or lozenge, then it could not have been produced *before* the registration date, unless a wrong number has be put on it, but it could have been made anytime *afterwards*. In view of the limited time for which registration gave protection it is highly probable that production would commence without delay, but for how long would it continue? Five, ten, twenty or what, years? Where the numbers are engraved or etched it is unlikely that the extra work involved would have been undertaken after the expiration of the protection date. This is not the necessarily the case with molded glass. If the numbers were stamped into the mould they will remain as long as that mould continues to be used. Moulds in good condition might have been put to one side and then brought out again years later. Certain anomalies that I have come across from time to time suggests that in some examples the actual production date may be significantly later than the design registration date. A piece which has no registration number, but is clearly a design that has been registered, may well have been made after protection period had expired. In many items of pressed glass the registration mark is faint and worn, perhaps this is because the mould had seen many years of use before the item was made. *It is important to remember is that the presence of a design registration mark only indicates the earliest date and not necessarily the actual date the article was made.*

Much the same applies to trade marks and signatures. If genuine and if not in error, these too can indicate a date band when the article was made. This is particularly the case when the mark is not molded in but separately applied. For example Pullin[4] illustrates four trademarks used by Thos. Webb & Son. they were in use at different times i.e. 1889-1905, 1906-1935, 1936-1949 and 1950-1966. Unfortunately some of these bands are rather broad!

It is often said that glass production techniques have changed little over the past centuries, this is largely true well into post war years when automatic machine production has taken over. Notwithstanding this some significant changes have taken place and these can provide benchmarks for dating an article. However it must be born in mind that when one glasshouse developed a new technique it would not be universally adopted through out the industry. The inventors may well take out patents and it could be some considerable time before a rival developed an alternative that did not infringe the patent. Equally I can well imagine that the "not invented here" syndrome operated in the past just as, or even more effectively, than it does to day. There would be considerable opposition to changing practice just because the place down the road was now using some new newfangled gismo! So again I use caution when applying these benchmarks in time.

For dating purposes I have used the following changes in production techniques to act as benchmarks for the different periods. In some cases there appears to be disagreement between authorities on when the changes were introduced.

The Pontil Mark

The consensus of opinion seems to be that until the beginning of the nineteenth century, except in very high-class ware, the pontil mark was left ungrounded and the foot domed to lift the jagged edge clear of the surface upon which the piece would stand. As the 1800s got under way the fashion became one of grinding off the pontil. Although this is just outside my period of study, I have found no evidence to doubt the theory. However it is clear that in many cases the ungrounded pontil continued until the pontil itself was displaced by the gadget. I conclude that while the ungrounded pontil generally means the item dates up to the mid-1800 this alone should not be taken as a date benchmark. The ungrounded pontil only means the article was made before about 1890 or even 1900. *The absence of a pontil mark is more significant* as it indicates the earliest the article could have been made.

The Gadget

This is a device intended to replace the punty. During the finishing stages of a wine glass, or other item that has a foot, instead of holding it with a punty iron attached to the underside of its foot, it is held, again by the foot, with a metal clamp on the end of a pole' known as a "gadget." The practice reduced manufacture costs and removed the need to grind off the pontil mark. In the earlier days the gadget was liable to leave marks on the bulk of the foot, where the clamp held the glass. It could also leave marks on the underside of the center where the clamp part is attached to the pole.

According to Wills[5] the gadget started to make its appearance after about 1800. Wilkinson[6], suggests that the gadget appears about 1830. These claims are not supported by my observations and I get the impression that the gadget did not come into common use until around the 1870s. Hajdamach[7] shows an 1806 print of stages in blowing a goblet, there is no gadget amongst the tools. He goes on to state that a large number of patents were taken out for this type of equipment in the 1860s and illustrates one by Ed. Moore, which was not taken out until 1893. *Thus, for the purpose of dating glasses and other ware, I make the assumption that an article made using a gadget would not be earlier than 1870.*

As the gadget came into general use attempts would have been made to reduce its shortcomings, namely the marks, especially the disfiguring ones. This was achieved by using asbestos lining on the jaws of the gadget to provide a soft surface and so reduce or eliminate these impressions. Again not every glasshouse would adopt this practice simultaneously but *for the purpose of dating, I assume it came into general practice about 1890-1900.*

Making the Foot

I have had some difficulty in discovering just how the foot on a wine glass was formed at the beginning of the 19th. century. Most authors seem to gloss over the subject but I have concluded there were probably three basic procedures that I will describe in the following paragraphs. In discussion with other glass collectors I realize my terminology might not be universally accepted. I am mindful of what my science teacher told me many years ago, "*you can use any phrase or name you like so long as you define it*" So in describing the type of foot on wineglasses etc, I will define what I mean as follows.

The Hand-Shaped Foot

The first, I will call the shaped foot. Here, having formed the stem, a knob of glass would be attached to its end and then worked it into the shape of the foot using pucelas, a sort of long fingered tongs, in conjunction with a flat piece of wood. Inevitably this would give rise to a thicker, less delicate foot with a squared or thickly rounded edge where the excess metal had been cut away and the final shaping done. See photo 6. Further more, depending upon the skill of the glass worker, the foot may not be perfectly circular, see photo 7.

Photo 6. The edge view of the foot of a wine which has probably been hand shaped rather than blown or molded.

Photo 7. View of a hand shaped foot showing slight irregularity in its circumference.

Blown Foot.

An alternative is what I call the blown foot. In this case a gather would be blown into a spherical shape, attached to the stem, then opened out with the pucelas. Pellatt[8], 1849, describes this as the method of forming the foot on a wine glass. This process can usually be identified by three characteristics. The first is a mark on the flat part of the foot where the opening out process was started. This is often difficult to spot and despite my best efforts I have not managed to obtain a clear photograph. The second is the shape of the edge of the foot itself. Because the flat is being produced from a curved surface an element of this curvature is likely to survive the opening out process, consequently the edge it will be curved on the top and flat on the base and most wear is likely to be on this extremity, see photo (8). The third is the circular base itself. A blown foot which has been formed by opening out a globe may show slight deviations from being a precise circle where as a molded foot (see below), would be more exact. Both the shaped and blown foot were replaced by the introduction of the molded foot. Again it is difficult to tie down just when this took place. For the purpose of dating, *I assume that the molded foot was introduced from 1875.*

Photo 8. Edge of a blown foot showing how the top curves and the lower surface is flat thus forming a "sharp" edge.

Molded Foot

What I have chosen to call a molded foot was formed by squeezing the knob of glass on the end of the stem between two spring loaded pieces of wood which were slightly recessed. Hajdamach[9] reproduces a patent design by J.H.T. Richardson dated 1876 which consists of a base board with a recess to form the foot and a spring loaded top board which is half the width. Wilkinson[10] shows a slightly different design. In either case the principle is the same. The knob of glass on the end of the stem is first squeezed then the glass rotated to form the circular foot. This process would leave characteristic tell tales, which distinguish it from its predecessors. Firstly, although there would be striations on the glass where it had been turned these would be smooth, regular and there would be an absence of tool marks. Secondly, where a batch of identical glasses were produced, all the feet should be exactly the same size. Finally the edge of the foot will have a different shape. The point of maximum wear may be set in from the extreme edge, which will be symmetrically rounded, this is illustrated in photo 9. *For the purpose of dating, I assume all glasses with these characteristics will date after 1875.*

Photo 9. The curved edge of a molded foot.

Jug Handles

Another aid to dating is the shape of the handle on a jug or claret. The earlier versions were formed by first fixing the handle at the top of the jug then bending it over and finishing at the lower end. This inevitably left a bit sticking out which was either cut or ground off or finished "pump handle" style. Later the process was reversed, the handle first applied at the lower end then taken up, curled over and tucked under itself as it was fixed to the top part of the jug. These styles are illustrated in photo 10. Wilkinson[11] suggests that by 1830 the change from "pump handle" to the present day style had taken place. I do not consider this to be the case. Pellatt[12], 1849, illustrates how jug handles are formed and shows the "pump handle" form. Also there are many examples of jugs that date well after 1830 that are in the old style. For example Design Registration 96703 by Benjamin Richardson, Stourbridge in 1854. Molineaux Webb designs of the 1851 era also show the lower end finish handles[13].

Photo 10. Two clear glass jugs. Left: Early "pump handle" finish. Right: Later handle as we see them to-day.

Another way to mount the lower end of the handle was to have it in the shape of a claw These can be seen in Design Registrations of the late 1860s. i.e. Thos. Webb & Sons, No 212674, 1867. A Percival Vickers catalogue of cut glassware, dated July 1881[14] appears to show a mixture of handle styles. Furthermore a Whitefriars catalogue of 1957 shows a series of jugs whose handles had claws at the top and pump handles at their lower end! *For the purpose of dating, providing other factors are consistent, I assume the "pump handle" style was in use up to about 1880, the "claw handle," came in about 1865, and the "present day style" came in about 1870.*

Acid Polishing

The cutting of glass takes place in three stages, the first is the rough cut done on iron wheels fed with a trickle of water and sand, next a finer finishing cut which left a matt finish. This was then polished first using wooden wheels and pumice slurry, followed by a brush wheel and finally a wood or cork wheel and putty powder. Cut glass polished in this way has two characteristics, namely the edge of the cuts are sharp and striations are visible on the cut area indicating the rotation of the cutting/polishing wheels. At the end of the 19th century a process of polishing with acid started to replace hand polishing. Thos. Webb & Sons produced their "first large piece by acid polishing" in 1889 but the process probably did not come into more general use until the early 1900s. The processes involve standing the items to be polished in a bath of mixed hydrofluoric and sulfuric acids. This slowly dissolves the surface of the glass, not leaving a matt finish as it would if the sulfuric acid was not present, but giving a nice clear shiny surface. Because the acid is dissolving the glass it tends to remove the cutting wheel striations and dulls the sharpness of the cuts. Initially the polishing time was carefully controlled to minimize this effect but in later years the glasses are treated in batches with set times and the effect of acid polishing is easy to see as it diminishes the quality of the cut. It is a process ideally suited to lead glass, I understand the barium glass is more difficult to polish in this way. As an aid to dating I make the following assumptions:

Where there is no evidence whatsoever of acid polishing, that is, the *striations are relatively deep and clear and the edges are sharp, the item is likely to be pre-1900.*

Where the *striation marks are non-existent and the edges of the cut are substantially rounded, the item will probably be post-1945.*

Sandblasting

This was introduced as a quick and cheap method of putting a decoration or inscription on glass and can be recognized by the coarse granular effect that is very different to the fine etching achieved by hydrofluoric acid.

However in later years the techniques have so improved that it has replaced acid etching. Photo 11 shows an early example of sandblasting and it is interesting to note that the tumbler is dated 1886 and has the inscription *"Sandblast Patent." For the purpose of dating, I assume that any item decorated by sandblasting will be post 1880.*

Photo11. An early sand blast pattern on a cheap tumbler. The date reads 1886 and the underside has an inscription "Sandblast Patent".

Pressed Glass

The production of hollow pressed glass got under way in the U.S.A. in the late 1820s but its development in the UK was probably retarded by the glass tax that was based on the weight of glass produced by the glasshouse. Only after this was lifted in 1845 was the English pressed glass industry able to make substantial progress. Pellatt[15] writing in 1849 is skeptical about the quality but refers to fire polishing as improving the finish, "Hence," he says, "it is now chiefly used for common or cheap articles." Initially only lead glass was used in pressed glass production but in 1864 William Leighton, an American glass maker discovered a mix using soda and lime. Slack[16] quotes from an article written in 1888 which refers to Sowerby's earlier metal saying many years ago, (which could mean almost anything), the Ellison Works, (Sowerby), introduced a cheaper metal than the hitherto full leaded mix, "in which there was only a small proportion of lead." The source of the writers intelligence is not known but if Sowerby and others were using a low lead metal then, judging from my density measurements, it would have been very low, less than 4% Pb. I do wonder if there is any lead at all, perhaps it was a story put around to mislead the opposition! I do not know when this started but I suspect it was about the same time as Leighton new mix. *For the purpose of assessing age, I assume that any pressed glass with a low density, i.e. less than 2.6-gr/ cc was made after 1865.* It should be noted that some pressed manufacturers continued to use lead glass well after that date.

Polishing Pressed Glass

Pressed glass did not need polishing in the sense that cut glass was polished. However the high pressure used in the molding process forced metal into the joins on the mould thus leaving a sharp tell tale over the length of the article. This was removed, or at least reduced to acceptable level, by "fire polishing." The article was taken back to the furnace and re-heated enough to remove these fins. To do this it had to be held on a pontil, (thereby leaving a pontil mark which was sometimes disguised), or held in a clamp like the gadget used for wine glasses. Lattimore[17], suggests this change came about in 1850, this is earlier than the date I put on the gadget but perhaps the gadget developed from the press-molded industries techniques. I do not know and it is not crucial to my study of uranium glass. *I therefore compromise and, for the purposes of dating, assume that a pressed glass article, which has been fire, polished without the use of a pontil post dates 1860.*

The process of fire polishing has another effect, which becomes apparent on the larger objects such as tazzas. As they are re-heated, on the end of the pontil or clip, they are rotated to stop them sagging and also ensure the heating is even. This can cause the object to twist and it is quite common to see fire-polished tazzas with slightly twisted stems. The process of fire polishing was phased out in the twentieth century, but I am not sure when. From observation of articles which have been dated by other means, and which have clearly been fire polished, I would think this phasing out came about around 1910 - 1920. However I am told that Bagley (Yorkshire), were still fire polishing pressed glass articles in the 1930s. *For the purpose of dating, I assume that a pressed article which has been fire-polished will not be later than 1930, and one which has not been fire polished will not be earlier than 1915.*

There is another aid to dating although it has nothing to do with glass techniques. Items such as salts, small bowls, tea and biscuit barrels, epergnes, etc are sometimes associated with silver or silver plate. It is well known that British silver is Hallmarked, indicating who made it, and where and when it was assayed. The interpretation of these Hallmarks is well published and available in most books on silverware. What is not generally appreciated is that silver plate may also be marked, not only with the well-known " E P N S" but also with the symbol of the firm that manufactured the silver plate. Unfortunately this has not been widely researched but E. R. Matheau-Raven has published a book on the identification of Sheffield Plate, which also covers a few Birmingham firms as well. The full reference is included in the Bibliography.

Whatever criteria are used for dating it is clear that there is always a degree of uncertainty. As with attribution it is desirable to appreciate just what is the likely margin of error. Dating is more complicated than attribution because periods rather than single dates are involved. It is quite possible that with a hand made item it was a "one off," or that it was only made over a very short time period. On the other hand, particularly with press-molded glass, it could have been made over a very extended period, perhaps as long as 50 years. In an attempt to be clear on what I mean when I have given dates I have adopted the following convention.

Where the article has a *Design Registration Number, or is identified in a catalogue/advert/pattern book,* then, in the absence of strong modifying information, *I quote the date of the source without qualification, irrespective of the period that I think it could have been in production.* It is in effect the earliest likely date.
Where the term ***about*** is used, it implies I consider the quoted date is the most probable, but could be + *or - 10 years.*

Where the term ***period*** is used, it implies I consider the quoted date the most probable, but it could be within a slot *of + or - 20 years.*
Theses ranges also imply that the item, or similar, could have been in production over a period of time.

The allotted date slot is done on the basis that I consider there is an 98% chance , i.e. 49 times out of 50, that it will be correct. However in some instances I do not have that degree of confidence in my opinion and I have therefore further qualified it using the terms, *probability, could be* or *best guess*. The same inference should be placed upon them as for Attributions.

[1]Angus-Butterworth L M - British Table and Ornamental Glass, fig 118
[2]Dodsworth R - British Glass Between the Wars, p53 -55.
[3]Hajdamach C - British Glass, p391 - 411.
[4]Pullin A G - Glass Signatures, Trademarks and Trade Names.
[5]Wills G - Antique Glass.
[6]Wilkinson R - Hallmarks of Antique Glass.
[7]Hajdamach C - British Glass. p34-36.
[8]Pellatt A - Curiosities of Glass Making p84-85
[9]Hajdamach C - British Glass p 33. Wilkinson, Hallmarks of Antique Glass, p 23.
[10]Wilkinson R - Hallmarks of Antique Glass, p 23.
[11]Wilkinson R - Hallmarks of Antique Glass, p 21.
[12]Pellatt A - Curiosities of Glass Making, p98.
[13]Molineaux Webb Catalogue in Manchester City Art Galleries.
[14]Percival Vickers & Co, Catalogue July 1881 p14 - 18
[15]Pellatt A - Curiosities of Glass Making. p31
[16]Slack R - English Pressed Glass. p 47
[17]Lattimore C - English 19th. Cent. Press-Molded Glass. p 21.

Section 2
Glasshouses and Their Uranium-bearing Products

Introduction
Items with Attributions

From my initial foray into the field of uranium glass it soon became apparent that the use of this element was not a rare and unusual event but was a relatively common practice on an international scale. I therefore decided to concentrate my study mainly upon English glass if for no other reason that it was easier for me to research. Never the less, I have, from time to time, added non British pieces to my collection, some I have been able to attribute, the majority I have not.

This section will describe those items that I have been able to assign a likely origin. The majority is English and I will give preambles to glasshouses from which they came. The others were really beyond the scope of my work but I include them giving what information I have.

Chapter 9

A Brief Outline of English Glasshouses During the Uranium Period.

The rise and decline of the glass industry in the United Kingdom is complex and largely lost in history. One of the major milestones was the development of leaded glass crystal, in 1673, by George Ravenscroft. Although others may have experimented with the use of lead in their mixes he is generally credited with being the Father of lead crystal. His first examples were prone to crizzling, i.e. the glass proved to be unstable, but by the end of the 1670s Ravenscroft's product were much improved and did not visibly deteriorate. These products were marked with a Raven's Head. They were produced at Henley on Thames, what to day I would loosely refer to as "the London area." It was not long before other London glass producers were making lead based crystal and by the start of the eighteenth century this type of glass was being made at many different sites around the Country. In the ensuing centuries it was to be a major influence on the type of glass produced in England for this high quality crystal became synonymous with English Glass. Eventually leaded glass became the specialty of the Midlands, though the reason for this is not clear. In particular Stourbridge with its high quality crystal, by the mid nineteenth century, was arguably the center of glass production in the England. Today lead crystal is still made there but the quantity is greatly reduced and the number of firms has waned to but a few. The quality of English crystal was due to the high lead content, usually greater than 33% wt Pb. It had the edge over the cheaper products which mainly originated from the Continent, and which had only about 25% Pb wt. Cut glass can and was made with metal which contains little or no lead but it lacks the quality and sparkle of its leaded counterpart and has no place in the English Midlands

In addition to the commitment to crystal, as we shall see in the following chapters, from the mid 1800s to the mid 1900s this area also produced colored decorative glass which also used a high lead mixture when it was probably unnecessary. Indeed, as far as uranium colors were concerned, it must have placed them at a disadvantage as the presence of lead appears to reduce the fluorescence in uv light. It also tends to darken the clear yellows and I find few examples of Midland glass that can match the brilliant, lively yellows from the North and the Continent.

Another major influence on the British glass industry was the introduction of the Tax in 1745. This was doubled in 1776. It operated on the basis of weight of raw material used and would clearly penalize the backbone of the British industry that worked with leaded glass. In retrospect I can see the stupidity of this tax. From 1780, Ireland was given an exemption and this put the mainland at a disadvantage and exacerbated the burden placed on the English producers when trying to compete with foreign products. One can not but help feel that if the Government of the day had deliberately set out to diminish English glass production it could hardly have done a better job. The tax was not repealed until 1845, which meant that for a critical 100 years the growth of English glass was stunted.

The development of pressed glass, generally agreed to have originated in the USA, in the earlier part of the nineteenth century was to play a major role in English glass in the following hundred and fifty years. It seems that although Apsley Pellatt may have experimented with press molding glass in the early 1830s (he registered a patent in 1831), it was probably not until the 1840s that pressed glass production became significant in the UK. Midland producers such as Rice Harris and Lancashire glasshouses such as Molineaux Webb were probably first to develop it commercially. Both these areas appear to have been obsessed with the use of leaded glass that was unnecessarily expensive. It should be remembered that the raison d'être for pressed glass was to reach the mass market and as such it needed to be cheap. To make it from unnecessarily expensive metal at least partly defeated this objective. When the northern glasshouses on Tyneside deployed a metal which could be pressed and which was lower or even free of lead the Midlands and Lancashire producers do not seem to have followed suit. Consequently their products, although slightly superior in quality, must have been considerably more costly. This probably explains why, by the turn of the nineteenth century the Lancashire firms were going out of business and the Midlands were not pressing glass.

Measurements of the density of glass, which I have already quoted, seem to indicate that the Lancashire houses eventually caught on to the idea but by then it was too late. As a result Tyneside and Yorkshire came to dominate the English pressed glass industry in the twentieth century Indeed the only major producer of domestic pressed glass ware in England to-day is the Corning Glassworks in Sunderland, which was formerly Jobling. As my interest centers on the use of uranium I will pick up the threads at the beginning of the 1800s and continue to post World War Two years.

Throughout this period there were numerous glass houses operating in the United Kingdom, even as late as 1948, Kelly's Directory lists some 50 manufacturers of glass. On the other hand if the question is asked of a collector "how many glasshouses were there in the UK during the first half of the twentieth century" the likely answer would probably be less than a score. The reason is that many have faded into obscurity or have not caught the eye of the collector / researcher. Only a few have become "household names." Because of this there is a tendency when attributing unmarked items to think they must be from one of these, especially if there are some common characteristics. Although the "household names" were prolific producers of glass items, and therefore the probabilities weigh in their favor, the possibility of other birthplaces must always be borne in mind.

There is still much work to be done to identify the lesser known and to determine more of the history of those who reached the degree of greatness for their products to be desired by current day collectors. This is not my area of research, my concern being primarily with the use of uranium to color glass. My study period is restricted to the nineteenth and twentieth centuries. In many cases I am able to make attributions to specific firms but where this is not possible, then to geographic areas. This should not be taken to imply that the product must have come from one of the known firms but I am not able to identify which one. It may also have come from one of the glasshouses that have now faded from our sight.

We must also bear in mind that it was not just the quality or quantity of the glass items produced that has caused the producer to be remembered. Perhaps the principle reasons items are "collectable" to day, is because they are identifiable and the history of the glasshouse has been researched. Both these require that some records are available to the collector / researcher. These include pattern books, design and patent registrations, advertisements and articles in such journals as The Pottery and Glass Trades Gazette. It is these factors more than the quality of the product, which has given them a place in history.

For the period of our study, as far as English glass is concerned, I will group the glass producers into the following areas:

- North East England, Tyneside and Yorkshire, with pressed glass
- The Midlands, including Stourbridge, with leaded glass
- Lancashire, with both leaded and non-leaded glass, with press molding and traditional blowing
- London, with both leaded and non-leaded glass

Bristol will not feature in our story, for although there had been much activity in that area with sites such as Nailsea, they were very much in the decline by the 1800s and I have no evidence concerning the use of uranium in that area.

Chapter 10

Glass from the North East of England

Much has already been written about this area. It is renowned for the production of pressed glass in the latter part of the nineteenth century and the first half of the twentieth[1,2,3,4,5]. Although pressed glass was produced in other parts of England, as far as the North East is concerned the glasshouses generally centered on Tyneside. Not withstanding in this grouping I am also going to include *Bagley & Co.*, otherwise known as the *Crystal Glass Company* of Knottingly, Yorkshire. Their products in the twentieth century shadowed those of Tyneside. The companies, which I have identified as using uranium in this area, are, Bagley, Davidson, Ed Moore, Greener/Jobling and Sowerby. When describing their products I will give a brief outline of their history. This does not mean that others did not use uranium but rather I have not found any identifiable examples. I have made density measurement on a limited number of non-uranium products from Matthew Turnbull, Thomas Gray, and Heppell, see under Section 1 Chapter 6. As already pointed out, the moulds of Thomas Gray and Heppell were purchased by Davidson in about 1884 so I cannot be sure that the specimens I have assessed were in fact made by the firms whose marks they show

[1] Slack R - English Pressed Glass.

[2] Thompson J - Identification of English Pressed Glass.

[3] Lattimore C - English 19th Century Press Molded Glass.

[4] Murray S - The Peacock and the Lions.

[5] Angus-Butterworth L M - British Table and Ornamental Glass.

Chapter 11
Bagley & Co., Yorkshire

Background

Perhaps one of the more prolific manufactures of British pressed glass that has escaped the attention of the collector is *The Crystal Glass Company*, of Knottingly, Yorks., more casually known as *Bagley*.

There appears to be some confusion over just when the business started. Angus-Butterworth[1] claims it originated with James Bagley sometime after he had completed his apprenticeship with the Leeds glassmakers, of Bower Smith & Co. in 1834. On the other hand a note produced by Rockware Glass in 1990 says the business was established in 1871 by John William Bagley and William Bagley, who was no relation and John Wild. They were practical glassmakers, and with others and traded as J W Bagley & Co. It became a private limited company in 1898, (Bagley & Co. Ltd.) making bottles.

At first their glass was melted in fireclay pots but later they introduced a continuous process and coupled it to a glass bottle making machine. Until the end of the 19th century all bottles were hand made, but a postmaster, Josiah Arnall in Ferrybridge, a village close to Knottingly, conceived the idea of a machine. This was developed by H M Ashley an engineer. The patent rights were bought by Bagley & Co Ltd., in 1899. A few years later these were superseded by the American Owens machine.

About 1912 Bagley diversified and started producing pressed glassware, particularly items used in the home. These amounted to a wide range of goods, including jugs, bowls, sundaes, butters, tazzas, salts, plates, dishes, tumblers, boudoir sets, ashtrays etc. etc. The Pontefract Museum has a good selection of Bagley glass as well as copies of some surviving catalogues from the 1920s and 1930s. It is interesting to note that these trade as "The Crystal Glass Company," (formed in 1913), Proprietors Bagley & Co. Ltd. During WW2 their production was directed towards the war effort with glass production aimed at satisfying the need for beer glass in the NAAFI.! After the war they returned to their normal production of decorative and domestic ware. The Company was taken over and became part of the Jackson Group in 1962 The new organization trading as White Rose Glass. Thirteen years later they were taken over by Rockware and shortly after production of their domestic and decorative ware came to an end. It is said that Rockware is now the largest British bottle producer and that a year's production would go round the world nearly four times.

It is not always easy to identify their products as the company was not shy about imitating the style of competitors, although they might have taken the view that it was their designs that were cribbed. In the case of unmarked items care has to be taken to distinguish between Bagley, Davidson and some Jobling products.

I have not been able to ascertain when Bagley first started using uranium to color glass, or to what extent it was used. I could speculate that it may have been when the Company took on a Chilean by the name of Branscombe who was a glass-coloring expert. The view has been expressed that that the use of uranium ceased after 1945 when the Government officials paid them a visit and took their entire stock, some 3 or 4 tons[2] . Notwithstanding I have found uranium-containing items with a Design Registration Number that dated 1950. It therefore seems likely that uranium was used after WW2, probably up to the 1960s.

All the samples illustrated are green. I have tested a large number of Bagley items with a Geiger counter and have only found the green shades to contain uranium. This does not mean that Bagley never used uranium in any other color but it would seem to indicate that if they did it was an uncommon practice. If a non-green piece of glass does contain uranium the odds would appear to be against it being from the Bagley factory.

A total of 14 examples of green Bagley glass have been examined. The average density is 2.49 g/cc with a range of 2.47 - 2.51 g/cc. with standard deviation of 0.013. This compares with the clear glass, average of 2.47 g/cc and range 2.45 - 2.48 g\cc. The uranium content averages 1.2 % wt, with a range 0.6% - 2% wt.

[1]Angus-Butterworth L M - British Table and Ornamental Glass, p 80 - 81.

[2]Dearden C P - Private Communication.

Photo 12 Trinket set, tray 30.5 cm x 17.75 cm, bowl 11.5 cm square, candlestick 11.5 cm wide x 12 cm high. Bowl marked "Made in England". Pattern No 3078. Date 1930-50. Value $35-50.

Photo 13 Large vase, 21 cm high, density 2.51 g/cc, uranium 0.12% wt. These are made in different sizes and may be clear or satin finished. Some have an insert for spacing flowers. They should not be confused with a similar design by Jobling. Date 1930-50. Value $20-35.

Photo 14. Right, flower trough, 15 cm wide, density 2.51 g/cc, uranium 0.08% wt. Bagley made a range of flower trough shapes from circular, diamond, straight, heart, semi-circle, curved and horseshoe. The one illustrated is *almost certainly* Bagley's and bears the marks, "Made in England" and "Patent Applied For". Date 1930-50. Value $5-15. Left, Ashtray, heart shaped, 8 cm wide, density 2.48g/cc, uranium 0.12% wt. One of set of "playing card" ashtrays, the others being club, diamond and spade shape. Not to be confused with Davidson who also produced a "playing card" set of ashtrays, however theirs did not have recessed cigarette rests. Date 1930-50. Value $10-15.

Photo 15. Biscuit Barrel, size 12.75 cm diameter. Density 2.49g/cc, uranium 0.09% wt. Unmarked but illustrated in an undated Bagley catalogue. Also similar to Bagley Design Reg. No. 849118. Date 1930-50. Value $20-30.

Photo 16. Leaf Dish, "Cocktail Time", size 23 cm x 22 cm.. Density 2.50g/cc, uranium 0.08% wt. Unmarked, but illustrated in "White Rose" catalogue 3055 and an earlier 1938 catalogue. Date *about* 1950. Value $30-35.

Chapter 12
Davidson's of Gateshead

The firm that I loosely and affectionately call "Davidsons" started from small beginnings in 1867 and became one of the major producers of pressed glass in the United Kingdom supplying not only local needs but also markets throughout the world. Its history and products have been well covered elsewhere[1,2,3,4]. It is not my intention to repeat the story here other than to provide a short synopses. My concern is with the use of uranium and this element certainly features dominantly in the products of George Davidson & Co. It is arguable that it played a major part in the Company's success.

George Davidson, born in 1822, was not a glass man. In fact it is likely he knew very little about glass manufacture when he decided to set up a glass factory in the Teams district of Gateshead on Tyneside in 1867. He had seen the need for the production of paraffin lamp glass chimneys, which were then being imported from the Continent. It is said that once established, production diversified into wine glasses and bottles which, in the absence of any information to the contrary, I presume were hand made. Unfortunately I have not seen any proven examples of this early work. In the 1870s Davidson entered into pressed glass production, four designs were registered in the two years 1877-8, which perhaps indicates the start of this method of production in the business.

When the founding George Davidson died in 1891 control of the business went to his son Thomas. He further developed pressed glass production to the exclusion of other products and introduced new designs. It was during this period that the famous Pearline glass was launched, see photos 17 - 34. The name came from the creamy white edging effect looking like a string of pearls. It was a great success and played no small part in the commercial viability of the Company. Of this, the Primrose (uranium) color was particularly popular. Pearline was a patented process that used a mix doped with just under 4% of arsenic. When an item made from this mix was reheated at a glory hole it turned to a milky color. In pearline production only part of the article was re-heated, usually the rim. It was also made in clear and blue glass. The Pearline patent was officially accepted in December 1889 but Davidson had advertised his new line as early as June of that year. Although patented, the process style was copied by others. It is claimed that the Burtles Tate & Co. "Topaz Opalescent" was, de facto, a copy. Greener also appears to have cribbed the idea see Chapter 14 photo 48. Both the density and uranium content of this jug are indistinguishable from a genuine Primrose Pearline. I have not had opportunity to subject it to gamma spectrometry.

From about this time, if not earlier, Davidsons also used uranium to produce a similar color but without the pearline effect, photos 35 - 38. They do not appear to have given it a specific name and perhaps it was a minor line. In the catalogues that I have seen, i.e. 1912 - 1940 I have not come across the color being described although greens, ambers and reds are mentioned. It seems that the Primrose Pearline was phased out of production in the second decade of the twentieth century. I have not found any Primrose Pearline in Registered designs after 1903, although I have found two other examples of the uranium yellow in designs registered as late as 1920 & 1923.

Many examples of Davidson's green glass, including all that on display at the Shipley Art Gallery "Davidson' s Glass, From Gateshead to the World" Exhibition of 1993, have been examined. Only two items, similar to photos 38 & 39, were found which gave significant Geiger counter readings, They also responded to both ultraviolet lights. It is difficult to understand why, when Davidson made so much green glass, only a very few items of this color contained uranium. Perhaps it was an experimental run in the 1920s or, it is just possible that these items were made, after the Company had ceased production, by another glasshouse that had acquired the moulds.

Thomas Davidson died at the age of 59 in 1937 and control of the Company passed to Claude L Fraser, the grandson of the founder. The Company was taken over by Brama in 1955.

While a modest number of designs have been registered, Davidson only used a trademark for a limited period from 1881 - 1890. It consisted of a demi-lion emerging from a mural crown. I have seen a lot of plain glass that bears this mark but I have not found any Primrose Pearline or other uranium glass carrying their trademark. This leads me to suspect that Davidson may not have used uranium before the late 1880s.

In addition to making their own moulds Davidsons

acquired moulds from other glass producers. These included those of Neville Glassworks in 1880 and Heppell in 1884. I have not found any items from these moulds containing uranium glass.

It is difficult to date Davidson's glass, especially in the period between the turn of the century and the start of WW2. This is because many of their designs were in production throughout this period. For example a cucumber dish, and the set of playing card ashtrays both appear in a 1912 and 1940 catalogue.

Their most collectable product is the Pearline and of this, arguably, the primrose is the most popular. The characteristics of 56 examples, which I consider to be in the highest two of my attribution confidence limits, have been examined. Their average density is 2.53 g/cc with a range of 2.49 g/cc to 2.57g/cc. and a standard deviation of 0.014. It is interesting to compare this with the density of the clear glass. The range is almost identical but the average has increased by 0.06g/cc. This may not be due only to the presence of uranium but to other elements in the mix, introduced to give the pearline effect. When I plotted density against the uranium content for these items there was some correlation. It suggested that 1% uranium increased the density by 0.07 g/cc. in this metal. This figure is much higher than I would expect and I think it likely that the increase in density is due to factors other than the presence of uranium.

Within these samples there is a considerable range in depth of color and uranium content. The latter varying from 0.22% to 1.36% by wt. This is well out side any error limits or reasonable random variation at the factory. The palest primrose only has 0.22 - 0.28% wt. U, then there appears to be a jump to 0.5% wt. U, which steadily increases to 1.36% wt. U. I cannot establish any explanation for this but only speculate. It could be that after the product was first introduced the uranium content was gradually reduced to save cost. This seems unlikely as a plot of uranium content against estimated date shows no correlation. Further more it does not account for the step change. My best guess at an explanation is that Davidson's deliberately made a pale and a deep primrose pearline and sold them side-by-side.

I have also examined nine examples of Davidson' s yellow glass which are not pearline and were probably made between 1910 and 1920. Their uranium content is about 0.66% wt. U with a range of 0.62% - 0.74% wt. U, and a standard deviation of 0.05. They have an average density of 2.49 g/cc with a range of 2.47 - 2.5 g/cc. and a standard deviation of 0.005. Compare this with the average of 2.47 g/cc, which I obtained for clear glass. It would appear to indicate that 0.66% uranium increases the density of the metal by 0.02 g/cc. which is very close to what would be expected on a straight proportional basis, (i.e. 0.016 g/cc). I have only measured the density of three pieces of Blue Pearline their average being 2.50 g/cc. This would appear to confirm that the Pearline formula increased to density of the metal by about 0.03 g/cc and uranium by 0.03 g/cc for each 1% of uranium.

In addition to green, a number of examples of Davidson's blue, pink, and purple glass have been checked but none showed any sign of bearing uranium. I think it highly probable that, with the exception of a few green items, Davidson used uranium only in their yellow (primrose) metal. This has always responded strongly to both short and long uv light.

[1]Lattimore C - English 19th Century Pressed Glass, pp 59 - 73.
[2]Slack R - English Pressed Glass, pp 66 - 85.
[3]Angus-Butterworth L M - British Table & Ornamental Glass, pp 71 - 74.
[4]Murray S - The Peacock and The Lions, pp 61 - 68.

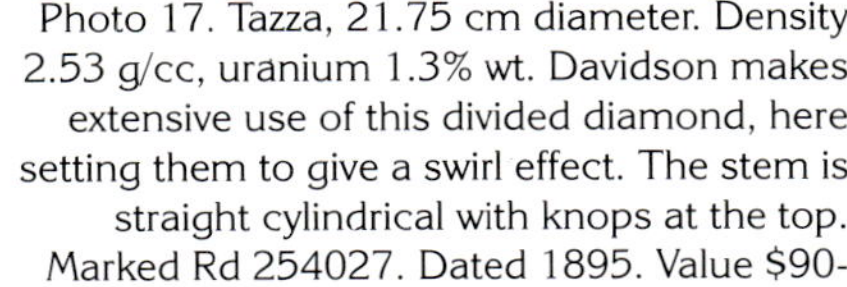

Photo 17. Tazza, 21.75 cm diameter. Density 2.53 g/cc, uranium 1.3% wt. Davidson makes extensive use of this divided diamond, here setting them to give a swirl effect. The stem is straight cylindrical with knops at the top. Marked Rd 254027. Dated 1895. Value $90-115.

Photo 18. Tazza, 21 cm diameter. Density 2.54 g/cc, uranium 0.99% wt. Marked Rd 285342. Davidson again uses a divided diamond but this time the shape is broken into nine equal pieces, almost like dots. Date 1896. Value $90-115.

Photo 19. Right, 8 cm high. Density 2.53 g/cc, uranium 1.05% wt. Rd 285342 .Date 1896. Value $35-50.
Center, Jug, 9.5 cm high. Density 2.53g/cc, uranium 0.25% wt. Not marked but pattern identical with Design Reg. 413701. This one of the "pale" primrose pieces. Date *about* 1910. The design has the heart shape together with the much-used divided diamond. Value $30-45.
Left, Jug 7.5 cm high. Density 2.52 g/cc, uranium 0.62% wt. Advertised in Pottery Gazette, 1. 4. 1893. Value $35-50.

Photo 20. Jug, 12 cm high. Density 2.56 g/cc, uranium 1.12% wt. Rd 32012? (the last letter of the Rd mark is not clear but this is clearly Davidson). Date 1898. Value $35-50.

Photo 21, Star dishes. Right, four points, 13 cm wide. Density 2.54 g/cc, uranium 0.87% wt. Rd 212864. Date 1893. Value $45-60.
Left, three points, 11.5 cm wide. Three point star dish. Density 2.52 g/cc, uranium 0.74% wt. Rd 212684. Date 1893. Value $45-60.

Photo 22. Boat dish, 19.5 cm long. Density 2.53 g/cc, uranium 0.68% wt. Rd 212684 Date 1893. This has the same registered design as the items in Photo 21, and provides a good illustration of Davidson's ability to take one shape and keep modifying it. Value $70-110.

Photo 23. Two troughs with handles. Right, length 15 cm. Density 2.5 g/cc, uranium 0.22% wt. Marked Rd 176566, this incorporates the Davidson daisy button pattern. Date 1891. Value $35-50.
Left, length 15.5 cm. Density 2.54 g/cc, uranium 0.93% wt. Marked Rd.217752. A good illustration of the divided diamond used alongside a solid diamond. An example of the "deeper" Primrose. Dated 1893. Value $45-65.c

Photo 24. Right, small tumbler, 7.5 cm high. Density 2.56 g/cc, uranium 1.24% wt. Not marked but *almost certainly* Davidson. Date about 1900. Value $20-35.
Center, Small handled basket, 10.75 cm long. Density 2.54 g/cc, uranium 0.81% wt. Design shown in Pottery Gazette 1. 9. 1891. Value $35-50.
Left, Salt, 7 cm diameter. Density 2.53 g/cc, uranium 0.93% wt. Rd 176566. Date 1891. Value $20-35.

Photo 25. Right, I guess this is a spill holder but it could also serve for toothpicks, as a posy vase or even a salt. Height 8.5 cm, density 2.55 g/cc, uranium 0.62% wt. Shown in Pottery Gazette April 1893. Value $45-60.
Left, ornamental basket, 8.75 cm high, density 2.52 g/cc, uranium 0.56% wt. Not marked but attributed as Davidson by reference to Pottery Gazette illustration 1.4 1893. Although press molded this piece, as with many other Davidson's items, had to be worked after removing from the mould. During this time it was probably held on a pontil, the mark subsequently being camouflaged by impressing with concentric circles. $35-60.

Photo 26. Butter dish with lid. 14.5 cm diameter. Density 2.52 g/cc, uranium 1.49% wt. Marked Rd 285342. Date 1896. Value $70-110.

Photo 27. Dish, 20.5 cm wide. Density 2.55 g/cc, uranium 1.12% wt. Rd No 237038. I have seen this pattern on jugs and tumblers. It should not be confused with Greener who also used interlocking circles but in their case they were rugby ball shaped and the circumference filled with dots rather than lines. Date 1894. Value $70-110.

Photo 28. Dish, 21.75 cm square. Density 2.55 g/cc, uranium 1.18% wt. Marked Rd 254027. Here the divided diamond is used in conjunction with a shell at the corners. Davidson "deep" primrose. Dated 1895. Value $70-110.

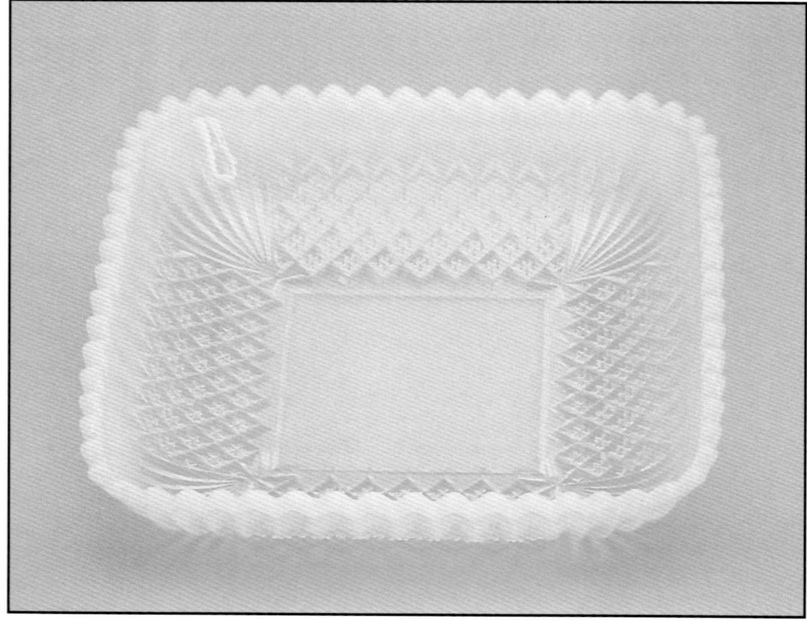

Photo 29. Dish 16.5 cm diameter. Density 2.54 g/cc, uranium 0.62% wt. Rd No 176566. Date 1891. Value $60-90.

Photo 30. One of a pair of rather battered knife rests. Length 7.5 cm, density 2.54 g/cc, uranium 1.12% wt. The pattern is a multiple divided diamond such as we have seen in Photos 17 & 28 but much smaller. Davidson was not the only glasshouse to use the divided diamond pattern, for example Molineaux Webb Registered Design No 352198 in 1900. Notwithstanding I consider this *almost certainly* Davidson, *about* 1890. Value, in good condition, $35-50 for a pair.

Photo 31. Epergne trumpet, 9 cm diameter. Density 2.54 g/cc, uranium 0.99% wt. It is unmarked. I have not seen anything like this shape attributed to Davidson and the pattern only has limited resemblance. It also lacks the wear I would reasonably associate with a piece of the Primrose Pearline era. *Could be* Davidson *about* 1910. Value $20-30.

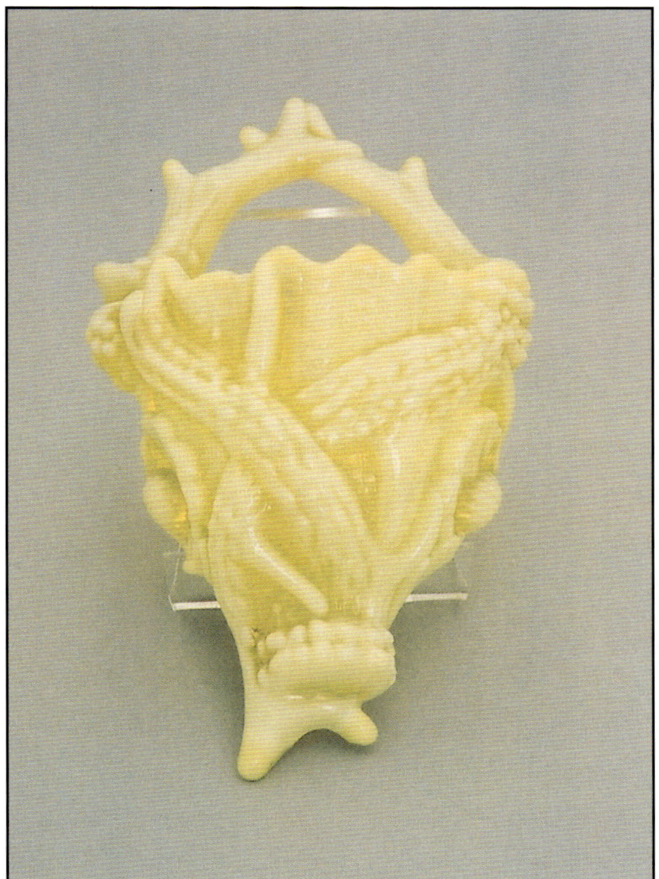

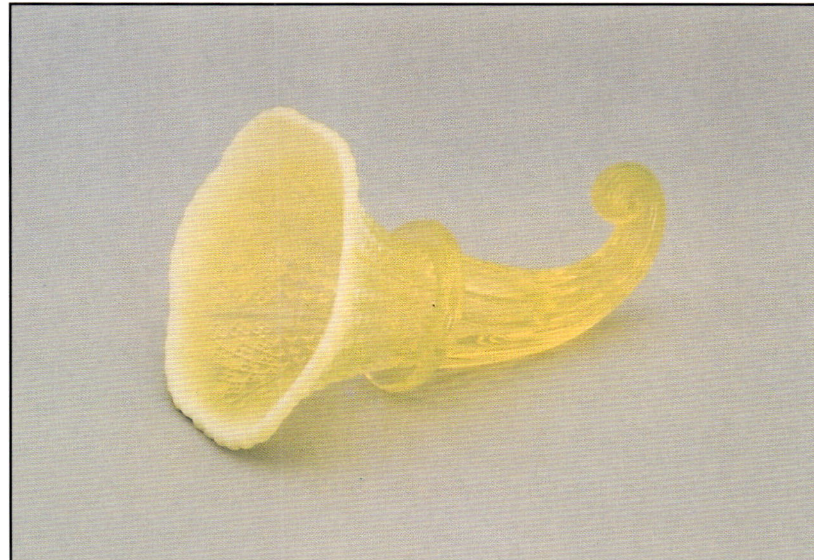

Photo 32. Wall vase, 18 cm tall. Density 2.55 g/cc, uranium 1.18% wt. This item is not marked and is not a pattern that has been known to be associated with Davidson. I have seen this type of basket in blue, similar to the Davidson blue pearline but not in any color I would not associate with Davidson. Finally its gamma ray spectrum did agree with that I would have expected from Primrose Pearline. *Probably* Davidson's Pearline *about* 1890. Value $35-60.

Photo 33. Tazza, diameter 15 cm. Density 2.49 g/cc, uranium 0.22% wt. Unmarked but pattern same as Rd 413701. This is a curious piece of Davidson's. The platform is too small for the size of the tazza and has no lip. Furthermore the edge appears to have been cut and fire polished which probably accounts for the slightly milky effect. I can only surmise that this piece must have failed after removal from the mould and a frigger rescued it. Its density is on the low end of the pearline range so perhaps it was made from a batch of metal which was on the limit of its specification or perhaps it was non-pearline. Value $35-70.

Photo 34. Right, a very pale pearline bowl, or was it used as a salt? *Almost certainly* Davidson' s although not marked with an "Rd", the pattern closely resembles other pearline examples. Diameter of bowl 7.5 cm, density 2.52 g/cc, uranium 0.26% wt. Marked on the base with concentric rings. Date *about* 1900. Value $20-35. Left, The same basic molding as the right piece but with no pearline effect. Diameter 9.5 cm, density 2.5 g/cc, uranium 0.62% wt. Could this be a piece of pearline that did not get re-fired, or was it intended as non pearline primrose? As other collectors have reported finding similar examples probably the latter. Date *about* 1910. Value $20-35.

Photo 35, celery, 17.5 cm high. Density 2.5 g/cc, uranium 0.62% wt. virtually identical to illustration in 1928 catalogue. *Almost certainly* Davidson *about* 1920. Value $30-45.

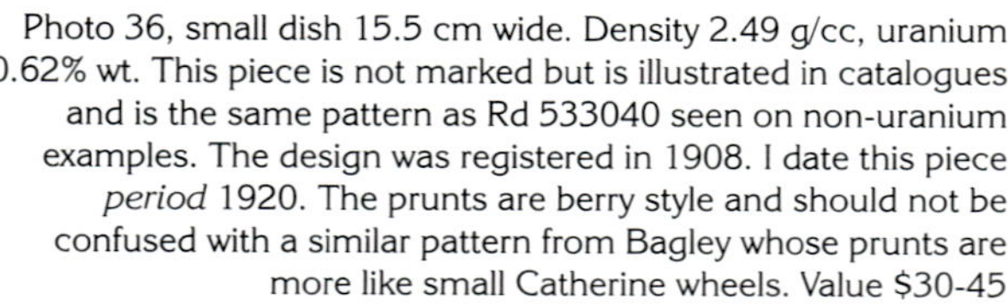

Photo 36, small dish 15.5 cm wide. Density 2.49 g/cc, uranium 0.62% wt. This piece is not marked but is illustrated in catalogues and is the same pattern as Rd 533040 seen on non-uranium examples. The design was registered in 1908. I date this piece *period* 1920. The prunts are berry style and should not be confused with a similar pattern from Bagley whose prunts are more like small Catherine wheels. Value $30-45

Photo 37, grapefruit or sweet dish, 12.5 cm diameter. Density 2.49 g/cc, uranium 0.74% wt. Marked Rd 695113. A range of products was made using this pattern, including plates, and bowls. Date 1923. Value $15-20.

Photo 38. Right, grapefruit or sweet dish with its own saucer underneath. Diameter of dish 12.5 cm., density 2.49 g/cc, uranium 0.74% wt. Marked Rd 695113. A range of products was made using this pattern, including plates, and bowls. Date 1923. Value $20-35.
Left, Another dish with the same pattern but, unusually for Davidson, in pale green metal. I do wonder if it was in fact made by that firm or whether it is from someone else who acquired their molds. If so it would be much later, *about* 1960. Density 2.48 g/cc, uranium 0.03% wt. Value $10-15.

Photo 39. Here there are two similar piano insulators of slightly different size. They would have been placed under the castors on pianos or other heavy furniture to prevent them cutting into the carpet. The pattern is illustrated in a 1928 catalogue. Right, 9.5 cm diameter, density 2.44 g/cc, uranium 0.25% wt. Value $10-15. Left, 9 cm diameter, density 2.47 g/cc, uranium 0.11% wt. Value $10-15. I have no doubt that Davidson did make the yellow insulator but again I have doubts about the green.

Chapter 13
Edward Moore & Co.

In 1860 a gentleman called Edward Moore took over the firm Shortridge, Sawyer & Co. who were located at West Holborn, South Shields, and so started another of the successful Tyneside glass manufacturers. The business, trading as Edward Moore & Co. at Tyne Flint Glass Works, were to send their pressed glass as far as Australia in the ensuing 53 years. Their products were of high quality and Pottery Gazette reports in July 1880, from their special correspondent at the Sydney Exhibition, "This firm have been recommended for a Second Class award." P.G adds "This is especially gratifying to them as we understand they do a good Australian trade."

A brief history of Edward Moore & Co. is covered by Slack[1] . With regard to their moulds there are two points to bear in mind. In 1888 they bought all the moulds of Coalbourn Hill Glass Works, Stourbridge, (Joseph Webb), which had ceased trading. It is therefore quite possible that items bearing Joseph Webb design registrations may have been made by Edward Moore. On the other hand when Moore closed down in 1913 their moulds were taken over by Davidson. However the Ed Moore factory had burned down in 1891 and it is not clear to what extent the earlier moulds survived.

Edward Moore undoubtedly made use of uranium to color his glass but marked examples are not easily come by. On the other hand it is still possible to find pieces of their marked flint glass at antique fairs and even car boot sales. Section 1 Chapter 6, on density, shows Moore's metal has an unusual constancy over the period 1865 to 1890. It indicates only low, or even lead free, mixes were used in their products. I have only found clear yellow and green uranium glass examples but Moore, in 1887 registered a patent, (4821), for an opaque glass in a soft shade of green which involved the use of uranium. It was called "Celadon." It is interesting to note that he records two methods of obtaining this color, one uses "oxide of uranium" and black oxide of copper," the other ,which is less expensive, used "peroxide of iron and black oxide of copper." Unfortunately I have not been able to find an example of this, which I could confidently attribute to Moore. The uranium mix in the patent would have had a uranium content of about 0.71% wt.

A number of Moore's designs made use of swirling gadroons and a saw tooth style finish on the lip of comports etc. It is true that other producers such as Walsh, Greener and Davidson all made use of the gadroon but they are much less common.

[1]Slack R - English Pressed Glass, pp 106 - 114.
[2]Thompson J - Identification of English Pressed Glass, p 88, photo 22.

Photo 40. Except for color, two identical vases. *Almost certainly* Edward Moore, following the attribution by Thompson[2]. Date about 1885. I note that their densities are not as I expected from that of Moore's flint glass. The addition of uranium alone is unlikely to account for the difference. Vase in yellow. Height 27 cm, density 2.52 g/cc, uranium 0.2% wt. Responds *strongly* to long wave uv but only *mildly* to short wave. Value $45-70.
Same size vase in green. Density 2.57 g/cc, uranium 0.2% wt. Responds *mildly* to long wave uv light and *weakly* to short wave. Value each $45-60. Note I have also examined a broken part of another Moore vase of similar green color and which was illustrated in their pattern book. In this case the item had a density was 2.55 g/cc and the uranium 0.25% wt. that is effectively the same as the above.

Photo 41. Three salts. Two are matching in pattern but one is green and the other yellow. They were bought at different times and places. They appear to resemble a Pervival Vickers & Co illustration in an 1881 catalogue but they also closely resemble an illustration in an Ed Moore catalogue. It is an example of different glasshouses making near identical products. However I consider that these are *probably* Ed Moore *about* 1880, a view reinforced by density. Left, (green), 11 cm wide, density 2.5 g/cc, uranium 0.12% wt. Value $15-20.
Center, (yellow), also 11 cm wide, density 2.5 g/cc, uranium 0.13% wt. Value $20-30.
Right, Diameter 9.25 cm, density 2.51 g/cc, uranium 0.18% wt. The pattern on the lower side is the same as that on the other two salts, and its density and uranium level are also close, but I have not found this item in any catalogue or pattern book. *Could be* Ed. Moore *about* 1880. Value $15-20.

Photo 42. Left, Candlestick 18.5 cm high, density 2.52 g/cc, uranium 0.17% wt. As far as I can tell this is the same pattern as an item in Ed Moore catalogue. However the drawing is small and I cannot be sure. The density and uranium levels are consistent with the other Ed. Moore items, which I have identified. *Probably* Ed. Moore, *about* 1890. Value $15-30. Right, I am less confident about this candlestick. Height 18 cm, density 2.51g/cc, uranium 0.17% wt. With its swirling gadroons it is difficult not to attribute this piece to Ed. Moore but instinct sounds caution. Perhaps it is because I have seen several examples in flint, which just look too new. Despite the density and uranium level at best I will give it a *could be, about* 1900. Value $15-20.

Photo 43. Small jug, probably for cream, height 6 cm, density 2.45 g/cc, uranium 0.5% wt. The style of the top with its swirling gadroons strongly suggests Ed Moore. The "pump handle" has been applied after the molding suggesting that it is earlier rather than later within the possible period. It has a perfect ground off pontil dimple. Despite the density and uranium anomaly with other Moore items I consider this *could be* Edward Moore, *about* 1870. Value $15-30.
Small bowl, 5 cm high. Density 2.45 g/cc, uranium 0.3% wt. The saw tooth top is in Moore's style and the square pattern on the body very closely resembles that of the jug. Again the base has a perfect dimple. *Could be* Ed. Moore, *about* 1870. Value $15-30.

Chapter 14
Greener and Jobling

The business was founded by Henry Greener and James Angus in the 1850s when they acquired the Wear Flint Glass Works in Sunderland, which was already producing bottles and other glassware. Henry, the son of Robert Greener a glasscutter, had been apprenticed to a glass manufacturer and later worked for Sowerby at Gateshead. James Angus was a glass merchant, and together the pair seems to have made a successful partnership. They traded as Angus and Greener until Angus died in 1869. Henry Greener then moved to a new site, still in Sunderland, at Alfred Street but continued the name Wear Flint Glass Works. He traded as Henry Greener. The firm expanded and produced a wide range of pressed glass goods in a variety of colors. Some of these undoubtedly included uranium.

Henry Greener died in 1882 but the business continued under the direction of his executors. However things did not go well and the company ran into debt. This led to it being taken over by a local industrialist James Jobling in about 1886. Jobling had been supplying chemicals to Greener & Co. and was one of the main creditors. Under Jobling's direction the company continued to trade as Greener & Co. until 1921 when he transferred the title of his Tyneside chemical business to the glass making side of his activities. It then became James A Jobling and Co.

Henry Greener had registered a trademark in 1876. It consisted of a demi-lion facing left and holding a five-pointed star. Although similar, it differed from the mark used by Davidson and is easily distinguished by the absence of the mural crown. One of Jobling's early changes was to modify the trademark. After 1887 the lion appears holding an axe.

During the 1870s Greener produced not only pressed glass but also blown table glass and cut and engraved ware.

Jobling's take-over of Greener and Co. was not an immediate success and despite attempts to introduce new equipment and products the Company was in financial difficulties by the turn of the century. This prompted Jobling, in 1902, to appoint his nephew, Ernest Purser as manager. Purser later took the name Jobling-Purser and played a leading role in turning the firm into profitability. Purser's background had been in electrical engineering with CA Parsons of Newcastle on Tyne. He instigated the modernization of the site but the rewards for this investment were interrupted by the 1914-18 war. Indirectly it may be that the war was to open the path to subsequent prosperity. Before 1914 the source of heat resisting glass had been Germany. The war terminated this and research was undertaken in the UK and USA to produce an alternative. By 1915 Corning had developed boro-silicate glass to help the war effort. It was given the name Pyrex. When hostilities finished Corning looked to exploit their wartime development and in 1921 sold the production rights to supply the British Empire (excluding Canada), to Jobling. In the following years this proved to be a mainstay of the Company's prosperity. However as far as I am aware uranium was not used in the coloring of Pyrex and its story is beyond the scope of this book.

Two of the original Greener notebooks for glass mixtures appears to have survived and are in the possession of the Sunderland Museum and Art Gallery's collection. I am indebted for the opportunity to study them, they make fascinating reading. The mixes used in glass making in the nineteenth and early twentieth century were closely guarded secrets. The recipes would be written in note books held close to the chest of the manager or "supervisor." They are therefore capable of telling something about the management of the glass house as well as the technology of its metal. In these two books which cover the period 1875 to 1897 and probably later, there are three changes of handwriting. The first appears to change in August 1884, the next after 1897. These dates bear a very close relationship to the management changes that I have already mentioned. The first is the take over by James Jobling, the second the appointment of Ernest Purser.

Interpreting the significance of these books is by no means straightforward and some uncertainty is involved. The first entry dated August 19th 1875 refers to "Flint Batch used in Akers Prussia St Glass Works." How this is related to Henry Greener's activities is by no means clear for I have not found it mentioned by other writers on Greener. It could however indicate some connection with the Lancashire glasshouses. There was a Prussia St Glassworks in Ancoats, at that time operated by Kerr Webb & Co. Also about that time there was a "William Akers glass and china dealer" in the area but not in Prussia Street. Furthermore, the notes for the 1875 - 1884 period contain a number of "Flint Batches" Some of these would have had a lead content of about 20% to 23 %, corresponding to a density of 2.85 g/cc - 2.9 g/cc. a metal more like Lancashire than Tyneside. However in my examination of clear glass items I have found only two examples with densities in this range, both had an 1858 "lozenge" registration mark. Some others in the books have much lower lead content and a "Common Flint Batch" of 1878 had only 4.5% lead, which would mean a density of about 2.55 g/cc.

It also gives the mixes used for uranium based "Chrysophis." The entries are sometimes for small batches of less than 20 lb., and sometimes for larger batches of about 500 lb.. These batches did not contain lead and would have had a uranium content of about 0.7% wt. None of these appear to match items I have examined. Unfortunately by 1879 a new unit of measurement, with which I am not familiar and able to equate, enters the formulae. It is "the barrow." However it makes only a passing appearance. But it would seem that "Pea Green" and "Pomona Green" were also colors bearing uranium. Dark Greens and Blue Greens did not contain uranium. There is no mention of Yellow, or Topaz.

The 1885 - 1897 mixes show Flint Batches with no lead and Best Flint Batch with as much as 26.5% Pb. It is difficult to reconcile this with the number of clear glass items that I have measured with densities between 2.5 g/cc and 2.65 g/cc. Perhaps Best Flint, as cullet, was frequently used in the other Flint batches, this would explain the wide range of densities found in the middle period Greener glass. Canary appears in 1885 with a uranium content between 0.1% wt and 0.18 % wt. Pomona in 1889 with a uranium content of 0.43% wt. Also in '89, Topaz with a lead content of about 11.5 % Pb, (density about 2.6-2.7 g/cc), and uranium content of 0.62% wt; Gold Yellow with uranium ranging from 0.69% wt to 0.87% wt; Victoria Topaz with about 8% Pb, (density about 2.6 g/cc.), and uranium of 0.65% wt.

Dated 16 July 1891, for the first time reference is made to "Primrose" with a note "Works well and if required a deeper color add one third more uranium." The expression "works well" is unusual, more normal to use words like "good color." If it was an experimental batch to imitate the Davidson Pearline, where the metal has to be reheated to obtain the milky effect, such an expression would be understandable. The uranium content of this batch would have been about 0.25% wt. An entry for June 30th 1897 is also for primrose. This time the uranium content works out about 0.58% wt, which is effectively the same as the item in Photo 48, a Pearline style jug! It therefore seems likely that this was the formula used by Greener to imitate the Primrose Pearline of their rival. It is not easy to read, the nearest I can get is;

Sand	500 lb.
Alkali	200 lb.
Limespar	12 1/2 lb.
Phos. Lime	106 1/4 lb.
? Soda (probably nitrate of soda)	125 lb.
Uranium	7 lb.
Antimony	2 lb. 5 1/2 oz.
Arsenic	9 lb.

The third set of recipes, which is in a different book to the foregoing, is in different writing and has no dates. The previous mentioned colors are included. Gold Yellow with a uranium content of 0.87 % & 0.68 % wt but both these involved the use of "cullet" and it is always possible that the cullet also contained uranium. Victoria Topaz with 10% Pb wt. and uranium 0.79% wt.. Topaz with 11% Pb wt. and uranium 0.62% wt. Pomona Green with 0.83% wt. uranium, which is significantly different from the mix, recorded in the other notebook. But most remarkable of all is what appears to be "Camalia" a color that I do not recognize. The mix is simply sand, lead, ash. saltpeter, uranium and a smidgen of copper. The lead content works out at 9.6% wt, (a density of just over 2.6 g/cc.), and uranium a staggering 7% wt. I keep looking but have not yet met up with any such specimen! It is just possible that this is a red color named after the red flower on the camellia tree. Weyl[1] reports a red uranium glass made in his laboratory in 1946, but it only contained 4% sodium uranate and had 71% PbO. Not at all like the Greener' s formulae.

Photo 44. Vase 18.5 cm high. Density 2.56 g/cc, uranium 0.19% wt. Design registration mark, (lozenge type), Angus & Greener 1867. Value $45-70.

Photo 45. Basket 12 cm diameter. Density 2.59 g/cc, uranium 0.25% wt. Design registration mark, (lozenge type), Henry Greener 1870. Value $45-60.
Jar 7.5 cm high. Density 2.45 g/cc, uranium 0.37% wt. Design registration No 182002. Henry Greener & Co. 1891. It is interesting to note that this is well after the death of Henry Greener and after James Jobling had taken over. While this metal has more uranium it is much less dense. Perhaps this change is not unrelated to the change of ownership. Value $15-20.

Photo 46. Left, basket 18 cm diameter. Density 2.63 g/cc, uranium 0.31% wt. No mark but some pattern similar to known Henry Greener designs, also density and uranium very close to right basket & Photo 45. *Probably* Henry Greener *about* 1875. Value $30-45.
Right, basket 17.5 cm diameter. Density 2.64 g/cc, uranium 0.26% wt. Design registration mark, (lozenge type), Henry Greener 1870. Value $45-60.

Photo 47. Basket 18 cm diameter. Density 2.59 g/cc, uranium 0.19% wt. Not marked but the pattern and style of fixing of the handle, as well as the edge of the dish, is strong evidence, as is the density. *Probably* Greener, *about* 1875. Value $30-45.

Photo 48. This is an example of Greener cribbing Davidson's Pearline. Jug 8.5 cm high. Density 2.53 g/cc, uranium 0.62% wt. Design registration No 262018, Henry Greener & Co. 1895. The coloring, the uranium content and density are typical of Davidson's Pearline. Value $35-60.

Contemporary with the Pyrex production, Jobling set about updating the design of their domestic and decorative ware. They were impressed with the quality of some French products, particularly Lalique, and made approaches for a British production license. When these came to nothing they decided to develop their own equivalent products in colored glassware. Some of these made use of uranium. The catalogues list their colors as being Blue, Green, Pink, and Amber in addition to Opalique and Jade. While I have not examined any Blue or Pink, (I would not expect uranium in these shades), I have found uranium only in *Green* and *Jade*. The story of Jobling is well covered by Baker and Crowe[2] .As has already been mentioned these authors give a formula for Jobling's *Jade* although they do not quote its origin. It is interesting to note the uranium is expressed as Uranium Trioxide ($U0_3$) which equates to 0.28% uranium by weight in the melt. The lead content of this batch is 8.7% Pb wt. that according to my graph Fig 1 Section 1 Chapter 5, would indicate a density of about 2.60 g/cc. Unfortunately the formula of the clear green is not given.

Jobling did not appear to use a trade mark, except for Pyrex, but a considerable proportion of their designs were registered and consequently often carry their Rd Number. I have noted on clear (flint) glass items bearing the Rd Number 724094, a Jobling registration of 1926, the words "British Make." Also a bowl similar to those in Photo 49 I have seen bearing "British Make." This is an unusual couplet, which I have not seen used by other glass-houses. The more common expression is "British Made" or "Made in England" I therefore consider it is supportive evidence of Jobling manufacture and have counted this when I attributed the tumbler in Photo 53.

I have examined 9 items of clear green glass which all have Jobling design registration numbers and found them to have a consistent uranium content of 0.12% wt. The average density was 2.47 g/cc with a range of 2.44 g/cc to 2.5 g/cc and a standard deviation of 0.02.

[1]Weyl W A - Colored Glasses, p207

[2]Baker J & Crowe K, - Jobling 1930s Decorative Glass.

Photo 49. Here there are two examples of Jobling's metal. The bowl on the plinth is translucent while the other is in their "jade". Both are the same size, 6.25 cm high, neither are marked but are clearly Jobling Catalogue No 2077. Lhs density is 2.6-g/cc and uranium 0.25% wt. Rhs density 2.61 g/cc, uranium 0.37% wt. The density of the Jade and the uranium content is in line with what I estimated from the formula of the melt. Date about 1935. Value $20-35.

Photo 50. Both these items have the Jobling "Fir Cone pattern". The plate is marked with the Registration No 777133. It is also catalogue No 5000. It is 18 cm diameter in clear glass. Density 2.47 g/cc, uranium 0.12% wt. The bowl is not marked and has a satin finish. Density 2.47 g/cc, uranium 0.12% wt. Both items date *about* 1935. Value in the UK for items of this size; Plate $10-15, Bowl $15-20. I have noticed that prices in Australia are significantly higher where Jobling glass of this type appears to be more collectable.

Photo 51. Jobling posy vase, density 2.44 g/cc, uranium 0.12% wt. Marked with Registration Number 800440. Catalogue No 2595. Date 1935. Value $15-30.

Photo 52. Water set with jug and tumblers. Jug 16 cm high, tumblers 9.75 cm high Densities range 2.49 g/cc - 2.5 g/cc, uranium 0.12% wt. Regd. No 783048, catalogue No 4050. Date 1933. Value for a complete set $35-60.

Photo 53. I have not found this tankard in any of the Jobling reference literature. It is 12 cm high, density 2.45g/cc, uranium 0.16 % wt. It is marked "British Make". I note the top of the handle is shaped very similar to shapes seen on Pyrex jugs and a product of this type would not be out of character with their production lines. I consider this *almost certainly* Jobling, *date* about 1935. Value $10-20.

Chapter 15
Sowerby of Gateshead

A comprehensive history of this Tyneside glass manufacturer has been written by Cottle[1] and Slack[2]. Like a lot of glasshouses the origins of what we now refer to as *Sowerby* is not clear-cut. Arguably it goes back to the 1770s but according to Cottle, the Sowerby Glassworks really started in Gateshead in 1807 and were established by two glassmakers who had come from Stourbridge. The site became known as the "New Stourbridge Glass Works" and the Sowerby family connection was to have Richard as one of the partners. The arrangements did not hold for long and the partnership was dissolved in 1809, which lead to Richard playing a more prominent role. He died young in 1811 and brother George took over and became the driving force in the company for the next two decades. By then his sons, John and George had become involved. Their father died in 1844 and John became the leading light and introduced pressed glass.

In 1846-47, Sowerby took over the "Gateshead Flint Glass House" and changed it to "Gateshead Stamped Glass" but it was closed down a year or so later.

A new venture was opened in 1852 with the Ellison Glass Works. As business flourished it became a major supplier of pressed glass and is probably the origin of the Sowerby items in my collection. The "New Stourbridge Glass Works" were no longer needed and closed in 1857. A hundred years later the Ellison works would be sold to Suntex as the Sowerby story came to its close. It is perhaps worth noting that the old Sowerby moulds were acquired by Nazing.

Little is known about the early products but I suspect that as they had their origins with Stourbridge glass workers, they were probably based on a leaded metal. No doubt such items exist, the difficulty is identifying them!

Much more is known about the pressed glass era and the products of that time. This is due to surviving pattern books, design registrations, the use of a trademark, (a peacock's head), and patents. It is probable that it marked the firm's first use of uranium. Samples that I have found date from the late 1870s and on the basis of these there would appear to be at least five uranium colors in production. (Four at the turn of the century and one in the 1930s). I would list them as follows, clear pale yellow, clear deep green, ivory (Queen's), opaque yellow (giallo?), and light (depression) green.

The yellows appear at two uranium concentrations, namely around 0.3% and 0.45% while the deep greens 0.35%. These figures should be regarded as indicative as only a small number of samples have been examined.

The ivory was the subject of a British patent taken out by John George Sowerby in 1878 (No 2156) under the title of "Improvements in the Manufacture of Glass of a Novel Color" Indeed the product as described in price lists referred to it as "patent Queen's Ivory" The patent describes the making of an opaque glass with "peculiar yellowish colour" which is termed "ivory." It states that an approximation to this color has been obtained by "adding to the usual ingredients of common flint glass, arsenic to make the glass opaque and uranium to give it the yellow tint." Sowerby then claims to make "a much finer body ... in fact a china like body by dispensing with the arsenic and substituting cryolite" (a sodium aluminum fluoride mineral) It continues "I am aware that cryolite is largely used in glass making, but not in conjunction with uranium..." A batch mix is quoted as follows;

	cwt	qrs.	lb.
Sand	12	0	0
58% Soda	1	0	0
Baryta (carb.)	1	1	0
Nitrate of Soda	1	1	0
Manganese			14

"To every 12 cwt of this batch I add 24 lb. of uranium and 1 cwt. 3 quarters, 8 lb. of cryolite."

John George Sowerby then goes on to qualify his mix by saying "I desire it to be understood that I do not restrict myself to the proportions above given, nor any particular relative proportion of cryolite to the uranium or any of the ingredients above enumerated..." This may well explain the variations found in the shades of Queen's Ivory items.

It is difficult to interpret this formula in terms of modern day chemistry. It is not clear what is meant by "58% Soda." Nowadays soda usually means sodium carbonate, as in washing soda, but in this case it more likely refers to sodium hydroxide, (NaOH), as this would contain about 58% sodium. Baryta, presumably refers to Barytes, which is the commonest barium mineral and is barium sulphate. On the other hand the "carb" might imply that it is barium carbonate but this mineral is generally known as Witherite[3]. We also see that the term "uranium" is used. As discussed earlier it is highly unlikely it means the bare metal.

Barium increases the density of flint but this may in part be offset by the presence of aluminum in the mix, we might therefore expect the density to be a little higher than for the basic flint mix, say about 2.5 gr/cc. The uranium content would be about 1.25%. u by wt. This is close to what I have found in a majority of samples examined although some have shown lower uranium levels. See Photos 61 to 67 and 68.

One item is widely different, it is more yellow than the ivory and has a much higher density. This is probably "Giallo" described by Cottle[4] as "a lemon yellow." Its uranium level is about the same as for Queen's Ivory but its density is much greater. In the absence of a chemical analysis I can only speculate. See Photo 70

The number of items of Queen's Ivory is sufficient for conclusions to be drawn. The densities are very consistent, lying in the range 2.49 - 2.53 g/cc, with a mean of 2.52 g/cc. Uranium has a wider range, 0.62 - 1.24 % wt. with a mean of 1% wt.

Murray[5] quotes from a loose sheet found amongst Sowerby records which also gives a mix for Queen's Ivory. It contains a small amount of china clay in addition to the cryolite but has a much greater uranium content, about 2.5%. I have not found any examples of opaque porcelain type glass that comes anywhere near this uranium level.

It seems that, from the samples I have studied, Sowerby used uranium in the 1930s but only for their green items. Uranium has not been found in their blues or ambers. However only a few of them have been studied.

[1]Cottle S - Sowerby Gateshead Glass, 1986.
[2]Slack R - English Pressed Glass, p 24-66
[3]Partington J R - General and Inorganic Chemistry. 1951 p 378.
[4]Cottle S - Sowerby Gateshead Glass p 58
[5]Murray S - The Peacock and the Lions p 31.
[6]Cottle S - Sowerby Gateshead Glass, p 71
[7]Cottle S - Sowerby Gateshead Glass p 78
[8]Cottle S - Sowerby Gateshead Glass, p 58

Photo 54. This is a two-part tazza the top resting on the lower support. Complete it stands 10 cm high and the diameter of the dish is 20.5 cm. Top and base respectively densities 2.49 g/cc & 2.48 g/cc, uranium 0.34% wt & 0.37 % wt. Trade marked with peacock's head. Date *about* 1900. Value $110-180.

Photo 55. Basket, 7.75 cm high, (incl. handles), density 2.57 g/cc, uranium 0.43% wt . Trade marked with peacock head and in pattern book 1882, item 11024. Value $30-45.

Photo 56. These two candlesticks come with the same pattern but different color. They are not marked but illustrated in Pattern Book XI (754), 1885[6]
Green, height 21.25 cm, density 2.58 g/cc, uranium 0.28% wt. Value $20-35.
Yellow, one of three candlesticks examined in this color. 20 cm high, densities 2.56 - 2.53 g/cc Uranium range 0.31 - 0.25% wt. Value $20-35.

Photo 57. the basket, 17 cm long, has a density of 2.57 g/cc, and uranium 0.28% wt. It is Lozenge marked, indicating Sowerby registered it on 1st June 1874. Value $50-70.

Photo 58, oval dish, 15.5 cm long. Density 2.57 g/cc, uranium 0.43% wt. It is press molded but not marked. A similar pattern has been seen with the Sowerby trademark. *Probably* Sowerby, *about* 1900. Value $20-35.

Photo 59, oval salt, 10 cm long. Density 2.55 g/cc, uranium 0.5% wt. This item is not marked but the pattern is identical to a round salt I have seen which did carry the peacock head trademark. *Probably* Sowerby *about 1910*. Value $20-35.

Photo 61, oval bowl in Queens Ivory, 21.5 cm long. Density 2.51 g/cc, uranium 1.1% wt. Lozenge marked for 1879, also shown in 1882 Pattern Book (item 1376). Value $145-220.

Photo 60, Vase and flower holder from the depression years. The vase stands 11 cm high. An identical vase and flower holder has also been examined. The vase densities are 2.47 g/cc & 2.46 g/cc., uranium in both is 0.074% wt. For the flower holders, densities are 2.49 & 2.45 g/cc, uranium 0.05% wt & 0.09 % wt. Not marked but design of both vase and flower spacer illustrated in Pattern Book, date 1933. Value $15-20.

Photo 62, box with lid, Queen's Ivory. Height 9 cm, both lid and box density 2.52 g/cc, uranium 1.18% wt. Trade mark and lozenge mark, 10th November 1879. Value $220-300.

Photo 63, trough in Queen's Ivory. 6.25 cm high, density 2.5g/cc, uranium 0.68 % wt. The item carries the Sowerby trade mark and is an example of their nursery rhyme series after Walter Crane. The curious thing about this item is its uranium content which is significantly lower than other Queen's Ivory items examined. I can only speculate on the reason, perhaps these items were aimed at the children's market and a cheaper version of the base metal was used? Value $70-145.

Photo 64, two baskets in Queens Ivory. Left, 7.75 cm high, density 2.53 g/cc, uranium 1.05% wt. has the Sowerby trade mark on the base. About 1885. Value $60-100. Right, Not marked but is identifiable as a Sowerby pattern. Density 2.53 g/cc, uranium 0.93% wt. Date *about* 1880. Value $45-70.

Photo 65, jug and bowl in Queen's Ivory. Jug carries both the trade mark and Registration Lozenge mark. The latter dates 1873, which is several years before the Queen's Ivory patent was lodged. I can only assume this item is from a mould made before the metal was invented. The jug is 4.5 cm high, has a density of 2.49 g/cc and uranium 1.24% wt. Value $60-90.
The small bowl is 4.5 cm high, carries the same trade and lozenge marks as the jug. Density 2.52 g/cc, uranium 0.99% wt. Value $60-90.

Photo 66, another two pieces of Queen's Ivory. The salt is 3.5 cm high, density 2.52 g/cc, uranium 1.12% wt. Lozenge and trade marked, the design being registered on 12th August 1878. Also illustrated in the 1882 Pattern Book. Value $45-70. The small bowl is 5 cm high, density 2.52 g/cc, uranium 1.12% wt. Trade and lozenge marked, 8th July 1878. Also in the 1882 Pattern Book.

Photo 67, small cream jug in Queen's Ivory. Height 5.5 cm, density 2.55 g/cc, uranium 0.99% wt. Item not marked but the design includes a peacock! It is illustrated in the 1882 Pattern Book.. Despite the lack of marking I have no hesitation in attributing it to Sowerby without qualification. Value $30-45.

Photo 68, I include this item here because it raises some interesting points. It looks like Queen's Ivory. The pattern is near identical to the basket weave designs shown in Sowerby pattern books and very closely resembles the basket 11371/2 in the 1882 book. Width 13.25 cm, density is 2.56 g/cc and uranium 0.43% wt. The pattern and appearance would lead to a confident attribution for Sowerby but ... The pattern is not unusual and does not have to be Sowerby. While the density is just about acceptable, the uranium is substantially low. This raises serious doubts. It might be Sowerby but *could be* a Sowerby look alike. Date *about* 1900. Value $20-35.

Photo 69. This little pot, which stands all of 6.25 cm high, is in Queen's Ivory. The unusual feature is the blue ring around its top. Two similarly ringed items are shown by Cottle[7]. It also illustrated in the 1882 Pattern Book. Density 2.52 g/cc, uranium 0.62% wt. Again although unmarked it is Sowerby *about* 1890. Value $20-35.

Photo 70, is an example of the well known Sowerby "Dolphin Bowl". It stands 13 cm high, density 3.24 g/cc, uranium 1.05 % wt. This often well illustrated Sowerby design is also shown in the 1882 Pattern Book, albeit in round rather than cocked hat shape. It has the Sowerby Peacock Head trade mark. This is not Queen's Ivory but Sowerby's Giallo, which was introduced in 1882[8]. Although the uranium concentration is typical of Queen's Ivory, the density is not. This suggests that the difference in color is not due to having more uranium but rather a different basic melt. The high density could be accounted for by use of barium or lead. I suspect the latter but without chemical analysis it is not possible to say. While both the Queen's Ivory and the Giallo have a strong to medium response to ultraviolet in the near region , the response in the far region is different, the latter giving, if anything, only weak response. Value $435-725.

Chapter 16
The Lancashire Glasshouses

Mention Lancashire and glass and the thoughts immediately turn to the giant Pilkington works at St Helens. However I have found no evidence that they ever used uranium and consequently they do not feature here. Instead I am concerned with the handful of businesses that grew in the mid nineteenth century and died at the end of it. They did use uranium but that was not the cause of their demise!

For at least part of the period that uranium was in use, the Lancashire glassmakers were major producers. However the industry started to fade at the turn of the nineteenth century and by 1930 all except Butterworths had gone. The two most prominent names were probably Percival, Vickers & Co. and Molineaux, Webb & Co. and they made a significant contribution to the production of glassware in the United Kingdom during that period. Among the smaller producers were John Derbyshire / Burtles & Tate / Andrew Ker & Co. / Thomas Kidd & Co / and Edward Bolton. I have only been able to find uranium colored examples of some of these glasshouses and they are shown in the following pages. Again it should be borne in mind that this does not mean that the others did not use uranium but rather that they have not yet been found out!

From my study of glass densities it would seem that the Manchester glass houses were using a part leaded glass up until about the 1880s. While this is not a fingerprint of glass from that area it does mean that any collector trying to attribute an item with a density in the range 2.7 - 2.9 g/cc might be advised to start by investigating there.

Chapter 17
Burtles, Tate & Co., Manchester

Compared with some other glass manufacturers, little has been written about this Lancashire company. Perhaps it is because their work is not so easy to identify or that they were not so prolific in the use of design registration. Up to 1900 they had registered only 35 designs, which is but a fraction of the numbers registered by producers like Sowerby and Davidson. Not withstanding they appear to have been a substantial glasshouse and had a showroom in London.

The Business was founded in 1858 and based in Poland Street, Oldham Road, Manchester. Thomas Burtles was a glassmaker who came from Glasgow. Matthew Butler Tate was also a glassmaker but was born in Newcastle-on-Tyne in 1814. By the 1880s they were also operating a factory at Bolton known as Victoria Glass Works. In 1887 they opened another factory in Manchester this time at German Street. Soon after that they closed down their Bolton operation. The business became a limited company in 1916. They advertised themselves as "Flint and Colored Glass, Also Ornamental Fancy Glass. Novelties of all descriptions for home and export trade."

Slack[1] refers to articles in Potter Gazette in 1891 and 1892 that refer to a "Topas Opalescent" being introduced by Burtles, the 1892 piece mentions a color called "sunrise" and says it has become as popular as their "uranium." It describes it as "deepening gradually from yellow or amber to pink with ruby edges." It sounds like a copy of Webb's Burmese but I have not found any examples to study.

It would be dangerous to place too much weight on one or two results but it does appear that, unlike other Lancashire manufacturers, Burtles were using a full leaded metal as late as the mid 1880s.

[1]Slack R - English Pressed Glass, pp 123-125.

Photo 71, The swan, size stands 8 cm high, density 3.29 g/cc, uranium 0.25% wt. Marked Rd 20086 within a rectangle. This design was produced in more than one size and the Registration dates it 1885. Value $60-90. The shell tooth pick holder, posy vase or what ever, 7.75 cm high, density 3.28g/cc, uranium 0.25%. It is not marked, press molded, completely threaded except for the feet. Based on similarity to the swan with respect to color, density and uranium content I would say *probably* Burtles, Tate & Co. I also have the feeling that this is the type of article expected from this glasshouse. Date *about* 1885. Value $35-45.

Chapter 18

James Derbyshire & Sons

To the collector the name Derbyshire is synonymous with John Derbyshire, but in fact there were three Manchester brothers, James, John and Thomas. James set up a factory, British Union Glass Works, in 1858 at Hulme. Within a decade another factory, also at Hulme, had been opened, this time by the three brothers. Until 1870 they were trading as James Derbyshire and Brothers, then as J.J. and T Derbyshire. However in 1873 John set up the Regent Road Glassworks in Salford and (presumably) separated from his brothers. According to Slack[1] this firm lasted only four years. Thereafter the name John Derbyshire ceases. Lattimore[2] tell us that the original firm traded as James Derbyshire and Sons and continued to do so until at least 1881. After that no adverts appeared in Pottery Gazette. It is possible that after the period on his own, John rejoined his brothers, but this is not documented.

The first registered design was by James Derbyshire & Brothers in June 1864, the last by James Derbyshire & Sons in November 1876. During the period of John' s control of the Regent Road Flint Glass Works a trade mark, consisting of the letters J D back to back, blended into a fisherman's anchor, was used. It is not clear what happened after 1876 and whether the Regent Road moulds continued in use. Nor do we know what eventually happened to all the Derbyshire moulds. However we might reasonably expect that moulds which had seen only little use would be in good condition and have some commercial value. They may have been obtained by other glasshouses. If this is the case I would expect to find a wide range in the characteristics of the metal of items from Derbyshire moulds. I have not studied sufficient examples to draw firm conclusions but there are indications that this is the case.

Photo 72, the anchor and JD trade mark of John Derbyshire.

[1]Slack R - English Pressed Glass, p117.
[2]Lattimore C - English 19th Century Press Molded Glass, p92.

Photo 73. This jar probably started life with a lid of some description. It bears the John Derbyshire trade mark. Height 10 cm, density 2.57 g/cc, uranium 0.93% wt. On the basis of the foregoing I would date it 1873-76 but the metal is different to that of the items in Photos 74 & 75 I am inclined to wonder if it were made much later, possibly by another glasshouse using an old Derbyshire mould. Value $20-35.

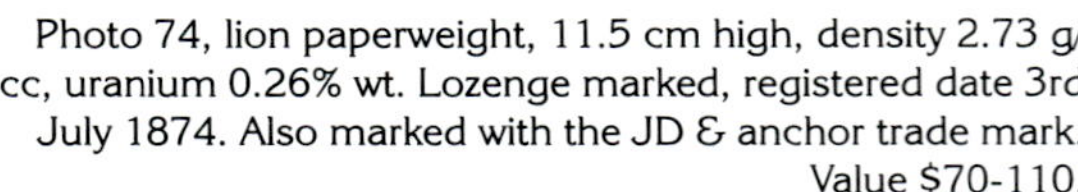

Photo 74, lion paperweight, 11.5 cm high, density 2.73 g/cc, uranium 0.26% wt. Lozenge marked, registered date 3rd July 1874. Also marked with the JD & anchor trade mark. Value $70-110.

Photo 75, press molded in three pieces. The base of this "hand" vase is identical to a design registered by J.J. & T Derbyshire on 11 the May 1872. It is however not marked. Height 21.5 cm, density 2.66 g/cc, uranium 0.26% wt. As this is not marked I will say *almost certainly* Derbyshire *and* suspect its date of manufacture was probably several years later than the design registration, *about* 1880. Value $70-110.

Chapter 19
Molineaux, Webb & Co.

I use the name for the generic group the origin of which probably goes back to 1827 when Molineaux, Webb & Co. established a glass works at Kirby Street, Ancotes, Manchester. The name has been spelt differently and had different additions over the years. Not a lot is known about its early history although Slack[1] is able to fill in some brief detail. He tells us that it started by making lamp lenses but by 1848 was producing pressed glass. The first design they registered was in 1864 and they continued into the twentieth century. It would seem that their products were mainly utilitarian domestic ware but in metal of high quality. Their Greek key pattern was introduced during this year and accompanied by a partly matt finish. It is thought that the Company also produced some decorative pieces by pressing or blowing. The Company continued to trade until 1929 The site was sold in 1932 and the moulds bought by Chance of Birmingham and Sowerby of Gateshead.

An identification of Molineaux Webb products is not always easy. Some are clearly marked with Design Registration but even in these cases it has to be remembered that moulds were eventually sold off to other glasshouses. As for pattern books, there is a bound copy of a book of drawings in the possession of the Manchester City Art Galleries which appears to contain extracts from a series of pattern books and which illustrate blown and pressed pieces. Because of its provenance it is thought highly probable that it does relate to Molineaux Webb, but that is not absolutely certain! In many ways there is a close similarity between the products of different Manchester glass producers and it is just possible it could be associated with another factory. In making attributions I have referred to these illustrations but *not* included any uncertainty in the attribution due to the slight doubt about their origin.

I understand that a recipe book for the period 1887 - 1889 does exist but I have not had opportunity to study it. However an extract has been seen and this appears to indicate that the units pounds (lb.) and grams were both used in the same mix! (An early partial adoption of SI units?) Accepting the usual uncertainty of not knowing exact chemical form of components, on the basis of this information, I estimate a glass of about 15% Pb (wt), which would mean a density of 2.75 g/cc. This is within the range of a number of samples that I have examined. Molineaux Webb did use uranium in their products but I have no reliable information on the mixes used. No examples bearing Design Registration marks that contain uranium have been found, although they are not uncommon in flint. The attributions that I have made in uranium glass are based on illustrations in the aforementioned pattern books.

The range of densities in the items illustrated is much the same as that found in examples of clear glass from this firm, Section 1, Chapter 6.

[1] Slack R - English Pressed Glass, p 120 - 123.

Photo 76. These two candlesticks have the same basic pattern the only difference being the finish of the candleholder. Left, height 19.5 cm, density 3.41 g/cc, uranium 0.5% wt. Illustrated as Regina 493, in the aforementioned catalogues. Although the top is slightly different to the illustration I can safely say Molineaux Webb without qualification. Date *about* 1850. Weak response to uv light. Value $20-45. Right, height 19 cm, density 3.3 g/cc, uranium 0.43 % wt. Attribution and date as above. Weak response to uv light. Value $20-45.

Photo 77. Left, I have examined a pair of these candlesticks, height 14 cm, density 3.39 g/cc & 3.4 g/cc, uranium 0.5% wt & 0.43 % wt. Again identified from the catalogues as, Florentine 494, date *about* 1850. Weak response to uv light. Value $20-45.

Center candlestick, height 17.5 cm, density 3.39 g/cc, uranium 0.46% wt. Identification as above Cambridge 495, date *about* 1850. Weak response to uv light. Value $20-45.

Right, candlestick, height 13.5 cm, density 2.47 g/cc, uranium 0.5% wt. This is the same pattern as the center 'stick and I would attribute it to Molineaux Webb. However contrasting density raises questions. The quality of the molding of this item suggests that it was made much later than the others. I date it *period* 1910. Does this mean the Molineaux went to a very low or even lead free metal for their pressed glass in their latter years? Or was the item pressed by Sowerby from an old mould, the snag with this theory is that the metal does not match any of Sowerby's which I have examined. Strong response to uv light. Value $15-30.

Photo 78. The common features of these three must link them together, all have the same style of top, two have common stems and two have the same pattern bases. They have different densities and uranium levels that rather support the idea that lead content was reduced as years went by.

Left, height 14.5 cm, density 2.68 g/cc, uranium 0.26% wt. This is similar to the other two in style, the only real difference being the stem. *Almost certainly* Molineaux Webb and, on the basis of wear and quality of item, *period* 1900. Moderate response to uv light.

Center, height 11 cm., density 2.44 g/cc, uranium 0.3% wt. This again contrasts sharply with others and I can only speculate as before. *Almost certainly* Molineaux Webb date *period* 1910. Strong response to uv light. Value $15-20.

Right, height 14.5 cm, density 3.4 g/cc, uranium 0.56% wt. *Almost certainly* Molineaux Webb, Balmoral 496. Date *about* 1850. Weak response to uv light. Value $20-45.

Below: Photo 79, a pair of knife rests. Length 8.5 cm, density 2.95 g/cc, uranium 0.31% wt. Closely resembles an illustration in the Molineaux catalogue, but with such a simple design this is far from conclusive. The density is within the expected range. *Could be* Molineux Webb, *period 1870*. Value as a pair, $20-30.

Chapter 20
Percival, Vickers & Co.

Very little has been written about this glass house, which was sited in Jersey Street, Manchester. Indeed both Slack[1] and Lattimore[2] put the firm in the category of "Minor Manufacturers," yet arguably they must have been one of England's most prolific producers of pressed and blown glass in the latter half of the nineteenth century. Up to 1900 they had registered some 70 designs but the catalogues that survive show a much larger range of products than these registrations suggest. These catalogues, which are in an unknown private collection, form the basis of an article by Barbara Yates[3]. I have been fortunate to have access to photocopies. These six trade catalogues cover the period 1846 to 1902 and show the company made a wide range of cut and pressed glassware, even extending into glass shades for electric lights. They only represent a snapshot of the Company's products. The 1846 catalogue illustrates nearly 300 decanter designs, 51 tumblers, and 300 wine glasses! By 1881 their molded products extended from bird glasses through a variety of tumblers, wines and goblets, to egg cups, finger bowls, candlesticks, piano feet, pots and jars, and even inkwells. I have not been able to find any surviving recipe books but examples of their ware, which I have identified, clearly indicate that uranium was used extensively in their products. The Company was liquidated in 1914. I do not know if any of their moulds were taken over by other glasshouses.

According to Barbara Yates the firm was founded in 1844 by Thomas Percival, William Yates, and Thomas Vickers, the name changed to Percival Vickers & Co. on incorporation in 1865. The first of the aforementioned catalogues is not dated but is thought to be 1846 and included both molded, cut and engraved ware. It would appear that the cut predominated and it is not clear whether the molded was blown or pressed. The same author also argues that there was close co-operation between Manchester firms despite them appearing to be in competition. She points to an example where cut "tankard" jugs, advertised by Burtles & Tate in Pottery Gazette (1888), were identical with some illustrated in the Percival Vickers 1881 catalogue. This would suggest that firms may have sold each others' products under their own name, or sub-contracted out production to others who might be thought of as rivals. We must bear this in mind when trying to interpret the density and uranium content of attributed items.

As with Molineaux, Webb & Co., I find the density of the clear glass to be significantly less than that generally associated with Stourbridge and Birmingham, see Section 1 Chapter 6, and generally lies within the range 2.63 g/cc to 2.93 g/cc. I have been told of an analysis of one item with a Registered Design No 115077,(i.e. 1885), which gave a density of 2.95 g/cc. and a lead content of 21.3% . It was reported that the item was crizzled. This density is marginally higher than I have found for around that date but none were crizzled. I can only guess at an explanation.

Although I have had no difficulty in collecting pieces of clear glass with Percival Vickers' Design Registration marks, I have found only one item of uranium glass so marked. For other identification I have had to rely on the catalogues. This is satisfactory where the illustrations are clear and the pattern complex but in other cases it is always possible that other companies may have made very similar articles. This is especially the case with wine glasses, tumblers, etc.

In the following illustrations it will be noted that there is a wide range of densities and I am left wondering whether this is due to change in their basic metal with time, or whether it was other glasshouses using or copying their designs.

[1] Slack R - English Pressed Glass, p 126

[2]Lattimore C - English 19th Cent. Press Molded Glass, p114.

[3]Yates B - Glassware of Percival Vickers & Co. Ltd.

[4]Arnold K - Australian Glass p54.

Photo 80. Here we have three piano feet insulators all of the same pattern, which appears in the Percival Vickers', catalogues but did that firm make them all? Let me start with the one in the center. Diameter 10 cm,, density 3.0 g/cc, uranium 0.22% wt. It has Design Registration Lozenge mark equating to registration No 120613, 8th July 1859. The deposition says *"Made and Registered by Percival, Yates, & Vickers for Thomas Dawkins Little Warner Street, Clerkenwell London."* It would therefore seem that the item was made for Dawkins but who owned the moulds? This is not a matter of academic interest for the situation became more complex as I investigated. It was not uncommon for Percival Vickers to illustrate Design Registry marks in their catalogues. This piano insulator is shown in the *"1893 Supplementary Catalogue of Molded, Cut, Engraved, and Etched Flint Glass."* but not with the lozenge mark. The item next to it in that catalogue is also an insulator but has an illustrated mark, which equates to Registration No 119975, 20th May 1859, Davis, Greathead & Green, Flint Glass Works, Stourbridge. My searches appear to indicate that while this pattern is not uncommon all the other examples I have found, whether or not they contain uranium, do not have the lozenge mark they also have a different base. Furthermore I have also seen a similar item portrayed as made by the Crown Crystal Glass Company in Australia[4]. I can only speculate that after producing for Dawkins in the 1860's, Percival Vickers later resurrected the mould but used a different plunger to make more for sale under their own name in the 1880's. These could include the other two illustrated in this picture. Then when the firm closed perhaps the mould was bought by the Australian company. Value $20-35.

Left, the top is slightly narrower than the above and the base has a pattern of concentric rings. I have examined two examples of this insulator, both are 10 cm diameter and both have 0.15% wt uranium, the densities were slightly different being 2.58 g/cc and 2.62 g/cc. *Could be* Percival Vickers, *about* 1895. Value $15-30.

Right, I have examined four of these insulators, all are 10 cm in diameter. Density is between 2.5 g/cc to 2.52 g/cc , uranium between 0.25% wt to 0.28% wt. *Could be* Percival Vickers, about 1895. However in view of the different characteristics of the metal it is difficult to accept that both the left and right pieces came from the same factory. Value $15-30.

Photo 81, two more piano feet insulators, but of differing patterns. The blue green one has a maximum width of 8.5 cm, density of 2.9 g/cc and uranium 0.06% wt. This is an unusual uranium color and it is just possible that the uranium is present by accident but somehow I don't think so. Responds to uv light. The density is what would be expected from Percival Vickers. This piece is identical to an illustration in their 1881 catalogue, (p 36, No 4), but I think it may be a little earlier. Value $20-35.

The yellow insulator, diameter 10 cm, density 2.53 g/cc, uranium 0.31% by wt. is illustrated in Percival Vickers catalogue 1893, (p6, item 9). Value $20-35.

Photo 82, finger cup, press molded with ground base and top. 13 cm diameter, density 2.94 g/cc, uranium 0.23% by wt. Although illustrated in 1881 catalogue, (p44 item 1), I would put the *almost certainly* qualification because of its simple design although its density and uranium are close to the Lozenge marked insulator in Photo 80. Again I think it may be earlier than the catalogue, *about* 1870. Value $45-70.

Photo 83, a press molded salt, 9.5 cm long. Two examples examined, densities 2.74 g/cc & 2.70 g/cc, uranium 0.31% wt & 0.28% wt. Illustrated in 1881 catalogue, (p33 item 1). Value $20-35.

Photo 84, a goblet, pressed in a three piece mould. It shows seeds and rough mould marks. Height 15 cm, density 2.89 g/cc, uranium 0.23% wt. Not marked but same as Design Registry submission No 221795, (9th Sept. 1868), also in Percival Vickers 1881 catalogue (item 54). This would appear to confirm that items first produced in the late 1860's were still being made 20 years later. The quality of the metal and molding suggest a date *about* 1875. Value $35-70.

Photo 86, another pressed tumbler. Height 10 cm, density 2.59 g/cc, uranium 0.27% wt. Shown in 1881 catalogue as item No 198. Value $30-45.

Photo 85, two tumblers with the same pattern but different sizes. The green one is 8 cm high, density 3.03 g/cc, uranium 0.22% wt. Pattern shown in 1881 catalogue. Value $35-70.

The yellow one is also press molded but 10 cm high. Density 3.16 g/cc, uranium 0.16% wt. Despite the appearance in the 1881 catalogue the quality of the molding says it must be much earlier. I put it *about* 1860. Value $35-70.

Photo 87, press molded candlestick. Height 20 cm, density 2.94 g/cc, uranium 0.26 % wt. Shown in 1881 catalogue, (p 40). Value $30-45.

Photo 88, it is unusual to find a candlestick associated with a luster. Here the stick is press molded, 17.5 cm high and has a density of 2.48 g/cc, and uranium of 0.37% wt. Except for the top flange, this molding is the same design as Photo 87 but the density is significantly lower. *Almost certainly* Percival Vickers. I reckon the date to be *about* 1900. Value $70-115.

Photo 90, two wines in uranium topaz. Left, stands 12 cm high, has a blown foot, stem drawn from bowl both of which have six ground facets. Density 2.9 g/cc, uranium 0.68% wt. Closely resembles item 129 in 1846 catalogue. The density is what I have come to expect from Percival Vickers, (and other Manchester firms), but the uranium is higher than I have found in their molded products. *Probably* Percival Vickers, *about* 1860. Value $45-70.
Right, 11 .75 cm high, blown foot, seven ground facets on bowl. Density 3.26 g/cc, uranium 0.62% wt. Almost exactly the same as item 323 in 1846 catalogue. I am cautious over the density but there is some evidence to suggest that Percival Vickers early work used full leaded glass. I would attribute this as *could be* Percival Vickers *about* 1850. Value $45-70.

Photo 89. I always think of these as "take to bed" candlesticks. I recall from my childhood that when staying with my Gran. whose house did not have electricity, I would be issued with a short candle stuck in a stick of this shape to light me up the dark staircase. Be that as it may, these examples predate those years. At first sight they are very similar to an Edward Moore product and had I not seen the Percival Vickers catalogue then I may well have attributed to that glasshouse, however ....
Left, press molded, design appears in the 1881 catalogue (p40). Height 9 cm,. density 2.63 g/cc, uranium 0.22% by wt. Value $15-30.
Right, the same style but not the same pattern as the above and I have not found it in the Percival Vickers catalogues. Height 9.5 cm, density 2.63 g/cc, uranium 0.4% wt. The density says it is unlikely to be from Ed. Moore so I would give it a *could be* Percival Vickers, with the reservation that the top of the candleholder looks very similar to some Molineaux Webb pieces. Date *about* 1885. Value $15-30.

Photo 91, a green wineglass with hollow stem. Height 13 cm, 6 facets have been cut on both bowl and stem, the foot is blown. Density measurement is difficult as a correction has to be made for the hollow stem, I estimate it as 2.9 g/cc, uranium 0.25% wt. The design is very similar to item 184 in 1846 catalogue but it is not clear whether the illustrated item has a hollow stem. *Probably* Percival Vickers, *about* 1850. Value $30-45.

Photo 93, the distinguishing characteristic of this glass is the cut of the stem. It is however not unique to Percival Vickers. The shape of the entire glass is nearly identical to item 178 in the 1846 catalogue, although the item illustrated has some decoration on the bowl and does not appear to have a hollow stem. I estimate the density as 2.75 g/cc but this could have an error as I have to correct my measurement by guessing the volume of air in the hollow stem. The clear glass responds strongly to short wave uv light confirming that it contains lead. Uranium on the green part 0.28% wt. *Probably* Percival Vickers, *about* 1860. Value $20-35.

Photo 92, wine glass, 12.5 cm high, density 2.93 g/cc, uranium 0.23% wt. The foot is blown and the pattern closely resembles Nos. 298 & 368 in the 1846 catalogue. There are some small differences that could be significant especially as I know that Richardsons also cut similar patterns. However in view of the density and uranium content I consider this *probably* Percival Vickers, *about* 1860. Value $30-45.

Photo 94, two wines which, excepting their shade of green, look so similar that they must surely have come from the same glasshouse? I think not.
Left, has a blown foot, six facets with squared tops cut on base of bowl and top the of upper knop. Height 13 cm, density 2.96 g/cc, uranium 0.31% wt. Closely resembles item 36, p4, 1881 catalogue. *Probably* Percival Vickers *about* 1870. Value $30-45.
Right, This glass so closely resembles the other. Moreover the actual shape of the bowl more closely resembles the reference in the 1881 catalogue. It is difficult to be sure whether its foot was blown or molded but it does have the ground off pontil. The metal has some slight blemishes so I would date it *about* 1875. However the density is 2.56 g/cc and uranium 0.5% wt. Until I have some corroboration that Percival Vickers did make this type of metal in this period I can not attribute it to that firm. Value $20-35.

Photo 95, three more wines which may well have come from this firm.
Left, height 13.75 cm, density 2.81 g/cc, uranium 0.25% wt. The glass has a blown foot, the knops, stem and cuttings are the same as item 240 in 1846 catalogue. *Almost certainly* Percival Vickers, *about* 1855. Value $20-35.
Center, has a ground pontil and blown foot. Height 14.75 cm, density 2.94 g/cc, uranium 0.22% wt. The stem and 8 ground facets are identical to item 241 in the 1846 catalogue, although the bowl is a different shape. In view of the density and uranium content I consider this *probably* Percival Vickers, *about* 1850. Value $20-30.
Right, the shape of this plain glass is so common, the fact that it is identical to item 287 in the 1846 catalogue by itself does not justify an attribution. However the ground pontil and blown foot is consistent with that period. The density of 2.95 g/cc, uranium 0.28% wt is consistent with other attributed greens. On balance I would say *could be* Percival Vickers, *about* 1860. Value $15-20.

Chapter 21
London and the Surrounding Area

The association of London with glass making goes back a long time, long before uranium came into use. As already mentioned it was back in 1673 that George Ravescroft developed his lead glass, which was to put the British Cut Glass industry in the forefront of the world. My study of the origin of uranium glass also points to London being a major development center. Indeed, as home to the Royal Institution and other learned bodies it would be surprising if it were not. Yet on scanning through the Kelly's 1948 Directory, excluding bottle, jar and technical glassmakers, I see only two names, that of James Powell (Whitefriars), and Nazeing. Theses are the only London glass producers that I have identified as using uranium.

Chapter 22

Nazeing Glass Works

The origin of this small glassworks probably goes back to 1870 and a factory opened by Charles Kempton in Vauxhall, London. His sons carried on the business and eventually became involved with Edison & Swan making Electric light bulbs. In 1928 the glass works was established at Nazeing, Broxbourne in Hertfordshire and it continues in business today. This period represents the era to which I refer when I talk of "Nazeing." Not a lot has been written about this company but its history is currently being researched and perhaps one day the results will be published. Meanwhile its products are not on the "highly collectable" list, never the less it does attract some interest.

A short account of Nazeing is given by Frank Andrews in The Glass Cone[1] from which I gather they produced colored decorative glassware as well as pressed items such as ashtrays. Unfortunately a lot of their records were destroyed in 1973. According to Andrews their decorative glass had a "fairly high lead content" but unfortunately he does not tell us how high. They acquired the moulds from both Sowerby and Davidson when these firms closed. The Sowerby moulds have been totally integrated and Nazeing have no separate records identifying them. However over 80% of them were scrapped. One that was not was the Sowerby Signal Lens, it is still in use. Very few of Davidson' s moulds were kept[2].I wonder if any from Ed. Moore and Molineaux, Webb were amongst them?

The Company has used uranium as a coloring agent but mainly for making yellow glass. They ceased using it about 1982.[3] In the 1970s they were making ashtrays for the French Pernod Company. The example I show later under French glass was made in France but when that Company ceased trading Nazeing did two orders of about 5,000 ashtrays. Nazeing used their own mould and batch but the two products look very similar. There is a slight difference in the typeface[4].

[1]Andrews F - The Glass Cone, (Glass Association UK) No 24, Winter 1989/90.

[2]Pollock-Hill S - Personal Communication, December 1990.

[3]Pollock-Hill S - Personal Communication, February 1997.

[4]Pollock-Hill S - Personal Communication, November 1999.

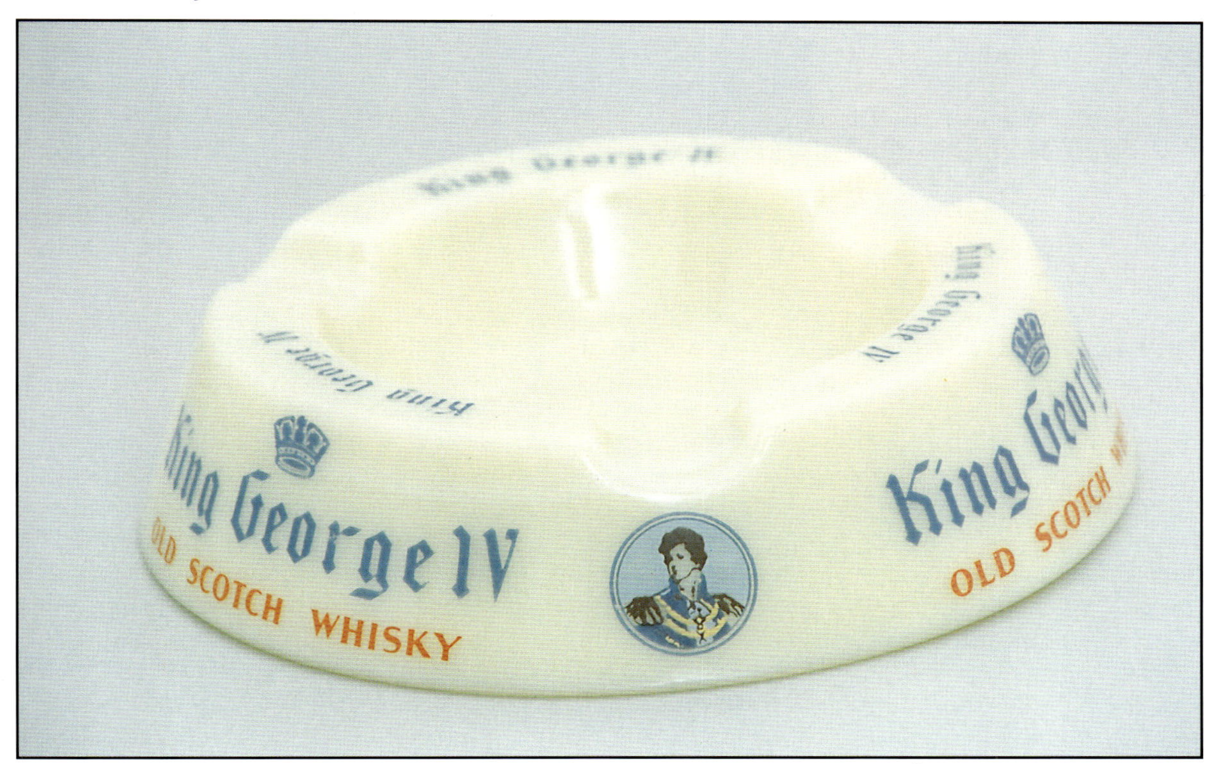

Photo 96. Ashtray, 15.5 cm diameter, density 2.51 g/cc, uranium 0.28% wt. The underside is marked "Nazeing." It was produced late 1950's or early 60's. and used a five color transfer. Later designs reverted to black glass and gold silk screened decoration. Value $15-20.

Chapter 23
James Powell, Whitefriars

It seems likely that a glass works existed on the Whitefriars site, which took its name from the lands originally belonging to the Carmelite Friars, as early as 1700, give or take a few years. The story of how this grew to become one of Britain's premier glass producers in the nineteenth and twentieth century has been well researched and is told in two comprehensive books[1,2]. Unfortunately the Company did not survive until the third millennium and closed in 1980. A good deal is known about this firm, especially from the time that James Powell bought the site in 1834. This is because records, workbooks, specimens and photographs have come into the possession of the Museum of London.

Whitefriars is of particular interest as it is the first recorded producer of uranium glass in the UK. (see Section 1, Chapter 1). Whether or not this was before Powell took over the glassworks, or whether the use of uranium was his innovation I cannot be sure. Notes in a batch book[3] indicate that on 4th July 1834 a batch was made containing "*Devon Ore*" that gave a green color. I have not been able to find out what "*Devon Ore*" is. At that time uranium was mined in Cornwall, although there were known deposits in Devon it is unlikely they were exploited. If this is the case then "*Devon Ore*" would not be a uranium source. The first mention of uranium is in a batch dated 12th Sept. 1835 when 12 oz. of "*uranium oxide from Johnson of Hatton Garden*" was added to "*3 qrs, 12 lbs. of Fritt & Metal*" and "*worked into goods of about 37 lbs wt.*" If this was the first production of viable uranium glass then it would be after Powell had taken over. A batch was made on 4th March 1836, some of which was subsequently made into candlesticks, which Lord Howe to presented to the Queen Adelaide.

That batch was the result of a cascade of other experimental batches, some of the cullet from one being used in the next. I have estimated, from data in the recipe book, that the uranium content would be 0.7%-0.8% wt U. (The arithmetic comes to 0.74% but there are some uncertainties such as the amount of water produced and lost during the melt and the type of uranium oxide used. I have neglected the former and assumed $U_3 0_8$). It is worth noting that some 248 lbs of the mix remained. The next mention of Whitefriars uranium glass comes in 1837. At a banquet given by the Corporation of London, for the new Queen Victoria, uranium glass "Topaz" finger bowls furnished her table[4]. Recipe 12 in the book gives the Topaz mix as being 11 oz uranium to 1 cwt of fritt. This I estimate would give a uranium content in the product of about 0.5%-0.6% U wt. (The arithmetic indicated 0.52%). I have had an opportunity to put the Geiger counter on three of these finger bowls. Two gave an indication of 0.6% wt U and the third 0.8% wt U. This would seem to indicate that part of the set was made from the Queen Adelaide candlestick batch and part from the Recipe 12.

An advertisement in the Connoisseur, (Nov 1907, Vol. xix, No 75), quotes from an advert in the Tatler of 8th August 1710 "*At the flint Glass House in White-Fryars near the Temple, are made and sold by Wholesale or Retale, all sorts of Decanthers, Drinking Glasses, Crewits &c. or Glasses made to any pattern, of the best Flint; as also all Sorts of common Drinking Glasses, and other Things made in ordinary Flint Glass, at reasonable Rates.*" It says this advert "*still holds good of the Whitefriars Glass Works*" and goes on "*James Powell & Sons. ..... their usual display of reproductions of 18th Century shapes and designs in Table Glass, are now exhibiting ....*" This not only indicates the age of the original glass works but also that in the early 1900s they were making reproduction Georgian table glass. We must bear in mind that some of this might contain uranium see Photo 101.

It is worth noting that the 1836 batch books refer to "common fritt" and "best fritt." The former has a lead content of about 29% and the latter about 31%, giving densities of around 3.1 g/cc and 3.18 respt. Evans et al[5] tell us that Whitefriars continued to make lead glass until the 1970s and their soda products from the late 1880s. They also say that there are some other technical signatures, namely optical molding which leaves a light ribbed pattern in the glass, mould patterned prunts, rigoree (a trail of glass with a milled finish), a collar with a zigzag trail, tears and trails. Before attributing every item with such characteristics to Whitefriars, it should be kept in mind that other glasshouses also produced similar effects.

Popular with the collector are their "straw" items, which are illustrated in Photos 98, 99 , 100. I have examined 7 of these. The average density 3.185 g/cc with a standard deviation of 0.053. The average uranium was 0.115% wt with a standard deviation of 0.03.

There is a curiosity with Photo 136 shown in chapter 27. The dark amber vase is clearly illustrated in the 1931 Whitefriars catalogue but I am not happy to attribute this item to that firm. The vase also is in Stevens and Williams pattern book as item 53254 and is discussed in that chapter.

Being in the forefront of uranium glass technology it is likely that Whitefriars continued to exploit their advantage, but for how long I have little idea. I have only been able to identify relatively few of their items.

[1]Jackson L - Whitefriars Glass, Art of James Powell & Sons.
[2]Evans W et al. - Whitefriars Glass, James Powell & Sons of London,
[3]Whitefriars Recipe Book 1832, p 29. Museum of London.
[4]Evans W et al.- Whitefriars Glass, James Powell & Sons of London, p19.
[5]Evans W et al - Whitefriars Glass, James Powell & Sons of London, p 223.
[6]Evans W et al. - Whitefriars Glass, James Powell & Sons of London, p 241.
[7]Jackson L - Whitefriars Glass, Art of James Powell & Sons, p102.

Photo 97, This wine is of particular interest. Height 13 cm, 3.13 g/cc, uranium 0.62% wt. The glass has a ground pontil and a blown foot. An illustration, very closely resembling this item, is shown in an early pattern book[6]. The uranium content and density are consistent with the "Topaz Batch 12" formulae. These I regard as indicative rather than proof of origin. *Probably* Whitefriars, *about* 1850. Value $70-115.

Photo 98, a bowl in "Straw". Diameter 13 cm, density 3.22 g/cc, uranium 0.12% wt. Whitefriars are known to have made very delicate, straw colored with opal effect items such as bowls, plates, tazzas etc. This is *almost certainly* an example, about 1890[7] .Value $45-70.

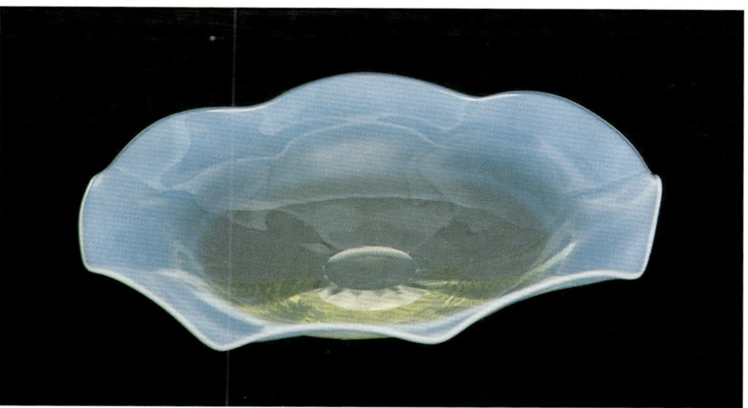

Photo 99, This time a plate in "Straw". Diameter 15 cm, density 3.12 g/cc, uranium 0.08% wt. *Probably* Whitefriars, *about* 1890. Value $30-45.

Photo 100, a tazza. in straw. 6.5 cm high, 12.5 cm diameter. Density 3.17 g/cc, uranium 0.12 % wt. *Probably* Whitefriars, *about* 1890. Value $45-60.

Photo 101, a claret, 13.25 cm high. Density 3.06 g/cc, uranium 0.22% wt. At first sight this item appears to be eighteenth century, it is dark green, hand made and has a broken pontil on the base, but there are give-aways. The presence of uranium is one, another is that the foot is molded. This item closely resembles Set No 2481 in the 1931 catalogue sheets. It was clearly intended to be repro. for the heading states "Based on Eighteenth-Century Originals". This type of repro. is not uncommon and is occasionally mistaken for the real thing. One should not jump to the conclusion that all such items are from Whitefriars, other glasshouses made them. Because this one has a close resemblance to the catalogue sheet, I would say *almost certainly* Whitefriars, *about* 1930. Value $30-45.

Chapter 24

The English Midlands

By the term Midlands I refer to that central part of England which encompasses some major industrial towns and cities and the counties of Warwickshire, Worcestershire, Staffordshire and Northants. Within this, for the purpose of studying glass manufacture, we are really only concerned with two locations, namely around Stourbridge and Birmingham. The term Stourbridge has to the collector wider connotations than the town itself and rather refers to the various glasshouses in that part of the world. They were, during the uranium age, the premier glass producers in the Country and of worldwide importance. Alas to day only a few survive. Of the famous names none are left in Birmingham and only Stuart Crystal and Royal Brierley remain in Stourbridge. At the time of writing the future of the latter is uncertain. Following financial difficulties the business was sold and the site scheduled for re-development.

Although a good deal has been written about some of the glass producers in this area, there is still much to be researched. Perhaps, as much as anything, there is a need for an overall picture to be painted showing how all those who participated in the development of the industry, grew, were inter-connected and eventually closed. Unfortunately such a work has still to be done.

There were glasshouses as early as the 1700s and perhaps earlier but records are scant and little is known of them. However by the start of the next century the business was building. The area would have had access to the rich Midland coalfields and the opportunity to exploit the new steam power technologies. Perhaps these were the reasons for the development of the cut glass industry, based on high lead content glass, rather than where this bright sparkling metal had been developed. Be that as it may, by the early part of the nineteenth century cut glass had become the mainstay of glass making in the Midlands and elsewhere in England. As the century progressed the Midlands also started to produce, in marketable quantities, fancy glass using color and trails, flowers, leaves etc. to adorn the basic item.

By the 1840s the American developed process of making items by pressing was attracting the attention of the English glasshouses. It is likely that some of the first pressed glass was made in the Midlands but it did not develop as it did elsewhere. Perhaps this was, at least in part, due to the areas fixation with its full lead crystal. Had it adapted, as the North East did, the history of glass production in Stourbridge and Birmingham may well have had a different outcome.

Identification is again a major problem. Some of Thomas Webb's pattern books are at the Local Public Records Office, albeit in varying states of decay. There are also two of Richardson's. Stuart Crystal is still in production and have their old books. The books of Stevens and Williams, now Royal Brierley, have survived and are currently in the care of Broadfield House Glass Museum. The story and products of Walsh have been researched and published[1]. Unlike the pressed glass manufacturers only a few products are marked with design registrations. I feel sure there are numerous surviving items from this area to which I am unable to attribute. I have grouped these into a chapter of their own.

As with the other areas I have to say that it has not been my intention to research the history of these industries but rather to identify their products which used uranium.

[1]Reynolds E - Glass of John Walsh Walsh.

Chapter 25
Richardsons of Wordsley

The business was started by two Richardson brothers, Benjamin and William Haden, together with Thomas Webb in 1829. After Webb left Jonathan joined his other brothers some time about 1840. The story of the "Richardson Dynasty" is told by Hajdamach[1] and merits a whole chapter of his book. Despite their success at the Great Exhibition of 1851 and the patronage they received, they went bankrupt in 1852. Not withstanding this the brothers Benjamin and Jonathan were soon back in business. In 1864 the name of the enterprise changed to Hodgetts, Richardson and Pargeter, then in 1870, when Philip Pargeter departed, to Hodgetts, Richardson and Son. Some time later, at the turn of the century the name Hodgetts disappears and the firm trades as H G Richardson & Sons. The business was taken over by Thomas Webb & Sons in 1930 who continued for a limited time, to use the Richardson name, but on products made by themselves.

It is arguable that Richardsons produced some of the finest glass in England and it may be that their preference for extreme quality rather than quantity contributed to their downfall. Never the less Manley[2] is forceful in maintaining that Richardsons' also made cheap glassware. Be that as it may examples of Richardson's glass, especially at affordable prices, are hard to come by. I have no doubt they used uranium in their wares but have only been able to find a few examples.

Some of their pattern books were rescued when the firm folded and are now held in the Dudley Archives. I have used these to help attribute items in my collection. They are difficult to date, but a "Lozenge" Registration mark in the middle of Book 2 dates it around 1870. This Book 2 has an entry by a salt that says "pressed not cut" which clearly indicates that they were making pressed glassware. Another interesting point is Pattern 5379, in Book 3, it shows a tumbler with the words "George Davidson & Co. No 27." Were Richardsons were making glass for Davidson to sell? Or did Richardsons cut a tumbler from which Davidson made a mould? The date would be about the time that George Davidson was getting into pressed glass. It can only be a matter for speculation.

On scanning the following results there appears limited consistency in uranium concentrations but taken over a hundred years of varying products this is not surprising.

[1] Hajdamach C - British Glass p95 - p130

[2] Manley C - Decorative Victorian Glass p35.

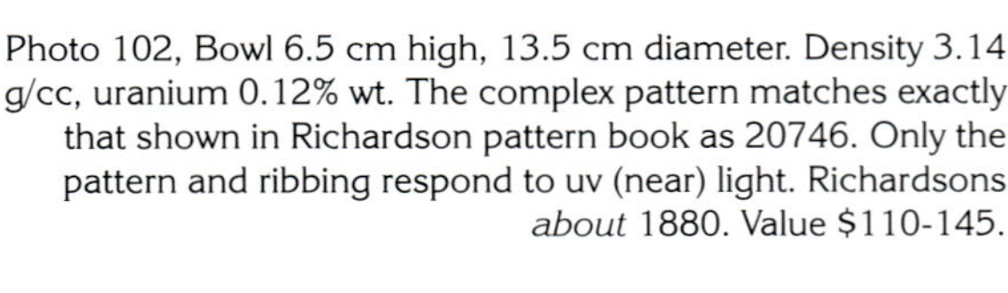

Photo 102, Bowl 6.5 cm high, 13.5 cm diameter. Density 3.14 g/cc, uranium 0.12% wt. The complex pattern matches exactly that shown in Richardson pattern book as 20746. Only the pattern and ribbing respond to uv (near) light. Richardsons *about* 1880. Value $110-145.

Photo 103, jam dish, in silver plate stand. Diameter 12 cm, density 3.14 g/cc, uranium 0.12% wt. Almost identical to item 19148 in Richardson's pattern book. The ribbing identical to that on Photo 102. Under uv (near) light, only the pattern shows. The stand is marked EPNS and RP (cross axes) L but unfortunately I have not been able to identify it. Richardson's, *about* 1880. Value $145-215.

Photo 104, posy vase, 10 cm high, density 3.24 g/cc, uranium 0.22% wt. This little beauty, perfectly shaped, is amberina in style and has faint gray vertical stripes joining up with the gray edging under the petal lips. The ruby is close to that of Photos 102 & 103. The shape of the petals is not dissimilar from a design registered by Thomas Webb but there is significant difference. The infill between them, which looks like a pair of eyes, match the design of one shown in Richardson's books, No 21163, and described as " the new leaf crimp." Richardson' s *about* 1890. Value $110-180.

Photo 105, I'm not sure how to describe this item. It could be a salt but with its folded sides I would not like to use it as such. The glass is just over 4 cm high and 7 cm diameter. The density is 2.97 g/cc, uranium is only on the crimped band and the raspberry prunt on the base. It is not possible to get a reliable reading with the Geiger counter. The crimped band is similar to that on Photo 102, furthermore Richardson patterns 18936&7 are very similar in style, including the raspberry prunt," but the top is different. The support carries the EPNS mark of Daniel & Arter, Birmingham. *Probably* Richardson' s *about* 1900. Value $45-70.

Photo 106. I had difficulty in distinguishing these two items from a similar one shown in a Stevens and Williams pattern book but the balance of evidence says they are not from that factory. Left a small salt perhaps. I suspect that it once had a metal support but it might have been intended for free standing. Height 4.5 cm, density 2.98 g/cc, uranium 0.13% wt. It has been made in a ribbed blow mould and has a perfectly round dimple where the pontil has been ground off. The metal has some very small trapped air bubbles. Identical to item 19382 in pattern book. *Almost certainly* Richardson's, *about* 1890. Value $35-60.
Right, bowl 6.5 cm high, 14 cm diameter. Density 2.97, g/cc, uranium 0.12% wt. Similar to the Richardson pattern and the density is the same as salt and Photo 105. The crimp work is also similar to items in Photos 102, 103, and 105. Its response to uv (near) light is very weak. *Probably* Richardson's *about 1890*. Value $60-90.

Photo 108, green wine with a Greek Key pattern. Height 12 cm, density 3.1 g/cc, uranium 0.28% wt. This type of pattern was used by a number of glass houses and by itself does not make for an attribution. However this one has additional scoring above and below the keys and also a ring of dots. On the basis of the more coincident detail the more reliable the attribution, the closeness of this to pattern 3583 leads me to say *probably* Richardson's and the blown foot with its ground pontil, *about* 1860. Value $15-30.

Photo 107, wine, 12 cm. high, density 3.17 g/cc, uranium 0.68% wt. Appears identical to item 915 in the Richardson pattern book. Although the elongated facets are not uncommon the double ring where the stem joins the bowl is unusual. I believe this justifies an *almost certainly* Richardson's attribution. As for date, the ground off pontil and blown foot says 1860 or earlier so I'll go for *about* 1850. Value $60-90.

Photo 109, although marked "Richardson's British and a Union Flag", see inset, this vase was probably not made by that firm. The likelihood is that it was made by Webb after they had taken over Richardson during the period they continued to use the Richardson name and trade mark. Height 17.5 cm, density 3.21 g/cc, uranium 0.99% wt. However some doubt lingers in my mind as the uranium level is a little below that I would have expected from Webb's "Sunshine Amber". *About* 1935. Value $45-60.

Chapter 26
Stuart Crystal

The origin of Stuart Crystal can be traced back to 1676 when a John Bradley started to build glasshouses at Wordsley. The Redhouse Glass Works, where Stuart Crystal started and is still based, was built by Richard Bradley in 1788. Redhouse Cone still stands to day and is one of only four surviving in the UK.

Aged eleven Frederick Stuart started work at the Redhouse Glass Works and eventually became its owner in 1881. During this time Philip Pargeter, who had been associated with the Richardson brothers, had a major impact on the business. He was particularly interested in colored glass and was a driving force to make a replica of the broken Portland Vase at the British Museum.

At the age of 83 Frederick retired in favor of his sons. Robert, the last survivor, died in 1946 and the management of the company continued under the grandson of the founder, another Frederick. The business expanded after WW2 and the 1960s saw another factory opened in Wales. In 1995 the Company became part of the Waterford Wedgwood Group.

Although today we associate Stuart with high quality cut crystal, in earlier days they were very much into decorative and colored glass. However products from that period are difficult to identify. Fortunately pattern books still exist and the Company has allowed me to look through them. Stuart's did use uranium. Old notebooks in the possession Stuart's archives give batch mixes for a variety of uranium-based colors such as Pomona, Canary, Chrysophis, Opaque Green, Opaque Blue, Opaque Yellow. Their origin is not clear, some may be recording mixes used by other glasshouses and brought by "poached" employees. However others are most likely the actual records of batches made up at Redhouse Glass Works and as such indicate that during the 1870-90 period uranium was used extensively.

Dated 13 2 1887 there is a trial batch for "Burmese Ware." At this time it was being produced by Thos Webb under license from Mount Washington Glass Company in the USA, see Chapter 29. Was this an attempt to break the patent and if so was it successful? It does not appear to be a copy of the patented formula having a uranium content of about 1.6% wt. Another interesting menu is in the 1890s book, a "Dark Topaz for Cameo Vases" has a uranium content of about 3.5% wt., which is slightly higher than any uranium glass that I have found.

Stuart[1] stopped making colored glass at about the turn of the century except for a small amount of green, amber, and blue that was produced in 1920/30

[1]Stuart Crystal - Personal Communication. 13/11/1989.

Photo 110, posy vase, 8.5 cm high, density 3.06 g/cc, uranium 0.1% wt. Neither the density nor the uranium matches any of the aforementioned formula but as these are incomplete that is not conclusive. The density is the same as that of some plain 1880 glass, which I considered, came from Stuart, and the crimping on the feet matches those in Pattern Book 4, item 7997. I put it somewhere between a *could be* and a *probably* Stuart's, about 1880. Value $45-70.

Photo 111, this wine appears to be an exact match with item 857 shown in Stuart's Pattern book. Close inspection reveals an anomaly, This glass has 11 rugby ball shaped facets on its bowl, while the pattern book says 12! If it were the one in the book it would date in the mid 1870's. The molded foot raises a niggle of a doubt. The density confirms that doubt. Perhaps Stuart reproduced their older designs in later years, more likely someone copied it. Height 13.5 cm, density 2.56 g/cc, uranium 0.31% wt. So when was it made? From the quality of the metal I would make a best guess of between 1890 and 1930, which is not very helpful. Value $15-20.

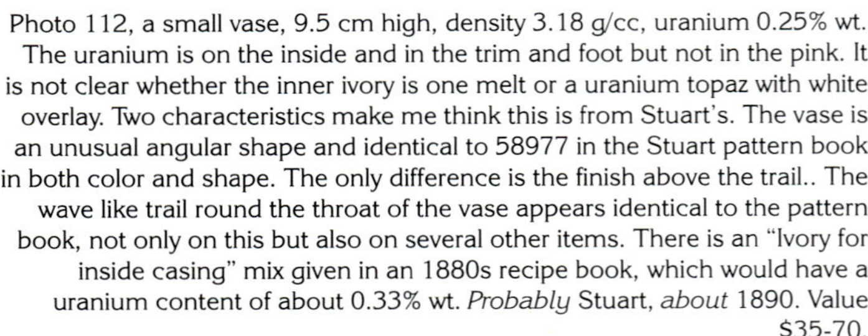

Photo 112, a small vase, 9.5 cm high, density 3.18 g/cc, uranium 0.25% wt. The uranium is on the inside and in the trim and foot but not in the pink. It is not clear whether the inner ivory is one melt or a uranium topaz with white overlay. Two characteristics make me think this is from Stuart's. The vase is an unusual angular shape and identical to 58977 in the Stuart pattern book in both color and shape. The only difference is the finish above the trail.. The wave like trail round the throat of the vase appears identical to the pattern book, not only on this but also on several other items. There is an "Ivory for inside casing" mix given in an 1880s recipe book, which would have a uranium content of about 0.33% wt. *Probably* Stuart, *about* 1890. Value $35-70.

Chapter 27
Stevens & Williams - Royal Brierley

The name of this glasshouse is legend amongst the other "greats" of the Stourbridge cum Birmingham area. According to its headed notepaper its origins go back to 1776. Little has been written about the history of this business, but quite a lot about its products. Dodsworth[1] writing an introduction for the Sotheby's catalogue for the Sale of the Royal Brierley collection, gives a short history of the Company. He tells us that the Williams-Thomas family, who have only recently sold out their interest, can trace their connection back to 1819.

The original glassworks was built in Moor Lane , Brierley Hill, but moved across the other side of the railway line in 1870 where it remained until the Receivership of recent times. The Company has now been sold and there is expectation that production under this proud name will start again but not on the old site. This, I understand, is up for re-development.

Like the other Stourbridge glasshouses Stevens & Williams were very much into cut crystal but they did not let this distract them from the production of colored and decorative glass, and for this they made liberal use of uranium. Perhaps the most notable period in their long history was when John Northwood joined them as Artistic Director in 1881. He had already been involved with the reproduction of the Portland Vase while at Stuarts. By the 1930s Stevens & Williams, now trading as Royal Brierley, were continuing with the use of uranium in their colored glass. From John Scrivers notebook in the Stevens & Williams records it would appear that uranium was first used in 1853.

Examination of the following examples reveals some interesting points. Items in Photos 116 to 119 all have densities 2.5 g/cc. This would indicate low lead metal. This is curious for a Stourbridge firm, especially as I find all their other metal of that vintage to have densities of 3 g/cc or more. I can only conclude that the off white mix is of quite low density possibly due to the opacifier. The uranium content of this group is all of the same order and the last three virtually identical.

Photos 132 to 134 show half a dozen of pieces with a white inner layer and a primrose yellow on the outside. All appear in the Stevens & Williams Pattern books of the 1920s. As far as I can determine the metal of these is identical to the "Primrose" products of Walsh Walsh, see Chapter 28. Walsh ran adverts of their product in Pottery Gazette. I do not know for sure that Stevens and Williams did not but I have never seen such an advert of theirs. So near identical are the items I do wonder if Stevens and Williams were making the product for Walsh.

In later years, see Photos 147 & 148 it would seem that some of their production was in low lead glass.

[1]Dodsworth R - Sotheby's Catalogue, 1998.

[2]Glass Collectors Digest, Marietta, Ohio, USA. Vol. II No1, June/July 1988 p 24.

[3]Manley C - Decorative Victorian Glass, pic. 117

[4]Thompson S - Museum Curator, Royal Brierley, personal letter to author 1992.

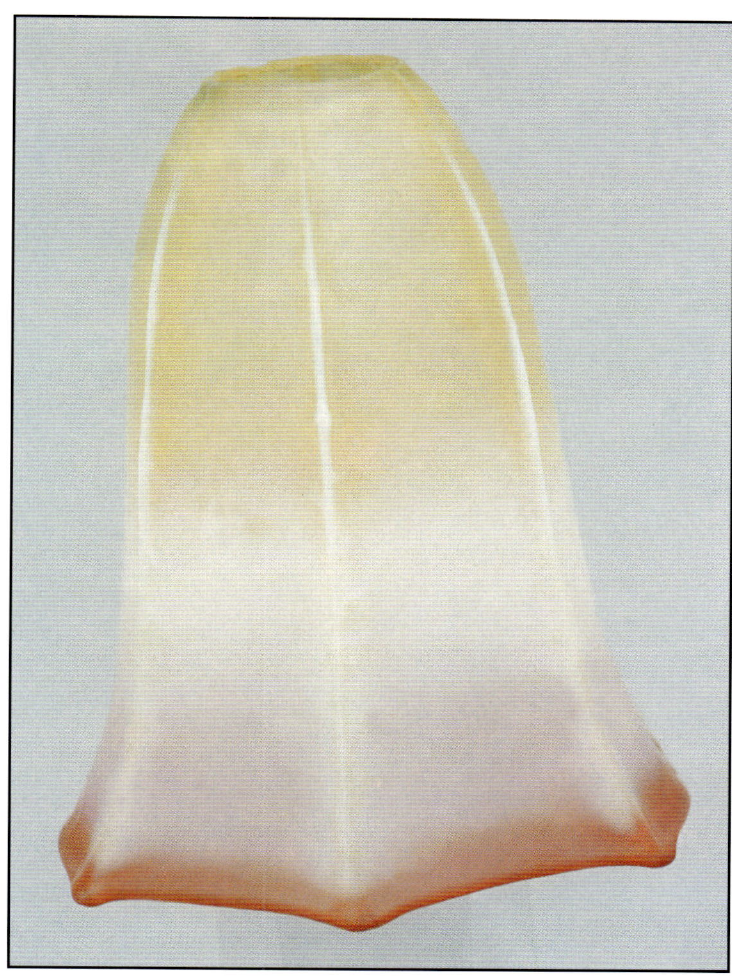

Photo 113, this delicate lampshade carries a Registration Mark. It is engraved "Rd 620799", which was registered by Stevens & Williams in 1913. Height 14.5 cm, density 3.23 g/cc, uranium 0.17 % wt. It is not clear whether all the metal contains uranium as the red areas are much less sensitive to uv light. Value $145-215.

Photo 114, I bought this dish at the sale of the Royal Brierley Collection in 1998. It was attributed by Sotheby's to Stevens & Williams, work of Pierre Erard, circa 1884. The dish is 14 cm diameter, has a density of density 2.97 g/cc, and uranium 0.31% wt. The uranium is probably in the ivory as the pink does not respond to uv light. Value $300-435.

Photo 117, the uranium is again in the "white" and not the trail work. Height 13 cm, density 2.5 g/cc, uranium 0.16 % wt. The "Flower" decoration identical to prunt on the vase in Photo 116. Impressed mark on base, which is unreadable, could be Stevens and Williams. The similarity of the metal, the mark on the base which compares with that on the item in Photo 115, and the "flower" all add up to *probably* Stevens and Williams *about* 1895. Value $70-145.

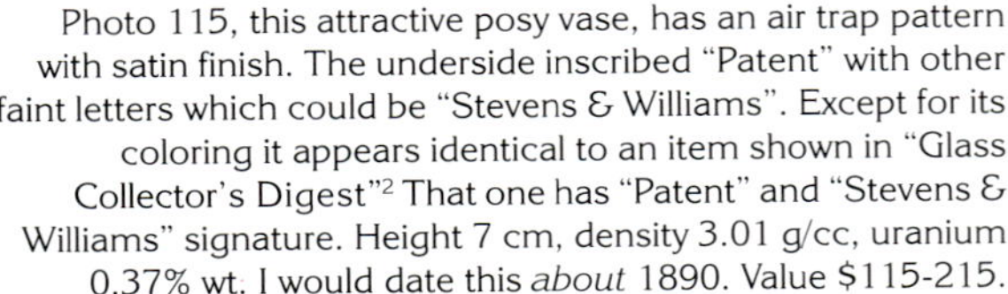

Photo 115, this attractive posy vase, has an air trap pattern with satin finish. The underside inscribed "Patent" with other faint letters which could be "Stevens & Williams". Except for its coloring it appears identical to an item shown in "Glass Collector's Digest"[2] That one has "Patent" and "Stevens & Williams" signature. Height 7 cm, density 3.01 g/cc, uranium 0.37% wt. I would date this *about* 1890. Value $115-215.

Photo 116, vase. 22.5 cm high, density 2.52 g/cc, uranium 0.25% wt. The uranium is in the ivory (almost white) outer layer. The amber trail work has no uranium. Similar item attributed by Manley[3] and by Thompson[4] (from photograph). The acanthus leaf with bent stem forming a foot appears a number of times in the Stevens & Williams pattern books of the 1880s. Prunt on pontil mark (see inset) is typical of other Stevens & Williams prunts. Stevens and Williams *about* 1895. Value $110-145.

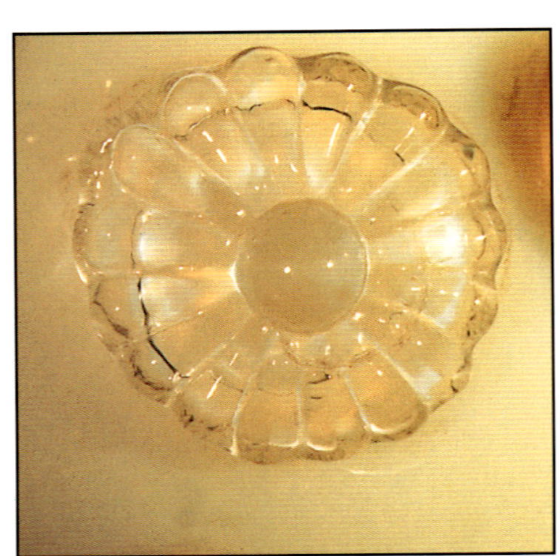

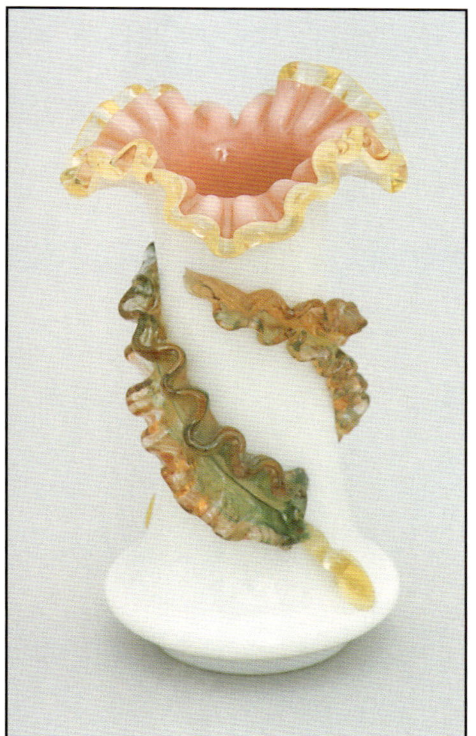

Photo 118, height 14.5 cm, density 2.49 g/cc, uranium 0.14% wt. The uranium is only in the ivory (almost white) outer layer. The top amber trail is identical to item in Photo 117 and there are traces of similar unreadable inscription on base. Acanthus leaf resembles Photo 116. *Probably* Stevens & Williams, *about* 1895. Value $115-215.

Photo 120, a jug vase that looks as if it came from the same glass house as items in Photos 116 to 119, but did it? Height 13 cm, density 2.38 g/cc, uranium 0.09% wt. The trail work looks like Stevens & Williams and so does the decoration but the density and uranium content, which is only in the white, are much lower than the others. I won't go further than say *best guess* Stevens & Williams *about* 1895. Value $45-70.

Photo 119, another decorated piece that has similar characteristics. Height 9.5 cm, density 2.5 g/cc, uranium 0.14% wt. Uranium only in outer layer. Top amber trail is the same as on Photo 117 & 118. Petal has same mixed color as the acanthus leaf on Photo 118. *Probably* Stevens & Williams, *about* 1895. Value $115-215.

Photo 121, two shell dishes which surely must have come from the same glasshouse. They closely resemble Stevens & Williams pattern 10938, which is dated 1881, as to justify an *almost certain* attribution. The mauve dish is 15 cm diameter, density 3.14 g/cc, and uranium on mauve 0.07% wt, and on the outside 0.22% wt. It is possible that the apparent uranium in the mauve is in effect shine from the outer layer.
The pink dish is 14.5 cm diameter, density 3.12 g/cc, and uranium on pink 0.2% wt and on the outside 0.22% wt. Value each $45-90.

Photo 122, a dish that closely resembles the shells in Photo 121. The shape appears as item 53130 in the Stevens & Williams Pattern books but as yellow primrose of the 1920s. Diameter 15 cm, density 3.16 g/ cc, uranium on the pink 0.19% wt, on the outside 0.22% wt. *Almost certainly* Stevens & Williams *about* 1885. Value $60-115.

Photo 123, the evidence for this attribution comes from its similarity to the items in Photos 121 and 122. I have not seen it in the Stevens & Williams pattern books but then only a sample has been searched. Maximum width 13.5 cm, density 3.15 g/cc, uranium in pink 0.2% wt, on the outside 0.22% wt. *Could be* Stevens & Williams *about* 1885. Value $60-115.

Photo 124, the crimp work on the top of this bowl is distinctly hunched and resembles that on items in Photos 118 & 119. Although its color is very close to the previous pieces it is not quite the same shade. More telling is the density, 2.5 g/cc, and uranium 0.17% wt on the pink and 0.2% wt on the outside. The density matches those pieces but the uranium does not. It does match items in Photos 121 & 122. Again we see the value of knowing the density and uranium level. In this case it raises serious doubts and I would go no further than saying it *could be* Stevens & Williams *about* 1885. Value $45-90.

Photo 125, salt, 4.5 cm high, density 3.14 g/cc, uranium 0.08% wt. The style looks much the same as the salt in Photo 106. Same size and number of ribs but the top is slightly turned over, the glass is thicker and the ribs much more pronounced. It is almost as if it had been pressed but there are no signs of mould marks. It stands on the end of the ribs, which have been ground however the dimple between the ribs is molded. Unlike the salt in Photo 106 it has only a weak response to uv (near) light. It closely resembles item 46,665 in the Stevens & Williams pattern book. dated 1914. So is it Stevens & Williams or Richardson's? The density and uranium suggest it did not come from the same glasshouse as the items in Photo 106, therefore I hazard *probably* Stevens and Williams *about* 1915. Value $45-60.

Photo 126, because it lacks finish or decoration I suspect this is a blank or a practice piece. However there are several illustrations in the Stevens & Williams pattern books, i.e. Nos., 12433, 14473, 14476, 15652 which show this style of top. Height 9 cm, density 3.32, uranium 0.6% wt. *Could be* Stevens & Williams *about* 1890. Value $20-30.

Photo 128 this topaz wine is shown in the pattern book as number 7716 and dates 1885. It is interesting to note that it has a molded foot and a ground off pontil, there are also seeds in the metal. The date seems to endorse my caution in assuming the date that the gadget came into common use. Height 12 cm, density 3.17 g/cc, uranium 0.46% wt. Value $70-110.

Photo 127, another is it, or isn't it conundrum. Both were identified by an authority on Stevens & Williams products as being an example of their "Rose du Barry," a poor imitation of Webb's Queen's Burmese. However I have not found the pattern in their books but then I have only been able to check a proportion of the many thousand entries! However I did come across a batch formula for "Rose Du Barry" which did not contain uranium but it is by no means certain that this formula was the one that was used in production. I have also examined another item which was thought to be "Rose Du Barry" and that did contain uranium at about the same level as these items. I'm not offering an attribution but an open mind. Left, height 11 cm, density 2.46 g/cc, uranium 0.19% wt. Right, height 10.5 cm, density 2.46 g/cc, uranium 0.22% wt. Both date *about* 1890, each value $35-70.

Photo 129, these three glasses illustrate the difficulty in dating. They were bought as one lot at a local auction and had probably come from a house clearance. As will be seen their uranium concentrations and densities are much the same. Their gold trim is also identical, the delicate yellowish green bowl on a clear stem are the same style. They surely must have come from the same glasshouse at about the same period. The stem of the center one has been cut whereas the other two have not. Perhaps the one on the left hand side was a blank. The right hand side glass has a straight stem and, unlike the other two has a ground off pontil., this would date it about 1880 while the others about 1920. However the shape of the left and center appears in the Steven and Williams 1934 pattern book as No 67554, with a note "new process" and "mould 2107". This puts them at 1933/4. But what about the right one with its ground off pontil? I wish they could speak. I'm *almost certain* they come from the same factory at the same time, *probably* Stevens & Williams. Value each $5-15.

Left: Photo 130, another eighteenth century repro. This shape is illustrated in Stevens & Williams pattern book as No 67723 but as "Bristol Blue", which dates 1934. It is 13. 5 cm high, density 3.29 g/cc, uranium 1.98% wt. To give it authenticity it has an ungrounded pontil and seeds in the metal. Apart from the uranium the give away is the molded foot. *Almost certainly* Stevens & Williams, *about* 1935. Value $30-60.

Above: Photo131, these two small bowls were bought at different times, the green one being in the metal basket, both are the same shape and size, i.e. 11 cm high. Both have perfect dimples where the pontil has been ground off.

The green bowl density is 2.8 g/cc, and uranium 0.05% wt. The measured radioactivity was confirmed to be uranium by gamma spectrometry. I puzzle why it is so low as dark greens can be produced without the use of uranium.

The blue bowl, which must have escaped from its holder, has a glossy inside but the outside satin finished. Density 3.03 g/cc, uranium 0.06% wt. The color is unusual for English glass. While I have come across many examples of different shades of radio active blue in continental glass, only infrequently have I seen it in what I believe to be English. An item of this shape appears in a Royal Brierley pattern book as No 47368, which dates 1914. With it there is a side note "Blue or Green". Also "W ? Baker, B'ham. N P". A firm W E Baker , Nickel Platters, in Birmingham, appears in the 1948 Kelly's Directory. On this basis I would say *probably* Stevens & Williams, *about* 1915. However I am puzzled over the different densities of these two. I wonder, if they were made for W E Baker, as seems likely, were Stevens & Williams the sole suppliers or did the nickel platers order their glass from several different glasshouses? So perhaps the blue was made by Stevens & Williams, but not the green. Value with the metal basket $30-45, without it $5-20

Below: Photo 132, width 15 cm, height 7.5 cm, density 3.27 g/cc, uranium 0.81% wt. Value $30-45.

Photo 133, Left, 6.5 cm high, density 3.29 g/cc, uranium 0.93% wt. Center, 5 cm high, density 3.04 g/cc, uranium 0.62% wt.. Right, 6.75 cm high, density 3.25 g/cc, uranium 0.74% wt. Value $30-45 each.

Photo 134, Left, 8.5 cm high, density 3.27 g/cc, uranium 0.93% wt. The EPNS cradle does not have a maker's mark. Right, 6.75 cm high, (excluding lid), density 3.29 g/cc, uranium 0.93% wt. The plated lid is not marked. Value $30-45 each.

Photo 135, this candlestick has an ungrounded pontil, folded foot and twisted stem, no doubt intended to give it a mid Victorian appearance. It is illustrated in Royal Brierley as pattern 53267, which puts it in the mid 1920's although it is quite possible it was made well after that date. It is an unusual design and has high uranium. It has to be Stevens & Williams / Royal Brierley dark amber, say *about* 1930. Height, 23 cm, density 3.29 g/cc, uranium 2.91% wt. Value $45-70.

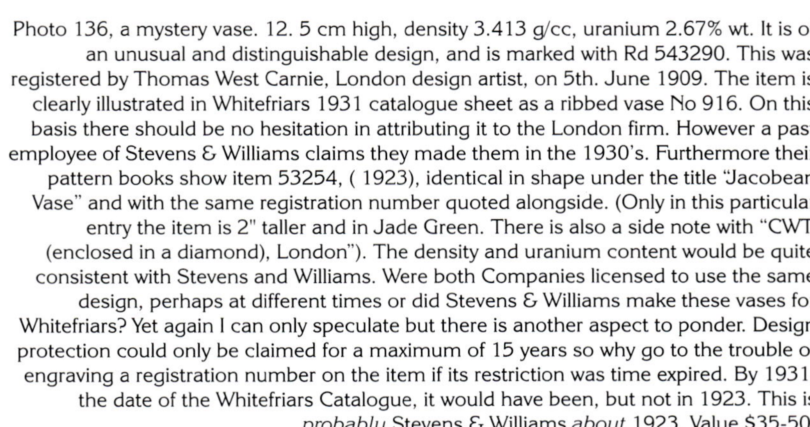

Photo 136, a mystery vase. 12. 5 cm high, density 3.413 g/cc, uranium 2.67% wt. It is of an unusual and distinguishable design, and is marked with Rd 543290. This was registered by Thomas West Carnie, London design artist, on 5th. June 1909. The item is clearly illustrated in Whitefriars 1931 catalogue sheet as a ribbed vase No 916. On this basis there should be no hesitation in attributing it to the London firm. However a past employee of Stevens & Williams claims they made them in the 1930's. Furthermore their pattern books show item 53254, (1923), identical in shape under the title "Jacobean Vase" and with the same registration number quoted alongside. (Only in this particular entry the item is 2" taller and in Jade Green. There is also a side note with "CWT, (enclosed in a diamond), London"). The density and uranium content would be quite consistent with Stevens and Williams. Were both Companies licensed to use the same design, perhaps at different times or did Stevens & Williams make these vases for Whitefriars? Yet again I can only speculate but there is another aspect to ponder. Design protection could only be claimed for a maximum of 15 years so why go to the trouble of engraving a registration number on the item if its restriction was time expired. By 1931, the date of the Whitefriars Catalogue, it would have been, but not in 1923. This is *probably* Stevens & Williams *about* 1923. Value $35-50.

Photo 137, Decanter set, tumbler, sherry glass, are all part of the Royal Brierley "Georgian" suit made in the late 1940's for a very short period. Decanter 20 cm high, density 3.3 g/cc, uranium 2.8% wt. Accompanying glass, 5 cm high, density 3.29 g/cc, uranium 2.8% wt. Sherry 8 cm high, density 3.42 g/cc, uranium 2.5% wt. Tumbler 10 cm high, density 3.4 g/cc, uranium 2.85% wt. All these items were traditionally hand made, the decanter set and tumbler have ground off pontil dimples. Values, Decanter and 6 spirit glasses, $45-60; sherry $5-15; tumbler $5-15.

Photo 138, height 8.25 cm, density 3.24 g/cc, uranium 2.91% wt. *Probably* Royal Brierley "Auburn" *about* 1945. Value $15-20.

Photo 140, although made in old style this goblet lacks a pontil mark. I have not seen this exact pattern in their books but it is probably Royal Brierley, "Cut Auburn" about 1945. Height 13 cm, density 3.26 g/cc, uranium 2.67% wt. Value $20-35.

Photo 139, height 10 cm, density 3.34 g/cc, uranium 2.91% wt. *Probably* Royal Brierley "Auburn" *about* 1945. Value $15-20.

Photo 141, this interests me. Height 10.5 cm, density difficult to determine because of the wide hollow stem but > 3.3 g/cc, uranium 1.18% wt. I first noted that the glass matches exactly an illustration in a Stevens & Williams pattern book, item No 15421, which would put it about 1888. This is much earlier than other examples of this type of amber metal that I have come across. Then I found it illustrated in a 1923 pattern book as "Cairngorm." So it looks as if an old design was pulled out of the files and re-used in the 1920s and later. The uranium is about half the level in the "ambers" of 1930 - 1950 period from this firm and is more like that of Thos. Webb's "Sunshine Amber". *Almost certainly* Stevens & Williams *about* 1925. Value $20-35.

Photo 142, sweet dish, intaglio cut, 9.75 cm diameter, Density 3.19 g/cc , uranium 3.0% wt. Illustrated under the heading "Cairngorm" in 1923 pattern book. *Almost certainly* Stevens & Williams. Value $45-70.

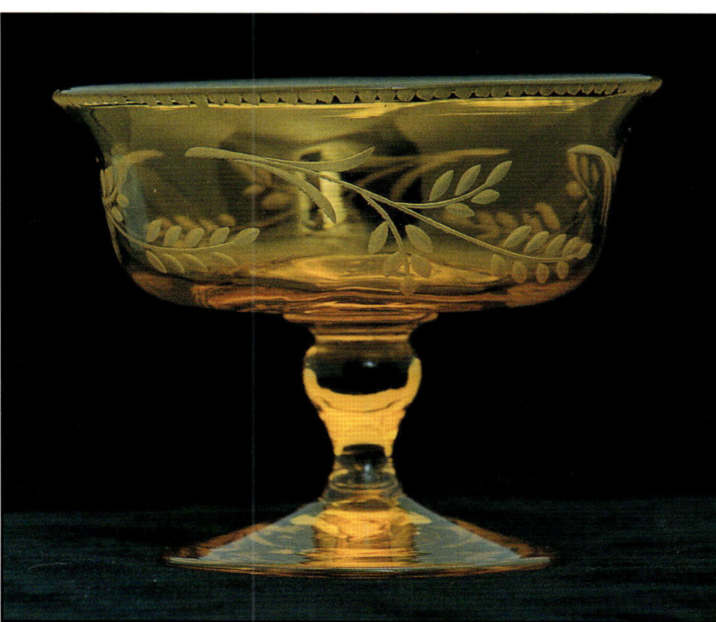

Photo 143, I have not identified this dish in the pattern book but the color, density, and uranium seem familiar! Diameter 10.5 cm, density 3.34 g/cc, uranium 2.79% wt. *Could be* Royal Brierley 1930 - 50. Value $15-20.

Photo 144, a sweet dish with a Grape Vine intaglio cut. Diameter 9.25 cm, density 3.32 g/cc, uranium, 2.91% wt. This pattern appears not infrequently in the Stevens & Williams' books. A similar one can be seen in Webb's but the uranium levels in these items are those of the former rather than the latter company. *Probably* Royal Brierley *about* 1935. $15-20.

Photo 145, cigarette holders like this would have adorned the more formal dining tables. Stevens & Williams made a number of different patterns and while I have not found this particular item in their books this is *probably* one of theirs. Intaglio cut, 7.5 cm high, density 3.31 g/cc, uranium 2.91% wt. Date *about* 1935. Value $45-60.

Photo 147, probably a tooth pick holder. Items in this style appear in the Royal Brierley patterns around the 60-70,000 Nos., i.e. about 1934. However I have not matched this particular cut, perhaps I should have looked harder! Originally the low density also concerned me, but with Photo 148 also having low density items I now think that Royal Brierley may have turned to low lead, lead free metal in some of their products. I'll say *could be* Royal Brierley *about* 1935. Height 7.75 cm, density 2.45 g/cc, uranium 0.09% wt. Value $15-20.

Photo 146, three simpler versions of cigarette holders, the shape is shown as Pattern No 65669 but those illustrated have been cut. From left to right the densities and uranium levels are, 3.31 g/cc, 3.22 g/cc, 3.17 g/cc; uranium 2.79% wt, 2.98% wt, 0.68% wt. Height 6.75 cm. The lower density of the green holder is probably due to the opacifier. Probably Royal Brierley, about 1935 - 1950. Value $15-35.

Below: Photo 148, these vases are examples of "ice" or "crackle" glass and *almost certainly* come from Royal Brierley *about* the WW2 period. The shapes of both are illustrated in their pattern books as Nos. D107 & D108. They have been hand made with ground off pontil marks. The densities are green vase 2.52 g/cc and yellow vase 2.58 g/cc. The uranium is, green vase 0.09 % and yellow vase, 0.43% wt. Heights are 17 cm and 14.75 cm. It would seem they were not produced after 1965. Value green vase $20-30, yellow vase $35-60.

Chapter 28
John Walsh Walsh

Little would have been known about this Birmingham firm but for the researches of Eric Reynolds. Now the story of the business with the strange name is told in his recent book[1]. Legend has it that John Walsh Walsh got his unusual name through a mix-up at his christening. It is not difficult to imagine how it could have happened, however there is no firm evidence for this. Although the firm traded as John Walsh Walsh collectors abbreviate this to Walsh, as does the trademark on some of the company's wares.

An advert in Pottery Gazette, (August 1880), claims the firm was established in 1801. This is being a little economical with the truth. It was in 1850 that John Walsh purchased the glass factory from Samuel Shakespeare that was located in Lodge Road, Birmingham. The founder appears to have had a relatively short life , but a busy one. He died in 1864. However the business stayed in the family through a daughter of his first marriage.

Unfortunately none of the pattern books from the days of John Walsh have survived nor for the years following his death until the mid 1920s. Those from then on are reproduced by Reynolds in his book. Thus virtually nothing is known about the products from the Shakespeare days and little from the earlier part of the Walsh era. I have no idea when uranium was first used on this site but it was certainly in use by the 1880s and continued until the 1930s and possibly later.

A colored advert in Pottery Gazette, Nov. 1883 for Walsh "Crushed Strawberry" and "Electric Blue" enables the identification of some items, see Photos 149 - 153. This and a few design registrations are all I have found to identify items from the first 75 years! There after some adverts in 1922/3 for their "Primrose Glass," (see photos 155 - 158), the Pattern Books reported by Reynolds, a pamphlet by Walsh[2] and some trade marks take us through the second quarter of the Twentieth Century.

In the 1930s Walsh produced their "Pompeian" glass. The metal was full of air bubbles, not in any pattern but rather as if it had been made of foam! The greens and ambers contained uranium, see Photos 162 - 165. I have not been able to find out how the effect was obtained but suspect it may have involved adding something to the mix to make it froth. It should not be assumed that this was unique to Walsh, other glasshouses may have made similar products. The Walsh pamphlet does say that "every piece is marked with the name Walsh." I have only found one such item, perhaps some were marked with adhesive labels, which have subsequently been washed off. The remaining Photos in this chapter show other examples of Walsh products, which I have found and examined.

[1] Reynolds E - The Glass of John Walsh Walsh.

[2] Colour in Glass, John Walsh Walsh Ltd, Birmingham Museums & Art Gallery.

Photo 149, the two basic shapes are shown in the Pottery Gazette advert of 1883, though the center one is in "Electric Blue" rather than the " Crushed Strawberry". Because of this an attribution for any one item would have to have been heavily qualified. It must be remembered that other firms made some similar shapes. For example left hand side item, looks very similar to Stuart's pattern 5402. However taken collectively with the other "Crushed Strawberry" examples there is much more confidence. A peculiar characteristic is that the items are made of several layers, perhaps as many as five where rationality says there should only be two, i.e. ivory on the inside and pink on the outside. On the left hand side item , which has a ground flat top, the following layers, starting from the inside can be seen. Clear pale yellow, ivory, clear yellow, pale ivory, pink. Undoubtedly there is uranium in the clear yellow and the ivory but it is difficult to be sure about the pink. The outside does respond to both uv (near) and the Geiger counter but this may be due to shine through the very thin pink layer. The uranium is difficult to estimate inside the narrow neck vessels and may be indicative rather than quantitative, the figures in brackets represent the Geiger reading on the outside measured in cps, see Measuring Radioactivity, Section 1 Chapter Four .
Left, 7.5 cm high, density 3.2 g/cc, uranium 0.56% wt, (5 cps), *Almost certainly* Walsh *about* 1885. Value $20-30.
Center, 12.5 cm high, density 3.21 g/cc, uranium 0.7% wt, (7 cps). *Almost certainly* Walsh, about 1885. Value $30-45.
Right, 8.5 cm high to top of silver, density 3.2 g/cc, uranium (6 cps). The silver top is hall marked Birmingham 1911. *Almost certainly* Walsh, 1912. Value $45-70.

Photo 150, these two bowls are not exactly the same but the differences, if you spot them, can be explained on the basis of different glass workers. Both are 11.5 cm diameter, both have densities of 3.18 g/cc, and uranium levels of 0.5% wt (5 cps) on the outside. These must come from the same glasshouse as those in Photo 149 The shape is illustrated in the 1883 advert but for an item in "Electric Blue" One of the interesting differences are the prunts over the pontil mark. Theses are shown in Photos 151 and 152. *Almost certainly* Walsh, *about* 1885 - 1915. Value $35-70 each.

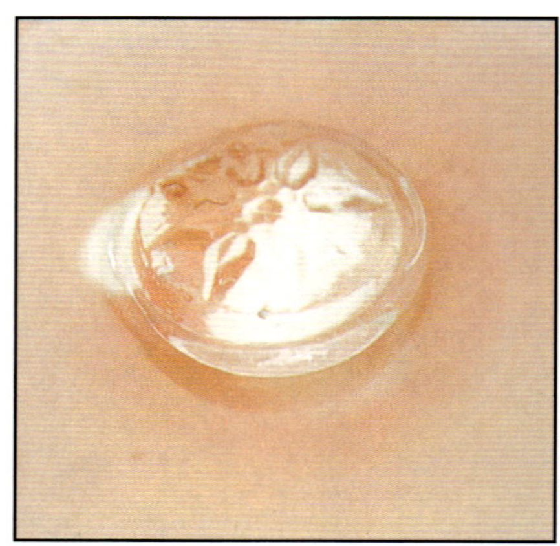

Photo 151, prunt on the left hand side bowl in Photo 150.

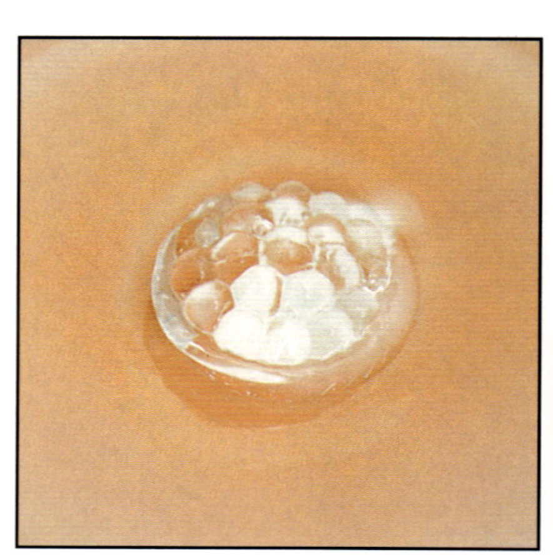

Photo 152, prunt on the right hand side bowl in Photo 150.

Photo 153, left, 8.5 cm diameter. Density 3.21 g/cc, uranium 0.42% wt, (4 cps). *Probably* Walsh *about* 1900. Value $30-45. Right, Sugar/jam dish, (probably had a lid). Silver plated band and handle. Diameter 8.75 cm, density 3.25 g/cc, uranium 0.5% wt (5 cps) on the outside. *Probably* Walsh *about* 1910. Value $35-60.

Photo 154, again this probably started its life with a lid. Height 8.3 cm, density 3.21 g/cc. The uranium is on the outside green only, the Geiger reads 5 cps, the layer is too thin to achieve the "infinite depth" required for estimating the concentration. The feet closely resemble those on both bowls inPhoto 153, there is a raspberry prunt on the pontil mark. On the basis of the density, feet and prunt I would say *could be* Walsh's "electric blue", *about* 1900. Value, if complete, $45-70.

Photo 155, this and items in Photos 156 - 158 are illustrated in at least two adverts in Pottery Gazette, (1922 &1923), as Walsh's. Other designs that I have identified are in the Walsh pattern books, (Photos 159 - 161). Similar color ranges were made by other glasshouses but not all their items contained uranium. It is not uncommon to find this primrose yellow (uranium free) on white. However, as mentioned in Chapter 27, Stevens & Williams pattern books also show "primrose on white," and, as I have described in that chapter, their products did contain uranium. From the point of glass density and uranium content they are indistinguishable from Walsh. This adds a little to our confusion for there are at least two items whose shapes are illustrated by both companies and a number that I have found not claimed by either! It is difficult to determine their construction but examination of items with ground tops indicates at least three layers of metal. The inner is opaque white, in most cases a brilliant white but in some examples a dull white, then a layer of clear yellow and finally a layer of slightly misty yellow. One might suspect this outer layer is the same as the clear yellow but with a little opacifier in it. However the uranium readings vary more widely than I would expect, this suggests that the outer layer, which is too thin to present infinite depth, has a higher concentration of uranium The readings then vary according to its thickness. Nevertheless I have quoted them as if they were measuring concentration. Height 14 cm, density 3.25 g/cc, uranium 0.62% wt. Value $45-70.

Photo 156, height with lid on 14.5 cm., density 3.22 g/cc, uranium 0.81% wt. Although I am including it here it is fair to point out that this shape also appears in a Stevens & Williams pattern book. Value $45-70.

Photo 157, two small vases. Left, 11.5 cm high, density 3.22 g/cc, uranium 0.81% wt. Value $20-35. Right, height 15 cm, density 3.35 g/cc, uranium 1.2% wt. Value $20-35.

Photo 159, this and items in Photos 160 & 161 are in Walsh Pattern Books of around 1925 as being in "Primrose". I have taken some license to include 161. Diameter 16.5 cm, density not measured, uranium 0.93% wt. Value, if complete with lid, $35-70.

Photo 158, diameter 31.5 cm, the density has not been measured, uranium 1.1% wt on outside and 0.93% wt on the inside. There is no outside white on this dish but it does seem that there is a layer of the usual white but this time trapped between primrose so that it only shows in trace at the ground pontil mark. Value $35-70.

Photo 160, Left, 10 cm x 7.5 cm, density 3.4 g/cc, uranium 1.2% wt. From the marks the silver plate was *probably* by John Turton & Co Sheffield.
Center, the sugar shaker, also appears in the Stevens & Williams pattern book. Height 18 cm, to top of silver, diameter 8 cm, density 3.03 g/cc, uranium 0.81% wt. The silver is plate. Value $35-60.
Right, 7 cm high, 9.75 cm base, density 3.34 g/cc, uranium 0.99% wt. Value $20-35.

Photo 161, I am not sure what this is although the auctioneer described it as a "goblet vase". Height 26 cm, density about 3.3 g/cc, uranium 1.2% wt. I have not seen this item, as such, in the patterns books, however there is a candlestick with the same base and stem. Add to this the color, density and uranium it is *almost certainly* Walsh. Value $45-90.

Photo 162, is a typical example of Walsh Pompeian glass. It is illustrated in the Walsh pamphlet already mentioned. As the mix is full of air I can not determine the density of the solid metal, the densities quoted are as they appear to be from treating the item as if there was no air in the glass. Height 18.5 cm, density 3.08 g/cc, uranium 0.31% wt Value $30-45.

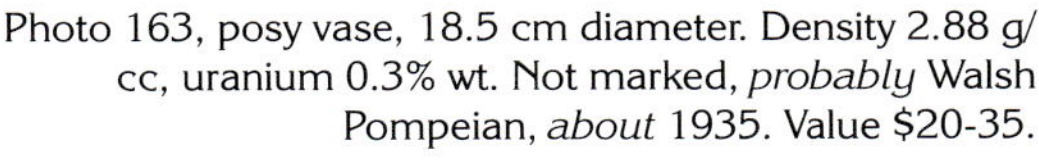

Photo 163, posy vase, 18.5 cm diameter. Density 2.88 g/cc, uranium 0.3% wt. Not marked, *probably* Walsh Pompeian, *about* 1935. Value $20-35.

Photo 164, 21 cm diameter, density 2.88g/cc, uranium 0.31% wt. Not marked, *probably* Walsh Pompeian *about* 1935. Value $15-30.

Photo 165, Left, 7.25 cm high, density 3.09 g/cc, uranium 0.5% wt. Shape shown in pattern book. *Almost certainly* Pompeian Amber *about* 1935. Value $15-30.
Center is also shown in pattern book. 14.5 cm high, density 3.08 g/cc, uranium 0.31% wt. *Almost certainly* Walsh Pompeian *about* 1935. Value $20-35.
Right, 9.5 cm high, density 3.06 g/cc, uranium 0.26% wt. Marked "Walsh England". Pompeian *about 1935*. Value $20-30.

Photo 167 can be identified as Walsh by the almost ghostly tulip silhouette, which is seen in the glass. The design was registered by Walsh No 375896. Height 8.5 cm, density 3.26 g/cc, uranium 0.16% wt. *About* 1910. Value $30-60.

Photo 166, this tall vase provides another puzzle. The shape is shown in Walsh pattern book but it is hardly a unique shape. It is too large for me to have determined its density and it has no mark except a rough pontil. I have not found anything to link this dark green with this Birmingham factory, hence my reservation. Height 25 cm, uranium 0.17% wt. *Best guess* Walsh *about* 1930. Value $45-60.

Photo 168, iridescent sweet dish, 7.5 cm high, density 3.19 g/cc, uranium 1.12% wt. Item marked "Walsh England". *About 1935.* Value $15-30.

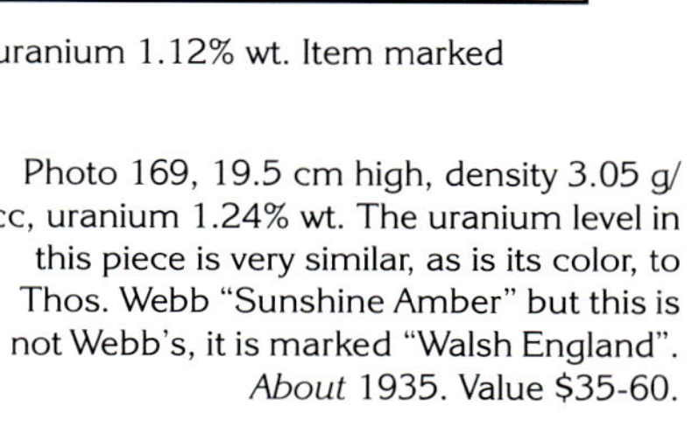

Photo 169, 19.5 cm high, density 3.05 g/cc, uranium 1.24% wt. The uranium level in this piece is very similar, as is its color, to Thos. Webb "Sunshine Amber" but this is not Webb's, it is marked "Walsh England". *About* 1935. Value $35-60.

Photo 170, according to the pattern book this tumbler should go with a water jug. Height 17.5 cm, density 3.14 g/cc, uranium 1.24% wt. About 1935. Value $15-30.

Photo 171, cut wine. 14.5 cm high, density 3.22 g/cc, uranium (on bowl only), 1.36% wt. The pattern is "Harlequin". It is interesting to note that the uranium content is close to the highest measured on the "Primrose" glass. Walsh *about* 1930. Value $30-45.

Chapter 29
Thos. Webb & Sons

The name Webb has been associated with several glasshouses and it is important to distinguish between them. Where in this book I have used Webb without a qualification or additional name I am referring to the firm that became Thos. Webb & Sons of Stourbridge. A good deal has been written about Webb but the two principle sources are probably Woodward[1] and Eveson[2] . In addition there are a large number of Webb's pattern books held in the Dudley archives.

The story is complicated from the beginning. Thomas Webb, the founder, started work with the Richardson brothers in 1829 to operate as Webb and Richardsons. He left them in the mid 1830s. However after he had joined the Richardson brothers, his father decided to go into the glass business and teamed up with John Shepherd to trade as Shepherd and Webb at the White House Glassworks. When his dad died in 1835 Thomas inherited his share in the White House Works and a year later, when Shepherd retired, quit the Richardsons and took over. Thomas Webb moved his business to Platts House in Amblecote where he built a new glass factory, which went operational about 1840. He retired in 1863 and his son Thomas Wilkes Webb soon became the driving force behind the business. It grew to exhibit at International Exhibitions and won awards for the quality of its products. He died on the first day in 1891.

Thomas Wilkes did not keep his works at Platts but moved to Dennis Hall in Dennis Park at Amblecote sometime in the first part of the 1850s. This was to be the final resting place of the business. It died in the last decade of the twentieth century. In 1886 the business became a public company with Thomas and his brother Charles as Managing Directors. Charles retired in 1900 and for the next twenty years the Managing Directorship was taken over by C W Jackson. In 1920 it became Thos. Webb and Sons Limited, a private limited company. This was followed by joining with Edinburgh and Leigh Flint Glass. It is noteworthy that Thomas Ernest Webb, the son of Wilkes, left the Company after his father's death, to start up Thomas Webb & Corbett Glass Works, which later adopted the trademarks "Webb" and "Webb Corbett."

Sven Fogelberg was appointed Managing Director in 1932 and he gave the Company a new lease of life taking it through the depression years and the war. In 1967 Crown House made a successful bid and took over the Webbs Crystal Glass Company. It again changed hands in the 1980s when Coloroll bought it, then later ceased production and closed for good when that Company went bankrupt.

The Webb name is legend and its products sought after by collectors. Cut crystal was always the mainstay of their business but they also produced large quantities of colored glassware, often cased and utilizing cameo or intaglio cutting. It is not clear when uranium was first used.

Eveson[3] says that he has found it mentioned in some 1880s Webb recipes, one of which was for a "very rich topaz" with 7.3% U wt. However other information provided by Eveson indicates that Amber and Canary were introduced about 1845. While the amber may well have been made without uranium it is unlikely that, in those early days, canary could have been. Furthermore this is about the time that the uranium was coming into popular use by most glasshouses. Photo 172 shows a wine that is identical to No 2665 in an old Webb pattern book of 1845. Alongside the sketch is the word "Canary" This would seem to confirm the use of uranium at that time. Eveson[4] gives the formula for a number of mixes used by Webb in the late nineteenth century and also in the 1930s. Using this data, on the basis described in the sections on density and uranium measurement, I have estimated these values for the different mixes. In some of these small amounts of barium are present and I have made an allowance for this in predicting the approximate density. Such mixes have an * in the comments column. The density figures may be a little low as I have neglected any water loss that would occur during the melt. These figures are shown in Tables 2 & 3.

Table 2. Estimated Density and Uranium Concentrations in Webb's Nineteenth Century Mixes

Color / Description	Est. Density g/cc	Est. Uranium % wt.	Comments
Lead Crystal batch	3.18	nil	
Gold Ruby for casing	3.1	nil	contains gold
Opaque Blue	2.55	nil	*
Alabaster	2.55	nil	*
Cyrysoprase	2.55	0.85	*
Lemon	2.55	1.1	*
Turquoise	3.15	nil	
Lemon	3.15	0.14	
Opal	3.56	nil	
Ivory	3.15	0.35	
Yellow Ivory	3.15	1	
Tricolor	3.45	0.26	contains gold
Carmine	3.43	0.41	contains gold
Convolvulus	3.43	nil	contains gold
Oriental	3.41	0.72	contains gold
Aquamarine	3.18	0.07	"Lead Crystal" based mix
Emerald Green	3.18	0.28	"Lead Crystal" based mix
Lavender	3.18	nil	"Lead Crystal" based mix
Rich Topaz	3.18	2.2	"Lead Crystal" based mix
Light Blue	3.18	nil	"Lead Crystal" based mix
Burmese	2.7	0.67	contains gold
Burmese opalescent green	2.72	0.49	No gold in mix
Lemon	3.18	0.13	
Opal for coating on brown	3.18	nil	
Russet	3.4	0.48	
Casing Blue	3.18	nil	"Lead Crystal"based mix
Dark casing green	3.1	0.26	"Lead Crystal" based mix
Casing purple	3.09	nil	"Lead Crystal" based mix
Olive green	3.12	nil	"Lead Crystal" based mix
Amber	3.1	nil	"Lead Crystal" based mix
Rich golden amber	3.1	2.3	"Lead Crystal" based mix
Royal purple	3.18	nil	"Lead Crystal" based mix
Black	3.08	nil	"Lead Crystal" based mix
Old bronzing green	3.12	nil	"Lead Crystal"based mix
Ordinary blue	3.16	nil	"Lead Crystal" based mix
Purple	3.16	nil	"Lead Crystal" based mix
Chrysoprase green	3.12	2.3	"Lead Crystal" based mix
Lemonescent	3.18	0.23	"Lead Crystal" based mix

Table 3. Estimated Density and Uranium Concentrations in Webb's 1930s Mixes

Color / Description	Est. Density g/cc	Est. Uranium % wt.	Comments
Flame	2.69	nil	
Sunset	3.12	nil	"Lead Crystal" based mix
Sap green	3.18	nil	"Lead Crystal" based mix
Amber sunshine	3.12	1.13	"Lead Crystal" based mix
Bristol green	3.15	1.15	"Lead Crystal" based mix
Eau de nil	3.18	0.23	"Lead Crystal" based mix
Amethyst	3.14	nil	"Lead Crystal" based mix
Marina green for casing	3.1	nil	"Lead Crystal" based mix
Black	3.1	nil	"Lead Crystal" based mix
Black	3.08	nil	"Lead Crystal" based mix
Casing opal	3.23	nil	
Opal for shades	2.78	nil	
Superlux opal	2.45	nil	

Webb were renowned for many of their products but for uranium glass there is one that stands out from all the others, namely "Queen's Burmese," see Photos 181 - 189. It is a delicate lemon that darkens to peach then finishes as a rich rose pink/red.. The change in shade is achieved by presenting the article, while it is being worked, to a "glory hole" where the reheat brings out the rose red. As the heating was not uniform only part of the color would change graduating according to the temperature The Burmese formula was first patented by Frederick S Shirley in America, in December 1885 (No 332294), for production by Mount Washington Glass Company. He took out a British patent in 1886 (No 8023), and allowed Webb to make it under license. I have already reported that Stuarts apparently experimented with a Burmese mix probably to emulate Webb production. It is also possible that Stevens & Williams tried to produce a Burmese. They did make a " Rose du Barry" which had some of the characteristics of Burmese. An oil lamp from the Royal Brierley Collection, (circa 1886), included in the Sotheby's sale[5] and described as "Burmese or Rose du Barry" did contain uranium. Indications were that it had about 0.3% wt uranium, however I cannot exclude the possibility that the item was cased and the uranium was hidden on the inside. A Rose Du Barry formula in the Royal Brierley records does not specifically mention uranium. Revi[6] states that Stevens & Williams did experiment with similar ware without infringing the Shirley patent but never marketed any. So whether or not Rose du Barry was an alternative Burmese is an unanswered question.

Webb continued production of this high quality product until the beginning of the 20th. Century, some items being left plain and some decorated in the department of Jules Barbe. The name "Queen's Burmese" was adopted after interest shown by Queen Victoria.

The original formula, patented by Shirley, is compared with that used by Webb; Table 4.

The uranium in the mix produces the lemon color, the gold, on re-firing the peach red, and the fluorspar and feldspar its translucence. In his patent application Shirley acknowledges Joseph Locke's Amberina but claims his invention involves the use of uranium as well as gold and aluminum. Shirley also indicates that the formula he quotes, and which I have reproduced above, can be varied in proportions.

Although these mixes are similar there are differences that could be of interest in making attributions. Using the simplified approach described in the earlier chapters I would expect Mt. Washington Burmese to have a density of 2.88 g/cc and a uranium content of 0.91%, while Webb's Queen's Burmese a density of 2.7 g/cc and a uranium content of 0.67%. I have not had the opportunity to examine bona fide examples of the Mt. Washington glass, but the values I have measured in Webb's glass are density 2.755 (range 2.78 to 2.74) g/cc and uranium content of 0.5% (range 0.52 to 0.46) wt. This makes me wonder whether the "uranium oxide" was in fact a diuranate, as such would give a uranium concentration near the measured 0.5% wt. In the later part of the production period Webb's reduced the uranium content of their Burmese perhaps by as much as half. However it may be that Mt. Washington's production mix was not the same as that quoted in the patent application, so this apparent difference should be used with caution when trying to distinguish between the two products.

Webb's records mention "White, Blue, and Lilac Burmese"[7] but I have not found any certain examples. It is difficult to anticipate what such items would look like. The term Burmese implies that they would have the rose reheat color. However the mix for "Burmese opalescent green" does not contain gold and would not therefore have a rose shading. It is quite possible that these other "Burmese" are without the red.

Despite the availability of the Burmese formula it has not been easy to emulate. Eveson tells me that Webb's attempted to reproduce their 19th century Burmese in the 1920s but the attempts failed. He speculates that this was because the Company had gone over to using lead oxide rather than the litharge used in earlier days.

One of the characteristics of Webb's products is seen in the grinding off of the pontil. This was always done by forming a perfectly circular dimple. Virtually all firms, at one time or another, ground off pontils but few made the effort to ensure this was a perfect circle. I am reliably informed that if its Webb's and it hasn't got a ground off pontil it was probably stolen!

Between the Wars Webb worked mainly in only three uranium colors, namely their Sunshine Amber, Bristol Green and Eau de Nil. These are illustrated in Photos 193 - 199.

[1]Woodward H W - Art Feat and Mystery.

[2]Eveson S - Sixty Years with the Crystal Glass Industry.

[3]Eveson S - Personal communication 1989.

[4]Eveson S - Sixty Years With the Crystal Glass Industry.

[5]Sotheby's Catalogue, March 1998, p 39.

[6]Revi A C - Nineteenth Century Glass, p 38.

[7]Eveson S - personal communication.

Table 4. Comparison of Burmese Formula used by Mount Washington and Thomas Webb & Sons

	Mt. Washington lb.	Thos. Webb & Sons lb.
Sand	100	500
Lead Oxide	36 (refined)	140 (litharge)
Potash	25 (Pearl ash)	130
Niter	7 (potassium nitrate ?)	30 (sodium nitrate)
Bicarb. of soda	5	35 (Soda ash i.e. carbonate)
Fluorspar	6	73
Feldspar	5	70
Uranium Oxide	2	8
Ironstone		3
Gold	1.5 pennyweights	7.5 pennyweights

Photo 172 has already been mentioned, this is an important piece for, if the attribution is correct, it confirms that Webb was using uranium in the mid-1840s and is probably one of their earliest pieces to do so. The glass appears identical to pattern No 2665. It is not only the positioning of the knop and the facets but the fact that there are 11 facets on the glass, which is the number, specified in the pattern book. Written along side is the word "canary". Even though the uranium does not match a formula in Table 2, on the basis of the pattern book I would say *almost certainly* Webb's, and date it 1845. Height 13 cm, density 3.1 g/cc, uranium 0.31% wt. Value $90-145.

Photo 173, an unusual vase. Height 15 cm, density 3.27 g/cc, uranium 0.31% wt. The base is marked Thos Webb & Sons set in a horseshoe. The vase has been intaglio cut, probably in Jules Barbe workshop, and appears to have been coated with a lacquer. Both density and uranium are consistent with the 19th century "Ivory" formula. The trade mark dates it 1887-8. Value $435-725.

Photo 174, a colorful jug that has been made from at least three layers of glass. Pink on the inside white in the middle and a different shade of crimson on the outside. The corrugated foot is the same style as the left item in Photo 175, which is seen on other Webb items. There is a perfect dimple where the pontil has been. Heavy gold work with a butterfly on the hidden side. Height 16.5 cm, density 3.25 g/cc, uranium on clear yellow, 0.62% wt, on crimson, 0.5% wt, and on inside 0.3% wt. The colors *could be* "Carmine" or "Oriental" or both! *Almost certainly* Webb's *about* 1890. Value $300-435.

Photo 176, is made from three layers of metal viz. Ivory - White - Ivory but the inside is slightly different shade from the outside. A shape closely resembling this is shown as number 14655 in a surviving Webb pattern book. There is a note "New Yellow". Diameter 11.25 cm, density 3.22 g/cc, uranium inside 0.93% wt, outside 0.5 % wt. Allowing for the uncertainty in measurement, the higher inside making a small contribution to the outside reading, these match closely the "Yellow Ivory" and "Ivory". Somewhere between a *probably* and *almost certainly* Webb *about* 1885. Value $60-90.

Photo 175, left, this unmistakable shape in Burmese used to be in a Webb's factory display. Height 10 cm, density 3.24 g/cc, uranium 0.29% wt. Both density and uranium are close enough to be Webb's "Ivory" *about* 1890. Value $110-145.
Right, is a small mug, which has a lot about it suggesting Webb. It has a perfect ground off pontil on the base. Height 6.5 cm, density 3.29 g/cc, uranium 0.37% wt.. The color, uranium and density all consistent with the Ivory formula. *Could be* Webb, *about* 1900. Value $45-60.

Photo 177 small threaded vase. 12.25 cm high, density 3.21 g/cc, uranium 0.17% wt. The petals on the top of the vase are identical shape to Webb's Design Registration 80167, although this item is not marked. *Almost certainly* Webb's Lemonescent, *about* 1890. Incidentally the threading machine, which would have made this item, was still at Webb's in the 1950's until sold for scrap! Value $100-145.

Photo 178, I thought at first this might be Whitefriars but then I found the pattern in Webb's, number 26695 which changes my mind to *probably* Webb Lemon date *about* 1900. Again the perfect dimple where the pontil has been ground off. Diameter 11.5 cm, density 3.26 g/cc, uranium 0.11% wt. Value $70-110.

Photo 179, two wines are as near identical in shape, size and pattern, as could be expected for hand made glasses. Both have a blown foot with a ground off pontil and I would date them *about* 1870. The pattern of the stem and on the bowl appears identical to 6391 in the Webb's Pattern Book, date 1860. Interesting are the density differences. They sold to me as a pair so the odds are they have spent most of their lives together although they were clearly not made as a pair. Look carefully the left hand side glass is slightly paler than the one on the right. Each is 6.75 cm high, but their densities are, left to right, 2.93 g/cc & 2.56 g/cc the uranium 0.25% wt & 0.5% wt. From this it looks as if one was a replacement, but which? If the left was the original, then it *could be* Webb's Emerald green, although the density is a little low. Value, each, $20-35.

Photo 180, this air trap pattern bowl is 8.5 cm diameter. It appears to have been made from three layers, pale ivory on the inside, then white and finally cased with canary yellow on the outside. Both inside and outside layers appear to contain equal concentrations of uranium although only the canary responds to uv (far) while both respond to uv (near). Density 2.89 g/cc and uranium 0.68% wt. Faint pencil like marks on the base have the No 15360 and m/6 yellow. The 15360 is a Webb design number and coincides with a "New Yellow". in 1885. Because of the construction, which traps air, I cannot place too much significance to the density. As with thin layered glass the uranium levels are also uncertain. The item would have been made by rolling the second gather over a diamond pattern grid to create indentations, then adding a third gather before blowing into shape. Webb's, 1885. Value $110-145.

Photo 181 this posy vase is typical Queen's Burmese. On the perfectly round dimple where the pontil has been ground off is the inscription "Patented. Thos Webb & Sons. Rd 80167" The Rd is the Design Registration number, which as mentioned in Photo 177 refers to the petal shape top. Height 6.75 cm, density 2.76 g/cc, uranium 0.43% wt. Date about 1890. Value $435-600.

Photo 182, another posy vase like Photo 181 and identically marked but with a the Red Berry pattern. Diameter 6.5 cm, density 2.79 g/cc, uranium 0.56% wt. Again date about 1890. Value $435-600.

Photo 183, also like Photo 181, identically marked but with the Hazel Nut pattern. Diameter 7 cm, density 2.78 g/cc, uranium 0.43% wt. Date about 1890. Value $435-600.

Photo 184, plain Burmese vase, 8.25 cm high, density 2.78 g/cc, uranium 0.47% wt. Marked as for Photo 181. Value $100-145.

Photo 185, a night light in two parts. Height 10.5 cm, marked on base "S CLARKE. TRADEMARK FAIRY PYRAMID". Density top 2.74 g/cc, base 2.78 g/cc, uranium (both) 0.37% wt. *Almost certainly* made by Webb for Clarkes *about* 1895. Value $215-300.

Photo 186 plain Burmese toothpick holder, 6.5 cm high , density 2.74 g/cc, uranium 0.5% wt. Not marked but well known Webb shape. *Almost certainly* Webb, *about* 1895. Value $70-110.

Photo 189, I am not sure for what this item was intended. It stands 24 cm high, marked "Webb Queen's Burmese Ware Patented". Density not measured, uranium 0.43% wt. It is a composite item and as such unusual. It was bought in Australia and there has been speculation that it may have formed part of Webb's display in the Centenary Exhibition held in Melbourne in 1888. Value $1100-1800.

Photo 187, another posy vase, 9.25 cm high, density 2.75 g/cc, uranium 0.28% wt. Although in Burmese style the colors do not blend in the manner normally associated with Webb's Burmese. The uranium is also lower than the other Webb Burmese items. Perhaps it was made later. These factors raise doubts but the shape is one used by Webb. *Probably* Webb Burmese *about* 1900. Value $90-130.

Photo 188, a small bowl, 6 cm high, density 2.73g/cc, uranium 0.43% wt. The crinkle work on the top is typical of some Webb's style. It appears that the item has been over heated at the glory hole so turning too much red and spoiling the overall effect. *Almost certainly* Webb's Burmese, *about* 1895. Value $115-145.

Photo 190, both these are effectively the same shape and size (6.75 cm & 7 cm) as the two pieces in Photo 191 and must surely hail from the same glasshouse. They appear to be made from three layers, inside pale ivory, then white and red outside. Uranium appears in both the outer and inner layer. Density 3.26 & 3.27 g/cc left to right respectively. Uranium, (on each), 0.5% wt. These levels would be consistent with Webb's "ivory" (inside layer) and "carmine" (outside layer). *Almost certainly* Webb's *about* 1890. Value each $70-110.

Photo 191, left, a posy vase, 6.75 cm high, density 2.84, uranium 0.26% wt. The shade, texture and perfect dimple where the pontil was ground off all say this is Webb Burmese without the red. The shape is the same as Photo 190. *Probably* Webb's, *could be* White Burmese, *about* 1890. Value $70-110.

Right, unfortunately this item is badly cracked. It is much the same size and shape as the left hand side vase. It has to be from the same stable. It is probably constructed in three layers but this time the outer layer is green. Density 3.29 g/cc, uranium 0.43% wt. The gold work is heavy and not a cheap transfer, there is a butterfly on the hidden side. *Almost certainly* Webb's *about* 1890. Value (if undamaged), $110-145.

Photo 192, this bowl vase has been made in a 10 pillar mould then hand twisted during the blowing stage. Basically dark green with a "bronzed" finish both inside and out. A perfect dimple where the pontil used to be. Density 3.21 g/cc, uranium 0.22% wt. It looks like Webb's bronze ware *about* 1900 but I think I would only give it a *best guess* at that. Value $45-70.

Photo 193, here we have three examples of Webb's "Sunshine Amber", which was marketed in the 1930's. There are other examples in Photos 194 -198. They are all marked "Made in England Webb" The color should not be confused with an amber of post WW2 years which does not contain uranium. Left, 8.5 cm high, density 3.3 g/cc, uranium 1.24% wt. "Drape" pattern. Value $15-20.

Center, 9 cm high, density 3.25 g/cc, uranium 1.24% wt. Value $15-20.

Right, 8.75 cm high, density 3.29 g/cc, uranium 1.12% wt. Webb "Ball" pattern. Value $15-20.

Photo 194, crackled posy ring, 15 cm diameter. Density 3.32 g/cc, uranium not reliably determined because of the shape the item presents to the Geiger but best estimate 1.3% wt. The crackling effect was obtained by plunging the un-cooled item into water into which a little potassium nitrate may have been added. Note the inner ring is rounded but the outer one ground flat. Also marked as "Made in England Webb". *About* 1938. Value $35-70.

Photo 195, posy vase 12.5 cm diameter in Webb Sunshine Amber. Marked, density 3.32 g/cc, uranium 1.2% wt. Date *about* 1935 Value $30-60.

Photo 196, intaglio cut bowl, 14 cm high, 25 cm diameter. Density 3.27 g/cc, uranium 1.12% wt. Marked as the above. Webb, Sunshine Amber, *about* 1935. Value $70-110.

Photo 197, sweet dish, 7.5 cm high, 11.5 cm diameter. Density 3.3 g/cc, uranium 1.1% wt. Marked Webb etc. Sunshine Amber *about* 1935. Value $20-35.

Photo 198, jug 14.5 cm high, density 3.1 g/cc, uranium 1.36% wt. Marked Webb etc. Sunshine Amber in Ribbonette Pattern. About 1935. Value $60-90.

Photo 199, two examples of Webb's Bristol Green in Ball Glass pattern Both are marked Webb etc. (see inset). *About* 1935. Left, height 11.5 cm, density 3.22 g/cc, uranium 1.05% wt.
Right, 7.5 cm high, density 3.2 g/cc, uranium 0.93% wt. Value, each, $20-35.

Photo 200, this is the only example of Webb's Eau de Nil that I have come across. It is has the Webb trade mark and of course a perfect dimple where the pontil had been. 4.5 cm high, 11.25 cm diameter, density 3.12 g/cc, uranium 0.19% wt. Date *about* 1935. Value $15-30.

Photo 201 shows two pieces from Edinburgh Crystal probably made. after they merged with Webb although clearly they are not made from Webb formula. Left, This green bowl is marked "Edinburgh Crystal". 9.25 cm high, density 2.75 g/cc, uranium 0.18% wt. Style says *about 1*930 the density indicates it is not Webb's Eau de Nil. mix. Value $5-20.
Right, Small cut glass dish, probably part of a set. Length, 10.75 cm, density 3.28 g/cc, uranium 0.81% wt. The mark has been partly worn away but is *almost certainly* Edinburgh Crystal. Date would be *about* 1930. Although the color looks close to Amber Sunshine the uranium level says it is not. Value $5-15.

Chapter 30

The English Midlands - The Remaining Items

As already mentioned the Midlands that is Birmingham and the Stourbridge area, were most important in English glass making during the uranium period. In the preceding chapters I have shown examples of the products of five of the more prominent glasshouses but there were more. Unfortunately I have not identified their products. There may also be pieces made by those five, in my collection, which I have not been able to attribute.

This area made particular use of high lead metal, i.e. generally about 30% Pb or more, and this is often the basis for my thinking a piece may have come from this area. Of course many other glasshouses used full lead crystal but other considerations such as technique, quality and color helps narrow the field of attribution.

In this chapter I have included all those items which I think have a sporting chance of having been born in the area. To avoid tedious repetition, unless stated otherwise, the confidence level should be taken as *probably* Midlands, in addition to any other possible attribution.

[1] Manley C, - Decorative Victorian Glass, p91

Photo 202, this wine has a very distinctive cut pattern. It is identifiable as Design Registration 214597, by Edward Webb, Wordsley, Stourbridge, 1867. Edward was part of the Webb family and at one time worked with his brother Joseph but this was well before 1867. *Almost certainly* Midlands and *best guess* is that this item was made at White House Glass Works. Height, 13.5, density 3.09 g/cc, uranium 0.68% wt. Value $35-60.

Photo 203, three wines with similarities. Left, has a vine pattern very reminiscent of Stevens & Williams but also of other glasshouses. The foot is blown and the pontil ground out. Height 14 cm, density 3.1 g/cc, uranium 0.43% wt. Date *about* 1860. Value $45-60. Center, wine with a grape vine pattern in dark green. This was probably a 1930's item cut in Georgian style. Not a fake but could be confused with the real thing. The uranium is the best indicator of this but despite the broken pontil the molded foot also gives it away. 11.5 cm high, density 3.3 g/cc, uranium 0.14% wt. Value $30-45.

Right, another repro *probably* from the Midlands. As before the uranium and molded foot are good indicators. Also the broken pontil mark looks just a little artificial., *about* 1930. height 11.25 cm, density 3.12 g/cc, uranium 0.62% wt. Value $30-45.

Photo 204, in view of the similarity in shape to Photo 170 I was tempted to attribute this to Walsh but it is repro. where as that item is not so I think just Midlands is more appropriate. Height 17 cm, density 3.1 g/cc, uranium 0.22% wt. Date *about* 1930. Value $35-60.

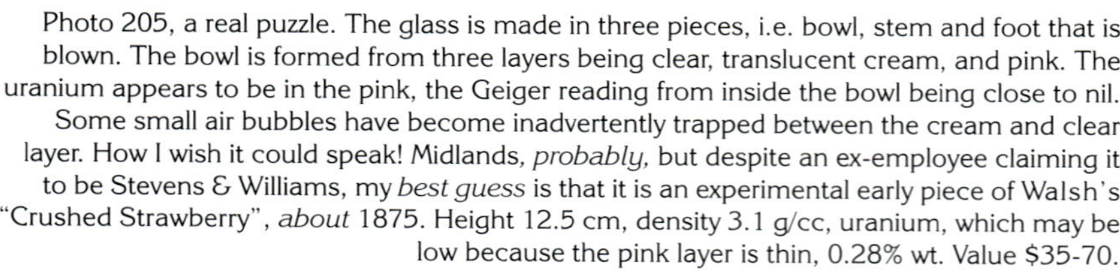

Photo 205, a real puzzle. The glass is made in three pieces, i.e. bowl, stem and foot that is blown. The bowl is formed from three layers being clear, translucent cream, and pink. The uranium appears to be in the pink, the Geiger reading from inside the bowl being close to nil. Some small air bubbles have become inadvertently trapped between the cream and clear layer. How I wish it could speak! Midlands, *probably,* but despite an ex-employee claiming it to be Stevens & Williams, my *best guess* is that it is an experimental early piece of Walsh's "Crushed Strawberry", *about* 1875. Height 12.5 cm, density 3.1 g/cc, uranium, which may be low because the pink layer is thin, 0.28% wt. Value $35-70.

Photo 206, left, made in three pieces with a blown foot. Hand cut and polished with ground off pontil. A lovely glass made by skilled craftsmen but difficult to know where. As I can not exclude the possibility of London or Manchester it has to be *could be* Midlands, *about* 1870. Height 10.5 cm, density 3.19 g/cc, uranium 0.07% wt. Value $20-35.
Right, a heavier glass than its companion, but there are similarities in style and construction. Height 10.8 cm, density 3.19 g/cc, uranium 0.34% wt. *Could be* Midlands, *about* 1870. Value $20-35.

Photo 207, 7.5 cm diameter, density 3.1 g/cc, uranium 0.31% wt. Ungrounded pontil. *About* 1900. Value $20-35.

Photo 208, these three tulip vases present something of a dilemma. Their densities are, left to right, 3.15 g/cc, 3.1 g/cc & 2.92 g/cc. The uranium content 0.28% wt, 0.15% wt. & 0.19% wt. The densities suggest that the right hand side one does not come from the same maker as the other two. They *probably* all come from the Midlands but which firms?. Manley[1] shows a photo similar to the right vase, the only apparent difference being that in his example the ruby is in clear flint. He confidently states "Richardson's were noted for their tulip ornaments..." but gives no basis for his attribution. All three date *about* 1900. I have little information as to the metal used by Richardson at that time but indications are that it would have a density about 3.1 g/cc. More to the point is that the feet on the center and right, closely resemble item 7997 in Stuart's pattern book. On the other hand the feet on left hand side vase look more like those on Richardson's "Sunflower" flower holder as advertised in Pottery Gazette Aug. 1906. However I would have expected a higher quality product from this firm. Height, left to right, 15.5 cm, 14 cm, 15.5 cm. Value, in same order, $90-115, $70-110, $115-145.

Photo 211, an epergne with a silver plate base. 9.75 cm diameter at the top, density 3.18 g/cc, uranium 0.14% wt. I bought this in Australia but I still think it came from the Midlands. The glass does show some resemblance to items made by Walsh. Date *about* 1900. Value $45-70.

Photo 209, tall vase 21 cm high, density 3.21 g/cc, uranium 0.16% wt. No pontil mark. Closely resembles an item in an advert in Pottery Gazette 1st Jan 1900. *Could be* L & S Hingley, Stourbridge, *about* 1900. Value $20-35.

Photo 210, from an 8 pillar mould. The foot is crudely made and has been badly held in a gadget. Perhaps an apprentice's piece. 18.5 cm high, density 3.1 g/cc, uranium 0.28% wt. *About* 1880. Value $45-70.

Photo 212, blown from an 8 pillar mould and twisted. The foot is molded and the pontil mark rough. Height 14.5 cm, density 3.23 g/cc, uranium 0.17% wt. I have a suspicion this might be Webb's Lemonescent, if it is the pontil mark says it was probably stolen before it was finished off in the works! *About* 1900. Value $60-70.

Photo 213, height 12.25 cm, density 3.15, uranium 0.09% wt. Date *about* 1900. Value $45-70.

Photo 215, the crimp feet on this item closely resemble the style in Photo 214, did it come from the same glasshouse? The density and uranium levels say probably not. Diameter 13.7 cm, density 2.95 g/cc, uranium 0.28% wt. Date *about* 1890. Value $70-110.

Photo 214, the interesting aspect of this vase, apart from its color, is the crimp work on the base. Petal shaped crimps with lines are common and were used by many producers but these crimps have a distinguishing small round "dot" of glass at the center of the top edge of each crimp. It is similar to illustration in both Stuart's and Webb's Pattern books. The shape is similar to Stevens & Williams pattern No 3530 from their 1873 book. Interesting but not sufficient even for a qualified attribution. Height 13.5 cm, density 3.18 g/cc, uranium on pale blue 0.05% wt, on feet approx 0.49% wt. Date *about* 1890. Value $45-70.

Photo 216, yet another piece of crimp work on the base that looks similar. Height 9 cm, density 3.25 g/cc. uranium, on inside and feet 0.43% wt, on outside nil. Date *about* 1890. Value $45-70.

Photo 217, The handle and foot of this basket are flint, the body is white opal cased each side with a uranium glass. Oddly, according to uv light response, the yellow trim does not have uranium, which makes me think it is younger than might otherwise be supposed. Diameter 11.5 cm, density 3.16 g/cc, uranium 0.28% wt. *Period* 1910. Value $60-70.

Photo 219, the uranium is in the inner layer of glass where it is hardly noticed! The pontil is left rough. I wonder if it is a frigger's piece. Height 13 cm, density 3.28 g/cc, uranium 0.43% wt. *Period* 1900. Value $45-60.

Photo 218, a characteristic of this item is that all the colors contain uranium. The cruciform shape is similar to Richardson's 5410 (Book 3), but the base is different and that item is a basket. Height 10 cm, density 3.1 g/cc, uranium 0.11% wt, 0.14% wt & approx 0.62% wt on inside, outside, and trim respectively. *Almost certainly* Midlands, *about* 1890. Value $70-100.

Photo 220, the pink is very thin on the yellow. The prefect pontil dimple is suggestive and the uranium would be about what I'd expect from "Yellow Ivory" so a *best guess* Webb *about* 1885. Height 8 cm, density 3.3 g/cc, uranium 1.1% wt. Value $45-60.

Photo 221, a most peculiar piece. The red splatter is sharp chips of glass. The pontil is rough. I cannot imagine anyone, except a collector of uranium glass, wanting to buy this. Was it a frigger's piece? The uranium is only in the ivory. Height 10 cm, density 3.5 g/cc (unusually high), uranium 0.3% wt. There is very little wear. As for date, if it is a frigger's handiwork then it could be anytime between 1890 and 1950! Value $5-70!

Photo 223, the trail work on this crinkle top bowl does not contain uranium, it is only in the ivory. 11.5 cm diameter, density 3.19 g/cc, uranium 0.2% wt. Pontil dimple is perfect in shape, the silver plate cradle was made by Joseph Deakins & Sons, of Sheffield 1886 - 91. *Almost certainly* Midlands, *about* 1890. Value $60-70.

Photo 222, 14.5 cm high excluding the metal work, density 3.11 g/cc, uranium 0.04% wt. The EPNS holder carries the mark of Francis Howard, Sheffield *about* 1885. *Almost certainly* Midlands but I can' t trace whom. Value $60-70.

Photo 224, these three items must come from the same source, the center and right match identical for colors while the right and left match identical in this unusual shape. The uranium on the first mentioned pair is in the base and the base and handle. In the left hand side piece it is on the base, handle and inside of the jug. Bowl 5 cm high, both jugs 4.25 cm high. Bowl density 3.27 g/cc, uranium 0.62% wt. Both jugs, density 3.18 g/cc, uranium 0.5% wt. *About* 1900. Value, each jug $45-60, bowl $35-50.

Photo 227, 5.5 cm high, 12.75 cm diameter, density 2.96 g/cc, uranium 0.09% wt. The perfect pontil dimple and the petals on the top both suggest Webb but I have doubts. *About* 1890. Value $45-70.

Photo 225, I doubt if this piece had any functional use although I suppose it could have held the odd small flower. It is a Victorian table piece. They were made with single or multiple stems, see Photo 226, and would have decorated the table on Sundays and other important dates. They were probably produced by a variety of glasshouses. Height 16 cm, density 3.24 g/cc, uranium 0.12% wt. Date *about* 1890. Value $30-60.

Photo 226, three more table pieces of different style. Although bought at different times their density and uranium content are practically the same. The right hand side piece is the more complex having three stems. Height 17 cm, density 3.24 g/cc, uranium 0.12% wt. Date *about* 1890. Value left to right, $45-70, $30-45, $70-110.

Photo 228, it is difficult to take this little piece seriously and I can't believe it is a finished item. The metal is thick, the top has been cut and the edges left sharp. *Best guess* is that an apprentice blew it in a pillar mould then took it home to show mum! Height 6.75 cm, density 3.17 g/cc, uranium 0.17% wt. Value, rummage sale material!

Photo 229, height 8.5 cm, density 3.3 g/cc, uranium 0.9% wt. The outside is Primrose and the inside plain white. The silver plate lid is marked EPNS but I cannot identify who did the plating. In all respects the glass is similar to the Primrose products from Stevens & Williams and Walsh, as already discussed in Chapters 27 & 28. Did this, and the items in Photos 230 - 236 come from either of those glasshouses? If not who did make them? *My best guess* is that they were made by Walsh or made for Walsh. *About* 1925. Value $30-45.

Photo 230, an electric lampshade in Primrose metal. Height 14 cm, density 3.33 g/cc, uranium 1.1% wt. *About* 1925. Value $30-45.

Photo 231, left, the silver is marked EPNS ABRA PLATE, which means little to me! Diameter 8.75 cm, density not determined, uranium 1.1% wt. *About* 1925. Value $30-45.
Right, marked EPNS on lid. Diameter 8.75 cm. density 3.33 g/cc, uranium 0.93% wt. *About* 1925. Value $20-35.

Photo 232, 10.25 cm high, density 3.26 g/cc, uranium 0.56% wt. *About* 1925. Value $20-35.

Photo 233, 9 cm high, density 3.3 g/cc, uranium 0.56% wt. *About* 1925. Value $20-30.

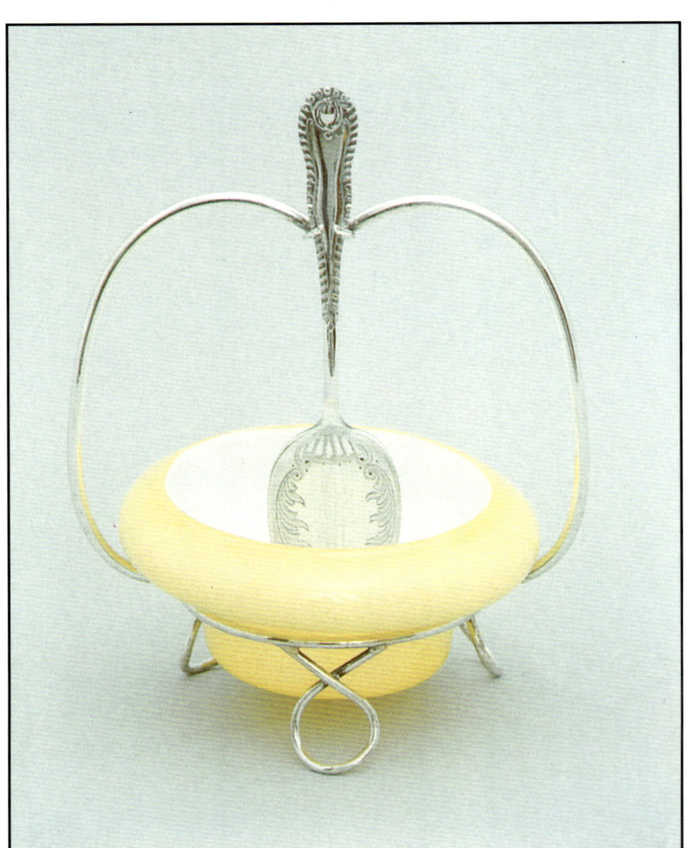

Photo 234, 12 cm diameter, density 3.24 g/cc, uranium 0.81% wt. The silver plate is marked but unfortunately unreadable! *About* 1925. Value $45-60.

Photo 235, the salt and pepper in the cruet set (center) are much the same as the two separate pieces. All are silver plate. I will not bore you with more densities and uranium, they are much the same as the predecessors. Diameter of salt/pepper in cruet set 4.5 cm, as separate items 5.5 cm. *About* 1925. Value, cruet set $30-35. Individual pots $20-30 each.

Photo 236, probably a commemorative mustard pot. It bears the inscription "Wembley 1924" which helps considerably with the dating! Density 3.28 g/cc, uranium 0.74% wt. Value $15-30.

Photo 237, this pepper pot is slightly different from the preceding items. It is a slightly darker shade of primrose and has a silver, (not plated) top. The hall mark indicates it was assayed in Birmingham 1921/2. Density 3.24 g/cc, uranium 0.93 g/cc. Value $45-60.

Photo 238, when I bought this vase I though it must be Walsh's Primrose but now I don't. The construction is different. It appears to be an opaque white, cased inside with a thin clear uranium yellow and outside with a much thicker layer of uranium yellow which has been given a satin finish by acid treatment. The broken pontil remains. Height 15.5 cm, density 3.2 g/cc uranium 0.43% wt. *Best guess* is that it is from a Midlands firm trying to imitate the successful Walsh *about* 1925.

Photo 239, plate with grape vine pattern in dark green. Another example of 1930's items cut in Georgian style. The uranium confirms this. 17 cm diameter, density 3.16 g/cc, uranium 0.6% wt. Similar vine patterns are in both Webb and Stevens & Williams pattern books however the uranium levels do not match any known for Webb's so the odds must favor them not having been made there. Perhaps Royal Brierley. *About* 1930. Value $30-60.

Photo 240, wine glass cooler. The difference between this and a finger bowl is that the coolers have lips, which support the wine glass stems as they are placed upside down in the bowl of iced water. The uranium tells us that it is not as old as might at first appear. The perfect round pontil dimple on this makes me think of Webb, but the uranium concentration says no, it's not! Diameter 12.5 cm, density 3.1 g/cc, uranium 0.62% wt. Value $60-90.

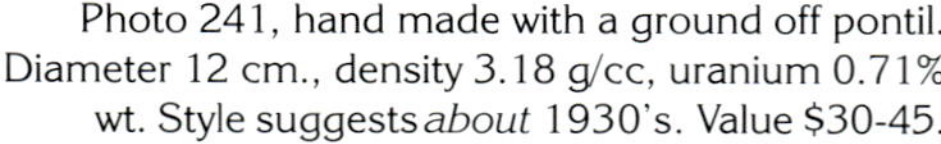

Photo 241, hand made with a ground off pontil. Diameter 12 cm., density 3.18 g/cc, uranium 0.71% wt. Style suggests *about* 1930's. Value $30-45.

Photo 242, another puzzle. The base is molded but it has a ground off pontil mark and the style is Deco, which says *about* 1930. Height 7.5 cm, density 3.17 g/cc, uranium 0.74% wt. Value $15-20.

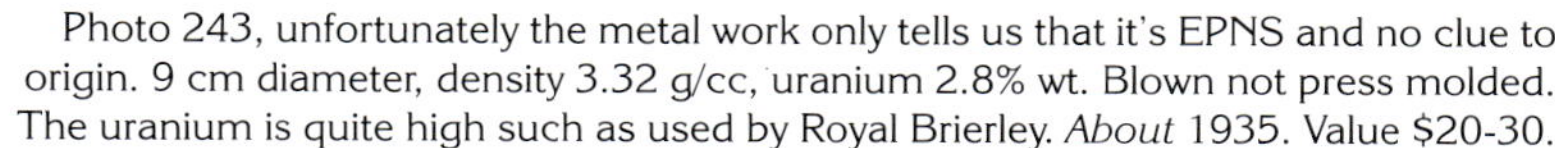

Photo 243, unfortunately the metal work only tells us that it's EPNS and no clue to origin. 9 cm diameter, density 3.32 g/cc, uranium 2.8% wt. Blown not press molded. The uranium is quite high such as used by Royal Brierley. *About* 1935. Value $20-30.

Photo 244, the pattern on the stopper and base is probably hand cut, but not acid polished. The bottle, (or is it a decanter?), is hand made. Height 23 cm including the stopper, density 3.32 g/cc, uranium, one of the highest I have recorded in glass, 3.1% wt. *About* 1930. Value $15-30.

Photo 245, the intaglio cut hunting scene is unusual. A similar design has been noted on a clear glass decanter which was signed W G Webb. There is no signature on this item. W G Webb, set up a small company with Samuel Jobe, called Jobe Webb in the Depression years. They bought in blanks and did their own engraving. Their workshop was situated close to Stuart's Crystal. Later Webb taught glass engraving at Stourbridge. This item looks like Thomas Webb's Amber Sunshine but the uranium level is too high for that mix. *Almost certainly Midlands, probably* Stourbridge *about* 1935. Height 9 cm, density 3.15, uranium 1.74% wt. Value $60-100.

Photo 246, intaglio cut vase with a grape vine pattern and blow molded with dimples. Height 20 cm, density 3.41 g/cc, uranium 2.7% wt. The uranium is such that this might be Royal Brierley Dark Amber. *About* 1935. Value $30-45.

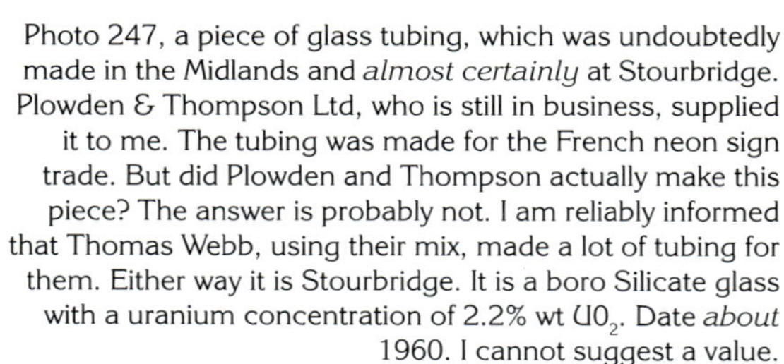

Photo 247, a piece of glass tubing, which was undoubtedly made in the Midlands and *almost certainly* at Stourbridge. Plowden & Thompson Ltd, who is still in business, supplied it to me. The tubing was made for the French neon sign trade. But did Plowden and Thompson actually make this piece? The answer is probably not. I am reliably informed that Thomas Webb, using their mix, made a lot of tubing for them. Either way it is Stourbridge. It is a boro Silicate glass with a uranium concentration of 2.2% wt UO_2. Date *about* 1960. I cannot suggest a value.

Chapter 31
American and Continental Glass

When I set out collecting uranium glass, I had no idea how extensively it had been produced. As this became apparent, I decided to restrict my researches to British glass, and English glass in particular. However, from time to time I have come across examples of products from other countries and, for various reasons, I acquired them. Those whose origin have been identified are included in this section; some of those that have not are included in Section 3.

American Glass

Photo 248, this and the items in Photos 249 & 250 all carry the Fenton name. This company started in 1907 and its story and products are well described by Heacock[1]. Specializing in art glass they have made considerable use of uranium. A lot of their production is styled on the Victorian era and could be mistaken for glass from that period. In particular they have produced Topaz, Burmese, Lime and may be other colors using uranium. Such items are not intended as fakes or even repro. but marketed in their own right. Their Burmese items are marked with their name but beware, I have seen the odd item where the "Fenton" has been ground off. If you look carefully a trace of the name usually remains after such treatment. The uranium concentration is about the same as Webb's but the density is much lower. It is worth noting that although the Burmese formulae were published (Frederick Shirley's patent), Fenton did not find it easy to reproduce. It seems that their glass chemist Charles W Goe had to experiment over a period of years. Fenton started to produce their Burmese line in 1970. At the time of drafting this book they use uranium for their Topaz, it is depleted UO_2. This item is 18 cm high, density 2.51 g/cc, uranium 0.62% wt. Fenton No 7359 BR, Pinch Vase. Plain items were not made after 1972. Value $30-60.

[1] Heacock W - Fenton Glass, (3 volumes).
[2] Glickman J L - Yellow Green Vaseline. Item 13.
[3] McKearin G S & H - American Glass p 421.
[4] Glickman J L - Yellow Green Vaseline Item 24

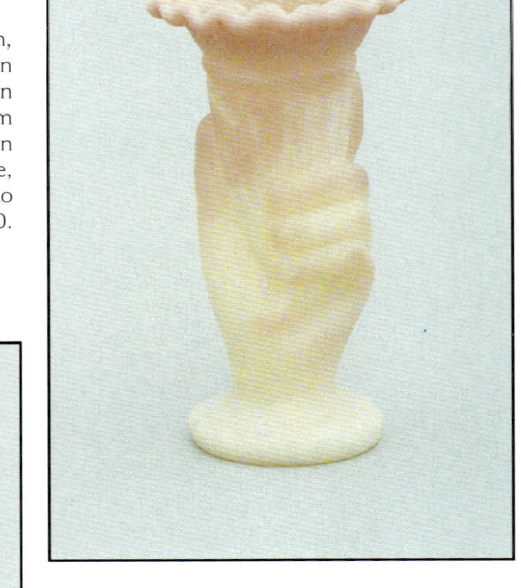

Photo 249, another Fenton Burmese. 9.5 cm high, density 2.57 g/cc, uranium 0.28% wt. Fenton C51531E, it was sold to QVC television network in October 1994 who showed it on a special program selling to homes all over the USA. At this time Fenton were reducing the uranium content of their Burmese, hence it is much less than in item the item in Photo 248. Value $35-60.

Photo 250, a Fenton Lime sherbet bowl, 8424LS Water Lily Three Toed Bowl. It is only one example of a range of products made in this color about 1977. Diameter 23 cm, density 2.56 g/cc, uranium 0.37% w. Value $50-70.

Photo 251, I bought this mixing bowl in Australia. It is not marked but I subsequently found out it was made by Fenton in the "Depression years". 16.5 cm diameter, density 2.52 g/cc, uranium 0.22% wt. *About* 1933. Value $15-20.

Photo 252. This doll's tea cup is marked with the Akro-Agate trade mark. This company started its life in Ohio in 1911 but moved to West Virginia in 1914. By the 1920's / 30's it had the largest slice of the American market for glass marbles. When they lost this they turned to children's wares around 1936. The Company closed in 1951. This cup and saucer are from their "Interior Panel in Jade Arko Luster". As will be noted the uranium level is extremely low and the items do not fluoresce under uv light. However the presence of uranium has been confirmed by gamma spectrometry, which suggested it was not depleted uranium. Therefore date *probably* between 1936 & 1942. Cup 3 cm high, saucer 7 cm diameter. Density 2.49 g/cc, uranium 0.06% wt. Value $5-20.

Photo 253, a small dish 10.5 cm diameter. Density 2.54 g/cc, uranium 0.25% wt. An example of "Custard Glass" which was made by a number of American companies. This is from Heisey *about* 1886. Value $20-35.

Photo 254, a Custard Glass plate by McKee and Brothers, Pennsylvania, *about* 1905. Venetian pattern. Length 26 cm, density 2.52 g/cc, uranium 0.19% wt. Value $30-45.

Photo 255, a pair of decorative vases, 20.5 cm high, density 2.44 g/cc, uranium 0.19% wt. Identical item attributed by Glickman[2] to Hobbs, Brockunier about 1870's and by McKearin[3] to the same firm but for 1883. Value $110-145 for the pair.

Photo 256, this sugar appears identical to one attributed by Glickman[4] to McKee *about* 1870. Personally I have doubts and would have put it much later, perhaps *about* 1910. Height 11 cm, density 2.43 g/cc, uranium 0.62% wt. Value $30-45.

Photo 257, I am taking a liberty by including this 6 cm wide dish. It is radioactive but not with uranium. It is marked with an "H" set in a diamond shape box, a mark associated with Heisey. The Geiger counter thinks it has 0.13% uranium by wt. It does not fluoresce, but then neither did the doll's tea cup (Photo 252). There is virtually no uranium in this item. The measured radioactivity is due to Thorium, but it needed gamma spectrometry to prove it. Value nominal.

Belgian Glass

Photo 258, the bottle has been made in a four piece blow mould. The base is concave and has been ground and polished. The stopper was made in a three piece mould. The four piece mould indicates it was not one of the early pieces. I have seen items with the same pattern press marked "Val St Lambert Belgique" I have also seen them in uranium green. This is 14.5 cm height but they come in a variety of sizes. The Company was founded in 1825 and is still an important glass producer now operating under the name "Crystallerie du Val St Lambert". Their products were not confined to pressed glass, they made, and still make, cut crystal. This may account for the high lead content in their pressed glass as it would seem that glasshouses had a tendency to stay with one basic mix. Density 3.14 g/cc, uranium 0.2% wt. *About 1910.* Value $30-45.

Czechoslovakian Glass

Photo 259, the ashtray bears the mark "Moser Karlsbad", see inset. It is 12.7 cm in diameter, density 2.45 g/cc, uranium 0.2% wt. Press molded then hand cut. Moser told me that there are no records concerning their use of uranium but it was probably not for any great length of time. They also made yellow-green glass using uranium. This item is about 1930. Value $20-35.

Finnish Glass

Photo 260, there is a damaged stick on metal label on the base says "Riihimaen .... Made In Finland" Riihimaen Lasi Oy Glass Works, Finland. Difficult to date but the label suggest it might be as late as post WW2. Height 17.5 cm, density 2.52 g/cc, uranium 0.47% wt. Value $20-45.

French Glass

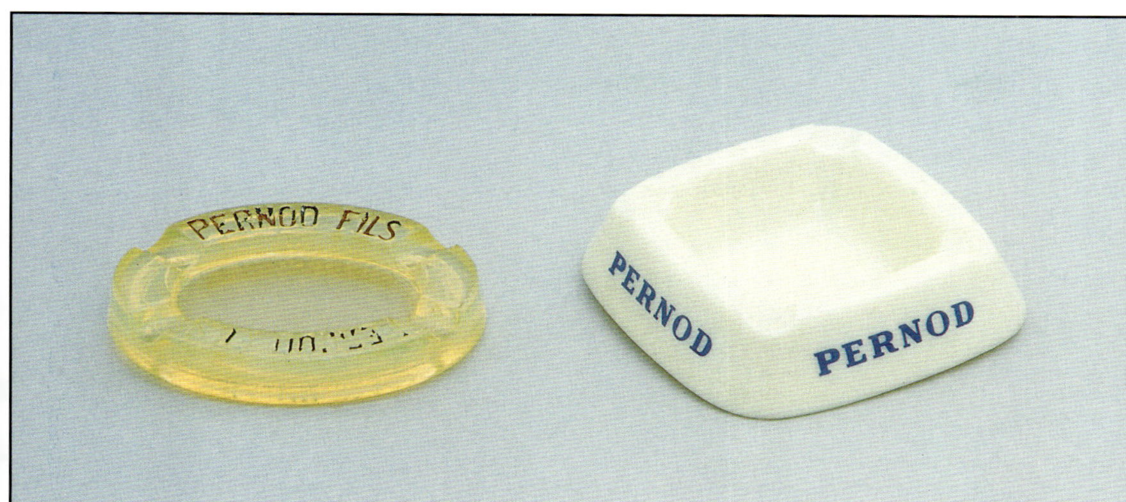

Photo 261, these two ashtrays have been made for Pernod at different times. Left, unfortunately Pernod have not been able to help me identify the maker of this piece. The top bears the inscription "PERNOD FILS" and the underside "DEPOSE MADE IN FRANCE 4692" 11.5 cm long, 9.1 cm wide, density 2.71 g/cc, uranium 0.28% wt. *Probably* before 1920. Value $20-45.
Right, was made for Pernod *about* 1970 by "Verrerie Louard" The firm closed down in 1979 and Nazeing took on orders for something like 5000 similar ashtrays but made from their own moulds. 12 cm square, density 2.48 g/cc, uranium 0.43% wt. Bears the legend on the underside "Opalex Made in France". Value $20-35.

Photo 262, a small, 4.3 cm high, press molded dish in a translucent jade green. Density 2.36 g/cc, uranium 0.17% wt. Inside of dish molded in relief, "BACCARAT". I won' t attempt to date it. Value $15-30.

Photo 263, the lamp shade was made for the English firm of "Christopher Wray Lighting Emporium Ltd." *about* 1985. It is their "Crimped Bell" pattern, part No 361/ANI. Although Christopher Wray now have their own glassworks in Wakefield, UK. this was made especially for them by Vianne in France. Height 15 cm, density 2.52 g/cc, uranium 0.37% wt. Value $15-30.

Dutch Glass

Photo 264, this honey pot is more unusual than it looks. It is an example of Graniver glass by Leerdam about 1925. The glass has a coarse ceramic like finish and is made by using coarse sand in the mix. It is always pressed. Height 14.5 cm, density 2.26 g/cc, uranium 0.87% wt. Value $60-70.

Section 3
A Miscellany of Interesting Pieces

Most collectors want to know who made the glass and when they did it. For most of the items in this section the first question will remain unanswered. But then I asked myself why, just because their parentage is uncertain, should they be treated as second class? They all attract interest for one reason or another and anyhow I love each and every one of them! I may not be able to attribute them but I can guess their date of birth and give the reader an assurance that they all contain uranium. Because they are a miscellany, it is difficult to sort them into logical groups; hence, I subdivide this section into categories, so that the order in which they appear is not entirely random.

Chapter 32

Pieces with Marks or Inscriptions

Photo 265, both these spirit glasses are Design Registry marked, 277168 and 404248 respectively. Each is 9 cm high. They date 1896 and 1902. Both are crudely made by press molding, the rough edges of the mould have not been polished off. Their densities are 2.41 g/cc and 2.5 g/cc while the uranium content is 0.5% wt. & 0.37% wt. The designs are registered by Jules Lang a company that is still in existence to-day trading in commercial catering equipment. They are not glass producers and with perhaps one small exception, never have been.

An advert in Pottery Gazette, (1st Feb. 1890) claims they had been established over 25 years and are "Glass and China Merchants, Shipper and Agents". It gives their address as 'Jules Lang & Co, 16 Hatton Gardens, London, with branches in Paris, Antwerp, and Amsterdam". Their "Specialties - Cut Tumblers, Wines, Goblets, Decanters, Jugs, Stone Glass Tumblers. Also Etched and Engraved Glass" They claim to be noted for their "thin lipped cut and plain tumblers." It would seem that they were wholesalers for distributors of "Belgian, French, and Bohemian Glass." For non-producers they registered a lot of designs, 26 between 1894 & 1900 and a further 194 before the outbreak of WW2. For a short time before WW1 they did have a glass factory in France but it closed after a disaster. It would seem that virtually all their glass ware was made by someone else. I have examined several other Design Registered items but they were in plain glass. These densities appear to break into two groups, i.e. 2.5 g/cc - 2.54 g/cc and 2.47 g/cc-2.48 g/cc covering a period 1896 to 1929. This would suggest they were using at last two suppliers. There is a reported connection between a Mr. Joseph Lang, (son of Jules Lang), in the 1940's and Nazeing glass Unfortunately the records were loaned to a glass collector some years ago and never returned.

The business was founded about 1858 by Jules Lang and Peter Brown and continued in the joint families until the 1950's when the Browns bought out the Langs although Brian (Jules Lang 's grandson) continued as chairman. It was incorporated in 1981. Harold Charles Brown died in 1991 The Company was acquired by its present owner Mr. Geoffrey Frost in 1994. It currently trades as a catering glass distributor. Value of each spirit, $15-30.

[1]Hajdamach C - British Glass p269-271.
[2]Evans W et al. - Whitefriars Glass, p30.

Photo 266, no doubt this press molded piece was specially commissioned for those who wanted to eat their egg out of a radioactive egg cup!. It is design registered No 711837, International Bottle Co. 1925. This company is listed in 1948 Kelly's under "Bottle Manufacturers" for "bottles for Food & Druggist Trades" and appears to be London based. Whether they actually made this egg cup and why they wanted it is not clear. Height 7 cm, density 2.49 g/cc, uranium 0.11% wt. Value $15-20.

Photo 267, a molded toilet water bottle Design Registry lozenge marked for 3rd April 1875 The deposition was by G V De Luca of 43 Wigmore St London. The 1881 census gives a Guiseppe de Luca as a General Merchant so presumably he did not manufacture this bottle. Height 13.5 cm, density 2.45 g/cc, uranium 0.31% wt. Value $30-60.

Photo 268, the mark on the neck says "British Syphon Co. London". The etching "Arnold & Co Lincoln" and the paper label "Quilter Mineral Waters Colchester" which adds there is a 3/- (three shilling) Deposit. I suspect this is post WW2 although the bottle *probably* originates in the late 1930's. Uranium 0.12% wt. Value $70-110.

Photo 269, I bought this rather battered powder (?) bowl in Australia. The dealer assured me he had brought it from Jamaica where he used to live. It is clearly marked with a Design Registration lozenge dated 14th February 1865. The deposition being by "Alfred Edward Edwards". Oddly the design is registered under glass, but this mark is for metal! The crown shaped lid which has lost a top piece, suggests that it was made to commemorate some Royal event but I have not been able to identify any of that date. Base 10 cm square, density 2.55 g/cc, uranium 0.4% wt. Value, if undamaged, $110-145.

Photos 270 & 271. I will discuss these two items together. They are of unusual construction best described as being double skinned with an air gap between, something like a modern "thermos flask". The glass has been silvered on the inside. The underside of each item a metal disc sealed in under clear glass. It bears the inscription "Varnish & Co, Patent, London". I have seen more elaborate examples of this type of glass.
Frederick Hale Thompson and Edward Varnish registered (London) patent No 12905 on 19th December 1849. The patent was granted on 19th June 1850. It was for "Improvements in the manufacture of Inkstands, Mustard Pots, and other Vessels of Glass". It says that "Our invention consists of blowing glass vessels so as to leave hollow spaces between the sides, so that the effect of silvering will be seen ..." It goes on to quote the formula for the silvering liquid which is poured into the hollow but it does not explain how the hollow shape was blown.
I have heard it claimed that the silvering liquid was mercury based. This may be because attempts were made to produce the silvering with mercury but it seems highly unlikely that Varnish glass came into this category. The Patent clearly indicates silver, as ammonical silver nitrate, was used with a sugar to cause the silver to plate out.
The bowl has a lid but I have not shown it because it is damaged. It had been sealed with a glass knob on its top rather than the metal disc, and this had been broken. Because of this I was able to measure the density of this lid. The uranium content of all three items is 0.62% wt, and the density of the lid 2.49 g/cc.
As far as is known Varnish was not a glass manufacturer and it is not clear who would have made these items. Hajdamach[1] describes an experiment into how such items may have been blown and states they were only produced for a few years. Evans et al[2] refers to a note in "Tallis's History and Description of the Crystal Palace" stating that most of the Varnish glass was manufactured by Messrs Powell & Sons. (Whitefriars). I do not think these two particular items were, for their density indicates that they are a non-lead metal, whereas, at that time, as already described, Whitefriars were using a basic fritt with about 30% lead.

Photo 272, we do not know how this piece started life, it has probably been corrupted to take an electric light fitting. It has a Design Registration lozenge in Category (iv), which is earthenware and indicates it to be an oil lamp base, registration number is 266628, deposited in September 1872. It does not indicate who would have molded the glass. Height, as shown, 24 cm, density 2.55 g/cc, uranium 0.43% wt. Dating depends on whether it started life as an oil lamp or whether it was deliberately made to take an electric fitting. Lets say between 1880 & 1910. Value $45-70.

Photo 273, On this item only the light green droplets contain uranium. Density 2.46 g/cc, uranium 0.15% wt, dark green density 2.51 g/cc, uranium nil. It is an American patent candle holder. The actual candle sits in the hollow stem and is spring loaded to poke its wick through the top, which bears the inscription "Greens Patent ARCTIC Candle Lamp. Pat. USA Sept. 1 98" Date about 1898. Value $70-145.

Photo 274, I do know what this is because I've read the inscription on the side but I still don't know how it works. "Maw's Registered Label Damper. S Mawson & Sons London" No clue as to date but it must be *about* 1930. Length 10.9 cm, density 2.48 g/cc, uranium 0.25% wt. Value $30-45.

Photo 277, unfortunately this little chappie has lost its stopper. The shape is the same as that shown in Design Registration 150513, 7th April 1862, by Cross & Blackwell. The difference between this item and the registration submission is that this container has a squatter body and shorter neck. Height 9.75m, density 2.78 g/cc, uranium 0.28% wt. The density hints that it may have been made in Lancashire *about* 1870-80. Value $35-60.

Photo 275, is a patented device for sharpening safety razor blades. It was sold with the slogan "Just ONE Blade and Lillicrap's Hone for Hundreds of Shaves" (Quite a contrast to the throw-away society of today!) A write up reads "Lillicrap's Hone embodies a scientific principle. Like many of the inventions, which have been great boons, it is simple in the extreme, but is perfectly effective. The Hone is made in Uranium Glass with a specially prepared surface. It is designed to conform accurately with the curvature of the Safety Razor Blade when this is fixed for shaving. The Hone was put on the Market in July 1930, and many shavers who have bought it have written to the makers to express their satisfaction."

The mention of uranium is interesting for it implies that it has imparted some special property to the glass. However I have examined several of these items and not all of them have contained uranium! As shown in Photo 276, they carry design Registration No 756950 and English patent No 346057 as well as numbers for other countries. Made for Lillicrap by "Wood Bros. Glass Co., Ltd., Manufacturers of Scientific Glassware, Barnsley, England. (Est. 1825)" Length 7 cm, density 2.56 g/cc, uranium 0.22% wt. Value $15-20.

Photo 278 & 279. These two talc bottles are much the same vintage but are from different firms and probably made by different manufacturers. No doubt the delicate uranium color added to the attractions of the talc they contained.

Photo 278, height 12.75 cm, density 2.54 g/cc, uranium 0.24% wt. Design reg. No 755481, label reads "Dubarry, 81 Brompton Road London" Date 1930. Value $20-30.

Photo 279, height 12 cm, density not measured as the bottle is full of talc, uranium 0.37% wt. Design reg. No 792836. label reads "Potter & Moore's Silk Sifted Talc. Made in England". Date 1934. Value, complete with box and talc, $45-70.

Photo 280 is another puzzle. The glass is very thin, only 0.05 cm at the top. The uranium is flashed on the inside. Base has been ground flat leaving a trace of a pontil mark. The top has been cut and ground before gilding. Inscription reads "Souvenir of Westgate on Sea" I date it *period* 1920 and make a *best guess* that it is Continental made for the British Market. Height 10 cm, density 2.52 g/cc, uranium 7 cps. Value $5-20.

Photo 282, I can date this accurately, the inscription reads "Souvenir of Auckland Exhibition 1913-1914". What is not clear is where it was made. Height 15.5 cm, density 2.68 g/cc, uranium 0.43% wt. Value $35-60.

Photo 281 it is somewhat unusual to associate pink with uranium, the exception being Burmese and its look alike. As explained that effect is obtained by adding gold to the mix and then reheating the article after it has been made. How this got its pink I do not know but it was probably not through reheating although there is a slight change of shade towards its base. To me it does not look like the rose pink associated with gold The base is hollow and the top ground flat. It also has a pontil dimple and a trade mark, Photo 281a, which I have not identified. The decoration is by transfer, which may have been fired on. But why a pontil not a gadget to hold it. Perhaps it was made relatively recently, when gadgets have faded from popularity, but from the wear I don't think so. Responds moderately to uv light. Height 12.5 cm, density 2.34 g/cc, uranium 0.28% wt. Value $20-30.

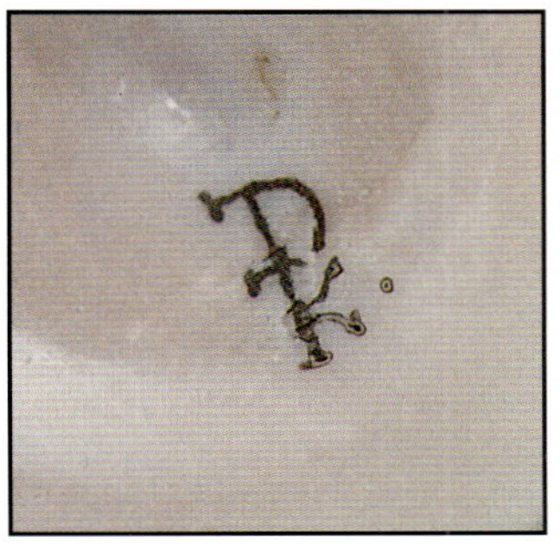

Photo 283, although it does not show up well on the photograph this wine bears a coat of arms. It has defied all my efforts to date and attribute although I originally thought it would be easy to so do. The inscription has the word IPSWICH but the arms are not correct for that Suffolk Town. This rules out the glass being part of the official regalia. The arms appear to be a compromise between those granted by Edward 111 and those of the present day. Either someone made a hash of the copying or, as seems more likely, they were never intended to be exact. The glass is hand made with striations on the mouth of the bowl. The foot is difficult to interpret but could have been blown. However there isn't a pontil mark. I'm going to date it between 1880 and 1930, which is not very helpful! Height 11.2 cm, density 3.14, uranium 0.09% wt. Value $20-35.

Photo 285, this studio made paper weight is signed but unfortunately I can not discern the first engraved name , the best I can do is "??dd?at & Johnson 1983" At least we know the date! Max. length 14.3 cm, density 2.5 g/cc, uranium 0.12% wt. Value $30-45.

Photo 284, a utilitarian piece in uranium glass. This lemon squeezer bears the words "Patent Applied For" but gives no other clue as to its origin or date. Width, from handle to stem 21 cm, density 2.55 g/cc, uranium 0.22% wt. Density and uranium are close, but not quite close enough to Jobling's, for a confident attribution so it is only a *best guess* and *about* 1935. Value $20-35.

Chapter 33

Radioactive Animals

This group is a collection of animals ranging from a reptile to a wingless swan. It is an illustration of how widely uranium has been used for decorative effect. They probably come from different "reserves," so I'll go through them one by one.

Photo 287, this Disney like creature has uranium only in its wings. Density 2.41 g/cc , uranium approximately 0.6% wt. Vintage *about* 1955. Value $5-15.

Photo 286, I love this little bird. It was one of my early finds when I rescued it from a "junk" shop for a very modest ransom. Years later it made an appearance in the BBC's "Birth of Europe!" series. It was to show that there were other uses for uranium as well as making bombs and power stations. Beak to tail measures 13.5 cm, density 2.51 g/cc, uranium 0.25% wt. Date *probably about* 1960. Value, after haggle I paid $1 for it and it is not for resale!

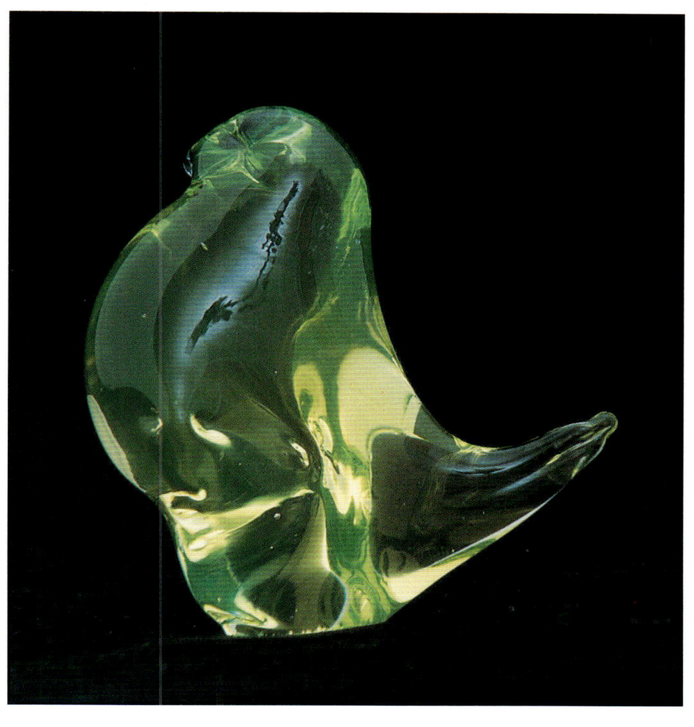

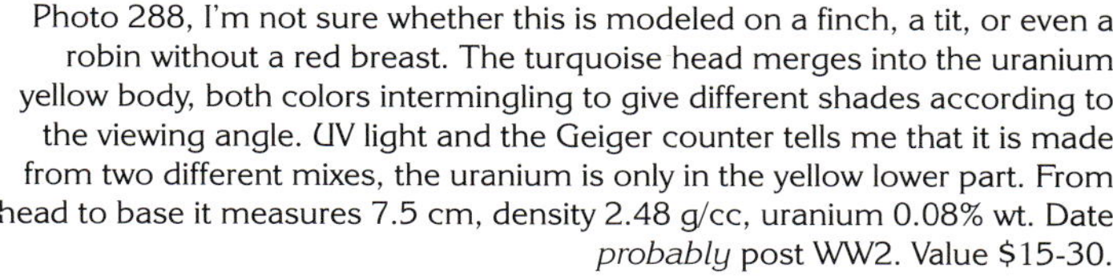

Photo 288, I'm not sure whether this is modeled on a finch, a tit, or even a robin without a red breast. The turquoise head merges into the uranium yellow body, both colors intermingling to give different shades according to the viewing angle. UV light and the Geiger counter tells me that it is made from two different mixes, the uranium is only in the yellow lower part. From head to base it measures 7.5 cm, density 2.48 g/cc, uranium 0.08% wt. Date *probably* post WW2. Value $15-30.

Photo 289, is big brother of the menagerie being 23 cm high from its waterline. Density not measured, uranium 0.6% wt. Gamma spectrometry confirmed that it is very low in potassium. Legend says an old lady saw it being made in Malta when she was on holiday in 1988, give or take a year. Value $35-60.

Photo 290, why would anyone want a miniature rocking horse elephant, especially a radioactive one? Perhaps it once formed the top part of a blotter but there is no evidence of this. It is press molded. Overall length 9.3 cm, density 2.43 g/cc, uranium 0.08% wt. Does not fluoresce with near uv but changes shade of green under far uv. As elephants live for a long time I am reluctant to date this one. Value $20-35.

Photo 291, height 7.25 cm, density not measured, uranium approximately 0.25% wt. Very thin delicate glass with gold speckles. Probably Venetian and anyone's guess about the date is likely to be as good as mine. Value $35-50.

Chapter 34
Curiosities

In this group are some odd items made from uranium glass; I am not even sure of the use for which some were intended.

Photo 294, it could be a candle drip although it has a metal center secured to a heavy base which in turn has a small threaded hole. My guess is that it came off a metal candle support such as used to be fitted to pianos. It is press molded, density 3.22 g/cc, uranium 0.25% wt. Despite its high density I do not think it old enough to be an early Stourbridge molding. Remember that Val St Lambert of Belgium was producing pressed glass with a density of 3.14 g/cc as late as 1908 (see Photo 258). By the look and style of this molding I would put it *about* 1890. Value $5-15.

Photo 292 The smallest piece in our collection. It weights only 16 grams, is 5 cm long. Density 2.38 g/cc, uranium approx. 0.7% wt. The white overlay has been cut away to reveal the yellow uranium. It carries an "M" like mark on the base, it has to be a seal. *Probably about* 1880. Value $30-60.

Photo 293, I have had several suggestions about this item, the most likely being that it is a pipe stand. Be that as it may it is a nice piece of uranium glass but who made it? Length 13 cm, density 2.45 g/cc, uranium 0.74% wt. It shows considerable wear so I date it *period* 1900. Value $20-35.

Photo 295, a draw handle 4.5 cm long. Density 2.6 g/cc, uranium 0.87% wt. *Period* 1910. Value $3-5.

Photo 297, is a thoroughbred chunk of uranium glass cut to make a paper weight. Height 6.25 cm, density 2.42 g/cc, uranium 0.5% wt. From the considerable wear that it shows I'd say *about* 1910, but it is so typical of yellow uranium glass it could be anytime since it came into fashion. Value $45-70.

Photo 296, the delicate color effect on this unusual paper weight is obtained by flashing a thin layer of uranium glass onto crystal then cutting back to make the port holes. Height 4.5 cm, density 3.08 g/cc, uranium 3.5 cps. (the U layer is too thin to provide infinite depth). It has been acid polished. The density suggests about 26% lead, which indicates it could be Continental or Midlands from more recent years. I wouldn' t like to say which but date it *about* 1980 Value $30-45.

Photo 298, any suggestions for what this little press molded piece of uranium jade was intended? I can only think it may be the inner part of an ink pot, or may be it was a bird feeder or may be.... It stands only 4 cm high, has a density of 2.35 g/cc, (which suggests that it may be a boro-silicate glass), and has 0.81% wt uranium. *Best guess* at the date is *about* 1930. Value $3-5.

Photo 299, just why such a mundane object should be made from a combination of pewter and radioactive glass I can not imagine. This jade like egg cup is fixed on a pewter mount so a density measurement is not possible. The uranium is 0.74% wt. and height 9.5 cm. Although I bought it in Australia my gut feeling is that it is French. As for date let's say *period* 1920, which gives quite a large margin for error. Value $30-45.

Photo 300, is not an egg cup. The turned over top would make it quite unsuitable for such a purpose. It is, perhaps, a toothpick holder. At one time it had a gold pattern but this is now almost completely worn off. It has been hand made, the pontil mark remains rough. I thought at first it might be Richardson's for they made similar shade white and green ware but the cheap gilding and low density says no. Height 10.25 cm, density 2.49 g/cc, uranium (green only), 0.62% wt. Date *about* 1880. Value $30-45.

Photo 301, there must be a use for a hollow green egg but I can't think what it is. It would be useless as a paper weight. It has been suggested it could be a hand warmer as used in the lace industry. I would go along with that if it was solid, but to have a hollow one made from uranium glass seems improbable. Longest dimension 8.75 cm, density not measurable, uranium 0.93% wt. As for date, sometime between 1880 and 1940, which is not very helpful! Value $30-60.

Chapter 35

Coralene Decoration

This is a technique for decorating glassware. Tiny glass beads are fixed to form the pattern. They may be colored, or if clear fixed over colored glass. The cheaper method of fixing was to use an adhesive but such examples have scarcely survived the passage of time unscathed. Frequent handling has dislodged the beads leaving only a trace where the original pattern has been. The better, and more costly, method of fixing was to reheat the decorated article.

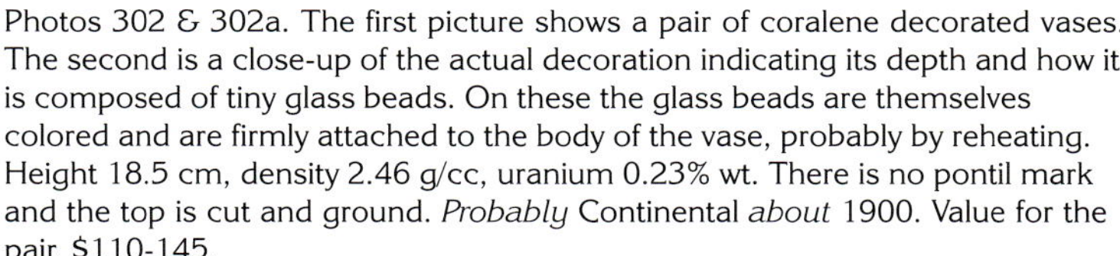

Photos 302 & 302a. The first picture shows a pair of coralene decorated vases. The second is a close-up of the actual decoration indicating its depth and how it is composed of tiny glass beads. On these the glass beads are themselves colored and are firmly attached to the body of the vase, probably by reheating. Height 18.5 cm, density 2.46 g/cc, uranium 0.23% wt. There is no pontil mark and the top is cut and ground. *Probably* Continental *about* 1900. Value for the pair, $110-145.

Top right: Photo 303, here it is clear that the beads were fixed over a colored pattern and with the passage of time most have fallen off. Although the item has a broken pontil mark I think it more likely to be Continental rather than English or American. Height 14 cm, density 2.44 g/cc, uranium 0.22 % wt. Value, as it is with much of the original decoration worn off, $30-45.

Chapter 36
Drinking Glasses

From my casual observations on the general availability of uranium glass I would think that it was used more often in making drinking glasses than any other group. I wonder what the folk who used them would have thought if they had known that the glass contained not only radioactive but a chemically toxic element As there is no evidence that it ever did them any harm they probably would not have been bothered! A sobering thought that for a hundred years or more the world's population has been supping from radioactive glassware. In Section 2 I have already shown examples but there are many more and to emphasize the frequency of the use of uranium for this purpose I now include a sample of others which I have not been able to attribute. They range from spirits to wines to tumblers. Some come from the last century but others were made within my lifetime. Uranium glass drinking vessels appear at most antique fairs in one form or another at a frequency which is certainly no less than other items.

Making reliable attributions for drinking glasses is full of pitfalls. There are only a few basic shapes that have to be shared between a very large number of makers. Think of a wine glass, it generally has a bowl, stem and base, (alternatively perhaps a cone shaped bowl and a foot), and the only opportunity for individualism is the pattern. Alter the size and it becomes a spirit or goblet. Where the pattern is likely to be unique because it is complex or unusual, then attribution may be possible, but in the majority of cases it is simplistic. I've lost count of the number of times dealers, (or inexperienced collectors), have named the maker on the basis that it has flats just like one illustrated in a particular book. A quick scan through pattern books will soon reveal that the idea was not the monopoly of one glasshouse. Although difficult to attribute, the wide variety of the uranium glass bearing examples are well worth collecting. The following represents some examples. If what is to be found at fairs and sales is anything to go by then there must have been many more "greens" produced than "uranium yellows."

[3]Journal of the Glass Association, Vol. 2, 1987, p32.

[4]Glickman J L - Yellow-Green Vaseline, No 194

Photo 304, two early wines in topaz. Left, this glass was surely intended for the discerning customer. Unfortunately I cannot find it in any of the pattern books that I have searched. I suspect that it came from one of the top Stourbridge glasshouses. Height 14.25 cm, density 3.15 g/cc, uranium 0.43% wt. Its blown foot, ground pontil prompts me to date it *about* 1855. Value $70-110. Right, also a quality wine. The stem is hollow and cut with 6 facets. The foot was probably molded and the pontil has been ground out. Height 13.75 cm, density 3.19 g/cc, uranium 0.22% wt. This could well be a product of the Midlands or London dating *about* 1875. Value $60-70.

Photo 305, the left and right hand side spirits are as near identical as are hand made glasses. Height 7.5 cm, density 2.47 g/cc, uranium 0.62% wt. Each has a ground off pontil and hand made foot, the eight facets have been hand ground and hand polished. They have to be *about* 1850. Value each, $20-35. Center spirit, height 7.25 cm, density 2.48 g/cc, uranium 0.62% wt. The similarity in density and uranium suggests this may be from the same stable as the other two. The foot is thick and hand made, it has a ground off pontil and the eight facets are hand cut and polished. *About* 1850. Value $20-35.

Photo 306, Left, another anomaly to my dating practice. The pontil mark is rough and has not been ground, the foot is probably blown. The lack of wear makes me suspect that this is another product of the 30's made in older style but I could be wrong. Height 11.75 cm, density 3.04 g/cc, uranium 0.2% wt. Value $20-35. Right, height 13 cm, density 2.49 g/cc, uranium 0.31% wt. It is difficult to be sure how this foot was made but the pontil has been ground off. I have some difficulty in dating so I'll go for *period* 1880. Value $20-35.

Photo 307. Left, the top and base of the styled rummer have been cut and ground, not a practice favored in the UK and probably indicates it was made down to a price. The top is too small for it to be a true rummer. Height 13.5 cm, density 2.4 g/cc, uranium, on bowl only, 0.43% wt. Dating is difficult and again I would not be surprised if it were some time after WW2. Value $20-35. Right, Large hollow stem rummer but it is not as old as first sight might suggest. The metal is virtually without blemish and the wear is slight. Density has not been determined because of the hollow stem, its height is 15.3 cm, uranium 0.5% wt. The top has been cut on a turntable then rounded with a flame. Difficult to date but I would not be surprised if it were post WW2. *Best guess*, it comes from the Continent but I have reservations. Value $35-50.

Photo 308, Left, I am not sure what purpose this vessel would have served. Its capacity is too large for a liqueur and too small for a spirit (shot) glass. It is press molded and has been fire polished. Height 6 cm, density 2.5 g/cc, uranium 0.31% wt. Date *about* 1900. Value $15-30. Right, A fairly crude press molded liqueur. I bought it in France and guess it may well be French. Height 8 cm, density 2.46 g/cc, uranium 0.9% wt. *About* 1910 Value $15-20.

Photo 309, height 4.75 cm, density 2.63 g/cc, uranium 0.5% wt. The base is well ground and concave. The 10 facets are hand ground and polished. The metal is of good quality. Date *about* 1880. Value $20-35.

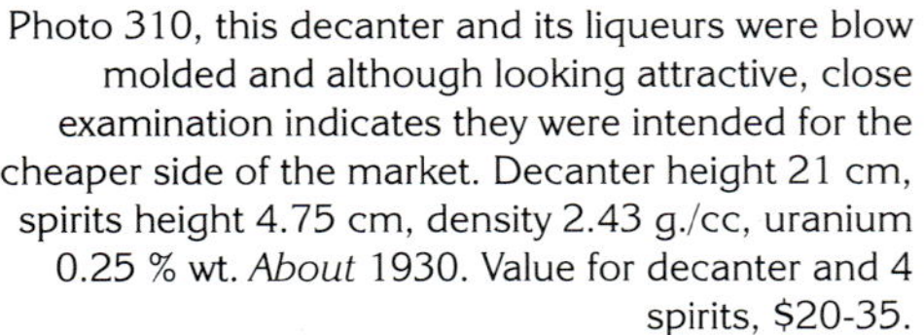

Photo 310, this decanter and its liqueurs were blow molded and although looking attractive, close examination indicates they were intended for the cheaper side of the market. Decanter height 21 cm, spirits height 4.75 cm, density 2.43 g./cc, uranium 0.25 % wt. *About* 1930. Value for decanter and 4 spirits, $20-35.

Photo 311, the pattern on the bowl of this wine has been cut and heavily polished. The foot has a ground off pontil but it is molded not blown. Height 11.75 cm, density 2.77 g/cc, uranium 0.62% wt. As for date let's say *about* 1875. The density suggests it might have come from the Lancashire area. Value $20-30.

Photo 313, two more engraved wines. Left, Another pattern I cannot trace. Blown foot, ground pontil, height 12 cm, density 2.68 g/cc, uranium 0.25% wt. *About* 1870. Value $20-35.
Right, drape patterns were not uncommon. I am not able to identify this one. Blown foot, ground pontil, height 12 cm, density 2.5 g/cc, uranium 0.16 % wt. *About* 1870. Value $20-35.

Photo 312, one of several examples of engraved patterns on the bowl of the glass. These can help identify the origin but this one escapes me. It's blown foot and ground pontil dates it *about* 1870. Height 12 cm, density 3 g/cc, uranium 0.25% wt. Value $20-35.

Photo 314, Left, wine has an interesting molded pattern on the bowl. The glass has been made in three pieces, the bowl blown first, then the stem added and finally a blown foot. There is considerable crizzling with mini internal cracks in the foot and the bowl going cloudy on the outside. The metal has not stood the test of time! Height 13 cm, density 2.5 g/cc, uranium 0.28% wt. Date *about* 1870. Value $30-45.

Center, the bowl on this wine must have started life in a dip mould, the foot is blown and there is a ground off pontil. Height 13.5 cm, density 2.85 g/cc, uranium 0.19% wt. Again the density and general appearance suggest Lancashire, perhaps Percival Vickers and the date *about* 1865. Value $30-45.

Right, like the center wine the bowl on this glass was formed in a dip mould but there the similarity ends. The cutting on the base looks as if it has been acid polished and it has an altogether mid twentieth century appearance. The density suggests it may have come from the Midlands but it is not marked. Height 13.75 cm, density 3.16 g/cc, uranium 0.74% wt. Value $20-35.

Photo 315, It is not crizzling that makes this glass look cloudy, it is how the maker intended although I am not at all sure how the effect was obtained. The metal does include a number of very small air bubbles but I suspect something else is responsible for the cloudy effect. Blown foot and ground pontil dates it *about* 1870. Height 13 cm, density 2.41 g/cc, uranium 0.56% wt. Value $30-45.

Photo 316. Left, the cut and ground top on this piece of deco says it's probably not made in Britain. Height 10 cm, density 2.42 g/cc, uranium 0.62% wt. *About* 1935. Value $15-20.

Right, typical deco or later. Height 8.5 cm, density 2.43 g/cc, uranium 0.25% wt.. Value $5-20.

Photo 317, Left, the six flutes which run from foot to bowl are unusual for they go deep into the bowl like an intaglio cut.. The base is blown and the pontil ground off. Height 12.5 cm. density 2.58 g/cc, uranium 0.37% wt. Date *about* 1870. Value $30-45.
Center, I should probably have included this in the "Midlands" section for I feel sure this is from where the glass came. Made in three pieces, blown foot and ground off pontil. The bowl despite the six large facets, is delicate at the rim. A glass of quality, *about* 1860. Height 12.3 cm, density 3.2 g/cc, uranium 0.87% wt. Value $30-45.
Right, The stem has two generous knops and the base of the bowl has been cut with 6 facets. The base is blown and there is a good dimple where the pontil was ground off. Height 12.25 cm, density 2.51 g/cc, uranium 0.43% wt. Date *about* 1860. Value $30-45.

Photo 318, this wine has seven flats ground out of the base of the bowl and carried down the stem. The foot is blown and the pontil ground out. Height 11.75 cm, density 2.49 g/cc, uranium 0.43% wt. Date *about* 1860. Value $30-45.

Photo 319, two wines with conical bowls. Left, has 7 flats, which run down the length of the glass. The stem is hollow, the foot is blown and has a ground pontil. It is heavily crizzled. Height 13.5 cm, density 2.88 g/cc, uranium 0.25% wt. It could have come from one of the Lancashire glasshouses, but then it could have come from a lot of places. Date *about* 1865. Value $30-60.
Right. Although closely resembling a Percival Vickers' glass illustrated in the Glass Association Journal[3] three things say it is not. This illustrates how easy it is to make a wrong attribution on the basis of a photograph. This glass has seven flats whereas the Percival Vickers one only has six, the density is too high and the uranium too low. My gut feeling is that this is a Webb. I have not found an exact match in their pattern books although items 2542 and 3546 are very close. Moreover the density and uranium match closely that of their "Aquamarine Green". The thick base has probably been blown and the pontil mark is ground off. Height 13.5 cm, density 3.14 g/cc, uranium 0.8% wt. I'd date it *about* 1865, (the Webb's pattern books are 1848). Value $45-60.

Photo 320, Left, a rib pattern like this is to be seen in the Stevens & Williams books but I don't think this is one of theirs, though I could be wrong. It has a good ground pontil but the foot is one of those difficult decisions, perhaps it was blown or perhaps it was molded so I have to be cautious on dating, say *period* 1900. Height 12 cm, density 2.49 g/cc, uranium 0.5% wt. Value $20-35.
Right, although not shown in the photograph, the metal has a number of very small seeds. The foot is blown but its edge has been ground. The pontil also. Height 13 cm, density 2.61 g/cc, uranium 0.22% wt. Date *about* 1860. Value $35-50.

Photo 321, Left, the delicate foot has been molded and is now showing signs of crizzling. It has a ground off pontil so I date it *about* 1875. Height 11.75 cm, density 2.74 g/cc, uranium 0.37% wt. Value $30-45.
Right, not the most attractive of wines but it is interesting. It has a broken pontil and a foot, which is molded not blown. If nothing else it only goes to show that an ungrounded pontil is no guarantee of an early birth. This piece was made in three parts. It could be a "repro" from the 1930's but I don' t think so. I would have expected better quality metal that would not lead to the extensive crizzling from which this suffers. Height 12 cm, density 2.63 g/cc, uranium 0.19% wt. Date *about* 1890. Value $20-30.

Photo 322, it was the color that induced me to add this to my collection. It has an unusual bluish shade of green. It is a high class piece with a drawn stem, blown foot and ground pontil. Height 13.3 cm, density 3.16 g/cc, uranium 0.12 % wt. Value $35-60.

Photo 323, Probably an "inexpensive" glass of its day. It is made in three pieces, the bowl is thick and heavy, the foot has been hand formed and made concave to accommodate the ungrounded pontil. The metal has a few seeds and a sprinkling of small air bubbles. The rich apple green color is unspoiled by crizzling . Perhaps it was intended as a blank and never cut? Height 13.25 cm, density 2.52 g/cc and uranium 0.68% wt. It could well have come from the Continent, I would date it *about* 1855. Value $30-45.

Photo 324 these wine glasses are identical in shape and size. The twisted stem design is unusual but not unique. Molineaux Webb did make similar shaped wines, it is therefore possible that these came from that firm. On the other hand Richardson's pattern book shows twisted stems on some of their glasses, the resemblance is so close that one might have no difficulty in attributing them to that firm. So take a closer look. Of the two illustrated, the one on the left is clear but the right one heavily crizzled. The densities are significantly different, being 2.65 g/cc and 2.49 g/cc respectively. Their response to long wave uv light was the same, i.e. strong, but different in the case of short wave uv. The former fluoresced with a distinct tint of pale violet blended into the uranium green. Both glasses have blown feet. Both wines were bought as part of a set and came from the same glasshouse, *about* 1860 but made from different mixes. Were the makers experimenting with low lead metals? If they were they would not have been aware of the crizzling problem as this probably only showed after many years. Height 10 cm. Value $20-35 each.

Photo 327, Left, a deco glass in amber. Height 11.25 cm, density 2.71 g/cc, uranium 0.37% wt. Value $5-15.
Right, the nearest illustration I can find to this glass is in the Stevens & Williams pattern book for 1936. However I don't think this is it. I think it possible that it comes from post WW2 years. Height 11 cm, density 2.64 g/cc, uranium 0.47% wt. value $5-15.

Photos 325 & 326.I will consider these four glasses together although they must come from different glasshouses. They are all in a style that could be mistaken for much earlier ware. All this amber, which is uranium based, does not appear until after the turn of the 19th century, more likely as late as the 1920's. To call them "repro" is perhaps too strong a term for it is unlikely that this color would have existed in Georgian or early Victorian times.

They are all made from leaded glass and have high uranium content. Looking through old pattern books it would seem that they could have come from a number of factories. Harry Powell, of Whitefriars, was very interested in older glass ware and on his travels, both in the UK and abroad, made sketches of items he saw in museums, paintings etc. These formed the basis for some of the designs produced later and became known as "Glass with Histories". They are characterized by rigoree and raspberry style prunts. But then sketches in other pattern books such as Stephen & Williams, Stuart Crystal, and Richardson's, to name just three, also show this styling. *Almost certainly* these are British *about* 1935, but that is far as I can go.

Photo 325, the prunts, rigoree and style are of an 18th century glass. It's color does not have the golden tint of those in Photo 326, nevertheless it is still a uranium amber but perhaps a little earlier than the others. Height 10 cm, density 3.12 g/cc, uranium 1.12% wt. Value $20-45.

Photo 326, Left, a tumbler with rigoree and trail work around the base, which is concave, ground and polished presumably because it had been worked on a punty. Height 9 cm, density 3.4 g/cc, uranium 1.24% wt. Value $15-30.

Center, 16.5 high, density 2.98 g/cc, uranium 1.8% wt. It has a folded foot, blown hollow stem and raspberry prunts. Value $35-60.

Right, one of a pair. The dealer who sold them to me insisted they were 1860. Nonsense. Like the others in this collection they are much later. Height 12 cm, density, (2 items) 3.52 g/cc & 3.58 g/cc, uranium (each) 1.18% wt. Value (each) $35-60.

Photo 330, left and right closely resemble the center in appearance, but their density is different and they probably do not come from the same glasshouse. They have numbers molded on their base, (4 & 3 respectively). It is interesting to note that the right is slightly darker glass than the Left, but it has less uranium. Their densities are 2.59 g/cc and 2.55 g/cc, uranium 0.25 % and 0.19% wt. . Height 7.5 cm, date *period* 1880. Value each $15-20. Center height 6 cm, density 2.45 g/cc, uranium 0.2 % wt. Crudely press molded, has a "2" on the base. An American shot glass perhaps? *About* 1880. Value $15-20.

Photo 328, a thick press molded goblet. Glickman[4] shows an identical piece which he describes as a "Russian tea glass ca. 1885". He does not give the reason for his attribution. I doubt the date on this example and, on the basis of lack of wear, would put it much later. Height 15.5 cm, density 2.46 g/cc, uranium 0.19% wt. Value $20-45.

Photo 329, if pattern is anything to go by this small tumbler could have originated at a number of different glasshouses. Derbyshire, Percival Vickers, Sowerby, to mention a few in the UK then of course it may have come from the USA. It has been press molded, is slightly lopsided and has seeds in the metal. Its density is high for pressed glass, which endorses my thoughts that it is *period* 1860. Height 12.25 cm, density 3.1 g/cc, uranium 0.14% uranium. Value $20-35.

Photo 333, water sets in uranium glass are not uncommon, especially the green ones which were produced in the Depression years. This set is particularly unusual because of its color. It is the only example of uranium glass I have ever seen with this pinkish amber tint. I have no idea who made it. Style says about 1935. Height of tumbler 11 cm, height of jug, 18.25 cm, density 2.43 g/cc, uranium 0.16% wt. Value of jug and set of 6 tumblers $35-50.

Photo 331, uranium yellow tumblers are not at all common and not as prevalent as their green counterparts. This one may well have been with a water carafe in its youth, now alas it stands alone. Height 8.5 cm, density 2.46 g/cc, uranium 0.87% wt. It has been hand made on a pontil and carries a considerable amount of wear. *Period* 1900. Value $20-30.

Photo 332, Is this a liqueur or a miniature tumbler from a salesman's pack? It is thin blown and the dealer claimed to have bought it in France. Height 4.75 cm, density 2.8 g/cc, uranium 0.18% wt. *Period* 1920. Value $15-20.

Photo 334, I am not sure whether these were intended for drinking or for use as a sweet. They are rather thick and heavy for the former and a little small for the latter. As far as I am concerned, to some extent this is irrelevant, because they have been colored with uranium. Left, there is nothing delicate about this piece, never the less I still think the foot is blown. The Stem and bowl have cut and polished facets. The pontil mark is ground off. Height 12 cm, density 2.67 g/cc, uranium 0.43% wt. Date *about* 1865. Value $35-50. Right, It wasn't until I tried drinking from this old timer that the thought came to me that it may not have been intended for such a purpose. More interesting is how it was made. The foot is blown. The hollow stem and bowl appear to have been cut and polished. Close examination casts doubts on this, for the usual associated striations are not there. The metal has seeds and is heavily crizzled. Perhaps this crizzling has destroyed or obscured the striations. The pontil mark has been ground off. Height 12.5 cm, density 2.88 g/cc, uranium 0.56% wt. Date *probably about* 1850. Value $35-60.

Chapter 37
Sweet Dishes

Uranium was also used to color sweet dishes. Examples are not hard to come by although they are mainly from the deco period or later.

Photo 336, this sweet looks very much like a piece from George Davidson but I think not. It is similar but not the same as pieces illustrated in their catalogues. Yet again it is another reminder that similarity is not good enough for attributions. Diameter 12 cm, density 2.61 g/cc, uranium 0.23% wt. Date *about* 1935 Value $15-20.

Photo 335, At first glance this metal looks the same as the Stevens & Williams green cigarette holder in Photo 146. The density and uranium tell a different story. This is difficult to date, it has a ground off pontil and a molded foot so I'm going to say *period* 1910. Diameter 9.25 cm, density 2.54 g/cc, uranium 0.5% wt. Value $20-35.

Photo 337, two identical sweet dishes from between the wars, or even just afterwards. Both have the same density but the amber has far more uranium. Height 9.75 cm, density (both) 2.64 g/cc, uranium 0.43% wt and 0.06% wt respectively. Value $5-15 each.

Chapter 38
Jugs

Photo 338, like a lot of jugs this was probably used as a vase. The lower part is badly watermarked. There are two types of water marking. The first occurs in areas of hard water and may form over a relatively short time. As the water in the vessel evaporates, perhaps because it is in a warm dry room, salts in the water deposit on the inside, rather like the scaling in a kettle. By a process of trial and error I have found that this can be removed by use of certain de-scalers, but I keep clear of those that require hot water. The other type of marking, the one which is affecting this item, is due to water over the years, etching the inside surface. This cannot be removed with descalant or any other cleaning process. Possibly it could be acid polished out but such treatment would dissolve the inner layer of metal and in my view destroy the item's originality. Like my receding hair I regard it as a mark of it's age and service.
The opaque milky yellow is reminiscent of Davidson's "Primrose Pearline" but the density tells us this is no way associated with that firm.
Height 14.5 cm, density 3 g/cc, uranium 0,25% wt. Date *about* 1900. Value in its present condition, $20-30.

Photo 339, Left, not a common color for uranium glass. It has been hand made, has a ground off pontil. It is crudely hand painted. I suspect it is early twentieth century. Height 15 cm, density 2.47 g/cc, uranium 0.12% wt. Value $20-35. Right, I have no doubt about the authenticity of this jug. It has the older style of "pump handle", shows moderate wear on the metal and a lot of wear on the gilt. Height 10.75 cm, density 2.42 g/cc, uranium 0.8% wt. *About* 1860. Value $30-45.

Photo 340, left, this opaque green jug has a perfect dimple where the punty was fixed and a pump handle. Could be mid to late nineteenth century but instinct tells me first quarter of the twentieth. Height 9.75 cm, density 2.47 g/cc, uranium 1.1% wt. Value $20-35.Center, the bowl of the jug was formed in a dip mould to give the ribbing effect, faint though it be. The foot shows signs of a gadget mark and the fact that it has a forward tilt suggests it was not made by the most skilled of blowers. An apprentice's piece perhaps? Height 10 cm, density 2.64 g/cc, uranium 0.26% wt. Date *about* 1900. Value $15-20.
Right, this jug is made from a press molded body and has an applied handle in the pump style. The base has a molded in star pattern and has been finished by grinding flat. I suspect the body was held on a gadget while the handle was applied. The molding is of good quality and probably acid polished. Instinct tells me *about* 1930 but I could be wrong. Height 9.25 cm, density 2.48 g/cc, uranium 0.87% wt. Value $5-20.

Chapter 39

Vases, Jardinières and Other Devices that hold Flowers

It seems only logical to follow jugs with vases as the former are often used as a substitute for the latter. In terms of uranium glass, use of the flower-holding devices would probably run drinking vessels to a close finish in a contest for the most common item. However unlike the former, which are much smaller the vase offers more scope for decoration, in glass, gilding or enamel. I have chosen a selection from my collection that I trust will illustrate this.

Photo 342, a large urn like vase. It has a hollow bases and ground top. There is no sign of a pontil mark. All the hall marks of late Victorian continental pieces. The color is very pale. The decoration appears to be hand painted. Fortunately this, unlike many others, has not been corrupted to take an electric lamp! Height 32 cm, density 2.52 g/cc, uranium 0.17% wt.
Date *about* 1890. Value $45-70.

Photo 341, Arguably some of the most fascinating glass work is to be found in epergnes. For the ordinary collector they present something of a problem. They are expensive and fragile. For those reasons I have only this one in my collection. As the pattern book of many glasshouses will verify, the epergne reached peak popularity towards the end of the Victorian era . Many were made using uranium for color with elaborate bases and multi trumpets. This is one of the simpler designs and *best guess* is that it is French. Height 31.5 cm, density 2.46 g/cc, uranium 0.28% wt. Value $145-215.

Photo 343, much of what I have said about Photo 342 applies to this piece. The light blue is more unusual. The gold decor at the neck has worn well but the same cannot be said of the white. Height 28 cm, density 2.5 g/cc, uranium 0.7% wt. Date *about* 1890. Value $45-70.

Photo 344, there is something classical about this shape but I do not think it was made as an expensive piece. The pontil has been ground and the base solid. The gold work is probably by transfer and shows signs of wear. About 1900. Height 26.25 cm, density 2.49 g/cc, uranium 1.24% wt. which is quite high for a dark green. Value $45-70.

Photo 346 shows two almost pure white vases. It is difficult to believe that there is uranium in their mixes. Left, looks like a jug or vase but I think it was intended as an ornament. It has glass flowers and trail work and an ungrounded pontil. UV light indicates that the clear metal is probably potassium based. Height 22 cm, density 2.46 g/cc, uranium 0.19% wt. It is difficult to date but I can see no point in putting uranium in the mix unless it was pre-gaslight days. So with some hesitation I say *about* 1890 Value $30-45.

Right. Another jug, vase or ornament. One of a pair with gilt decoration and a ground off pontil. The surfaces have been acid etched. The most striking thing is the whiteness which despite the presence of uranium, would do credit to any soap powder advert. Date, for the same reason as above, about 1890. Height 22.5 cm, density 2.45 g/cc, uranium 0.12% wt. Value $30-45.

Photo 345, if there were a prize for the ugliest piece in my collection I think this would be a contender, nevertheless it does contain uranium. It has a rough pontil mark and the "leaves" at the top have been added after the stem was formed. The white spatter was probably added after the item was formed and then melted in at a glory hole. Height 23 cm, density 2.42 g/cc, uranium 0.14% wt. I cannot make up my mind about the date. Value $15-20.

Photo 347, unlike Photo 346, these vases are not a pure white but carry a slight green tint which is due to the uranium in the mix. Left, has been made from three layers of glass, indications are that the inner one has the most uranium. Why use it on the inside is beyond my understanding. Height 18.75 cm, density 2.41 g/cc, uranium (outside) 0.25% wt, (inside) 0.37% wt. Again the hollow foot and cut top says its *probably* not British, date *about* 1930. Value $30-45.

Right, Blown in a mould then finished off on a pontil. The decor is hand painted. It could have come from an English studio but I doubt it. Height 16 cm, density 2.43 g/cc, uranium 0.31% wt. Value $30-45.

Photo 349, the hand painted turquoise vase is probably from the Continent. It has a hollow foot and cut top. Height 21.25 cm, density 2.47 g/cc, uranium 0.31% wt. Date *about* 1915. Value $20-35. The green vase has a hollow foot and cut top, its Continental origin is confirmed by the way the figure seven is formed on the underside of its base. No British house would have put the cross stroke on it. The painting and gold work are in good condition but there are moderate signs of wear. Height 22 cm, density 2.37 g/cc, uranium 0.43% wt. Date between the Wars. Value $15-20.

Photo 348, the interesting aspect of this piece, apart from the decoration, is its color. It is a pale gray. I can not imagine how uranium played any part in producing this shade but it is not unique. I have seen a number of examples like this which all have uranium in them. I am reluctant to hazard where it came from or its date of birth but I suspect it of being continental from between the Wars. Height 12 cm, density 2.5 g/cc, uranium 0.25% wt. Value $15-30.

Photo 350 shows another turquoise vase from the Continent. Height 20 cm, density 2.47 %cc, uranium 0.19% wt. Although similar style I consider this is a little older than the green vase in Photo 349. let's say *about* 1915. Value $30-45.

Photo 351 both these items must have come from the same glasshouse. A thin layer of uranium bearing green has been cased over white opalene. The outside delicately hand painted with a touch of coralene added to give some sparkle. Both have broken pontil marks. I wish I could give credit to the maker. The uranium layer is thin and may not have achieved "infinite depth" which would explain the slight variation between pieces so I will quote the figures in geiger readings.
Left, height 13.25 cm, density 2.43 g/cc, uranium 2.8 cps.
Right, height 14.5 cm, density 2.47 g/cc, uranium 2 cps. Date *about* 1910. Value each, $35-50.

Photo 352. The unexpected about this vase is that the uranium is in the cream not the yellow! Blown molded with a cut top. The design is hand painted. *Probably* a between the wars piece. Height 20 cm, density 2.48 g/cc, uranium 0.5% wt.

Photo 353, at first glance this might seem to be a piece from Stourbridge, it has some resemblance to Steven & Williams. But the quality is just not there. Most likely a cheaper Continental piece imported about the turn of the century. Height 14.75 cm, density 2.46 g/cc, uranium outside 0.29% wt, inside 0.18% wt, Value $30-45.

Photo 354, If this isn't late nineteenth century English then it ought to be! It has solid base with a nice round dimple where the pontil has been ground off. The snake is delicately wound round the neck of the vase. I would have liked to have thought this came from Richardson's, but the density says it probably did not. The uranium is only in the snake and difficult to estimate because of its shape. Height 18.5 cm, density 2.35 g/cc, uranium 4 cps. Value $30-60.

Photo 355, celery or vase? Is there a difference? Press molded and nameless. An example of the popular concept of what uranium glass should look like. The metal has little air bubbles and seeds. I would not be surprised if this had come from Ed Moore but that is not an attribution. Density 2.56 g/cc, uranium 0.37% wt. *about* 1880. Value $35-60.

Photo 356, these three press molded vases all have the same pattern but do not come from the same mould and may not have been made by the same glasshouse. Look at the vital statistics taking the order left to right. Diameter at top, 8.25 cm, 9.5 cm, 9.5 cm; Densities, 2.82 g/cc, 2.58 g/cc, 2.55 g/cc. Uranium 0.19%. 0.43%, 0.31% wt.. Quite clearly the left vase is different metal from the other two. These are the type of products I would expect from Tyneside, but the density of 2.82 g/cc arouses suspicions as it is more like that of Lancashire metals. It is just possible that two were made on Tyneside , then the moulds were acquired by a Lancashire glasshouse. Date *period* 1915. Value each $20-30.

Photo 358, I find this color attractive, alas I do not know from where it came. The base is solid and the vase has something British about it. Height 15 cm, density 2.44 g/cc, uranium 0.37% wt. Another piece difficult to date but I'll say *about* 1920. Value $20-35.

Photo 357, My *best guess* for this jade jug is that it hails from the USA. It has a ground off pontil and a rounded top. The gold bands have worn thin. I would say *probably about* 1910 but it could be later. Height 13.75 cm, density 2.42 g/cc, uranium 1.1% wt. Value $15-30.

Photo 359, I apologize for the reflection of the photographer but the color and shape of the vase made it difficult to avoid. Of all the pieces in my collection this is the only one where I consider the uranium may have got there accidentally, the concentration is so low it is barely detectable but is confirmed by reaction to uv light. It is the only example I have found with uranium that is deep blue. It has been blown from a dip mould and the top finished by hand while the body held by some form of gadget. It is too uneven for it to have been cut on a turntable and there is no pontil mark. Height 16 cm, density 2.66 g/cc, uranium 0.05% wt. Date *period* 1920. Value $15-30.

Photo 362, more of a jardinière than a vase it has an attractive and unusual cloudy effect. I have been unable to trace its origin but I would like to think it came from the British Isles. It has a ground off pontil and was hand blown. Height 13.5 cm, density 2.51 g/cc, uranium 0.14% wt. Value $20-30.

Photo 360, how did they get the air bubbles in the glass? The usual technique would be to roll a gather of glass on the end of its blow tube over a bed of spikes then, before the resulting indentations disappeared, take another gather on top so trapping air. The gather would be worked in the usual way as the item was blown into shape so the entrapped air expanded. On this item the air bubbles are smaller at the base than at the top. This is because there was more expansion as the vessel opens out. Whitefriars were renowned for their bubble glass in the 1940/50's but I think it unlikely this is one of their products. Height 20.25 cm, density (after making an allowance for the trapped air) between 2.7 & 2.8 g/cc., uranium 0.15% wt. Value $15-20.

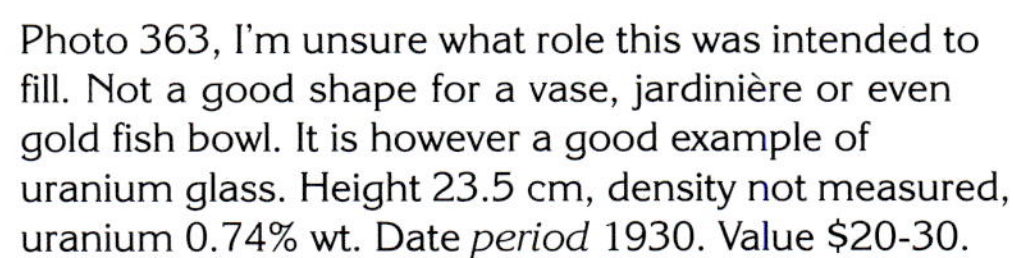

Photo 363, I'm unsure what role this was intended to fill. Not a good shape for a vase, jardinière or even gold fish bowl. It is however a good example of uranium glass. Height 23.5 cm, density not measured, uranium 0.74% wt. Date *period* 1930. Value $20-30.

Photo 361, these two may be the same shape but they are not from the same factory. The left piece has internal diagonal flutes, which means it was probably blown in a mould rather than pressed. The right is another example of crackle glass. Characteristics, left to right, Height 21 cm & 15.25 cm, densities 2.56 g/cc & 2.42 g/cc, uranium 0.09% wt & 0.15% wt. Date, *probably* post WW2, say *about* 1950. Value each $15-20.

Chapter 40
Oil Lamps

The use of oil lamps predates the days of Ali Baba and goes back to at least the 4th century BC. I am only concerned with those that were in use during the uranium era that was concurrent with the development of paraffin from mineral oil in the late 1850s. These lamps came first with a single burner then in 1865 Hinks introduced the twin burner known as "Duplex." While the burner may be a guide to the date and origin of the lamp it must be remembered that burners are largely interchangeable and are still available to day. When I bought Photo 366 I observed that the burner in it appeared to be of modern manufacture, the quality of the brass and the wick adjusting wheels are usual indicators of age, and I queried it with the dealer. "Oh " she said, "I've put a new one in that will take a globe, the original was only designed for a chimney and customers usually prefer to have globes." Fortunately she had kept the old burner so I bought the lamp! In the photographs I have removed the chimneys and globes where they were clearly not original and had no interest to my uranium glass collection. In most cases densities have not been measured and the heights quoted are as the lamp is shown in the photograph.

The use of oil lamps did not die entirely with the coming of gas and electricity. Many houses were using them as late as the middle of the twentieth century in older properties and areas where electricity was not readily available.

Photo 365, another quality lamp but the brass shade ring is only partly original. The ring itself should have been made from strip, this one is from rod and is a repair job. This burner has concentric drives for wick control, which I suspect is a later Duplex development. Again they bear the Hinks "Patent" inscription The paraffin container is separate from the body of the lamp. Height, 35 cm, uranium 0.68% wt. Date about 1890. Value, as shown, $145-215.

Photo 366, a cheaper lamp than the two predecessors, the paraffin holder is mounted directly onto a cast iron base. The burner controls are simple brass wheels and bear the inscription "English Made Duplex". It is not intended to carry a shade, only a chimney. The base carries the Design Registration Number 313891. This was registered in 1898 by "John Harper & Co., Albion Works, Willenhall, Staffordshire. Iron Founders and Manufacturers." The firm was still in existence in 1948. Height 33.5 cm, uranium 0.31% wt. Value $145-215.

Photos 364 & 364a, this I suspect is one of the more expensive and earlier Duplex lamps. The burner has two side by side wick controls, bearing the words "Hinks & Sons Patent" , (see Photo 364a). Both the paraffin container and body of the lamp are decorated glass. There is a heavy base comprised of brass and marble. I do not know the purpose of the two thumb nuts on the side. They mount into a fragile brass ring and I would have thought too weak to have been lamp supports. Perhaps they may have supported a shade? Date *about* 1880. Height 47 cm, uranium 0.16% wt. Value, as shown, $110-215.

Photo 367, this is probably only the inner paraffin holder of what was a two piece lamp. It has twin wicks with quality brass wheel controls set side by side. They bear the inscriptions "Patent Duplex Quality" with a "No 2" in the center and "Wright & Butler Birmingham". I have shown this mainly because of its drab gray/green color. Again it is another example where the use of uranium seems to be a waste. When I bought it an enterprising dealer had mounted it in a wrought iron wall mount pot holder! Height 170 cm, density 2.5 g/cc, uranium 0.62% wt. Date *about* 1895. Value $30-60.

Photo 368, the shade not the lamp has the uranium. It has a single unmarked burner which could well be the original. The shade is 15.25 cm diameter, has a density of 2.42 g/cc, and a uranium content of 0.09% wt. It is another of those items which I have difficulty dating, let's say *about* 1915. Value, lamp with shade $80-150.

Photo 369, two lamps from the deco period. Left, made with a uranium based opaque metal. The wick control on the burner bears the legend "British Make" but there is no clue as to who may have made the glass ware. Diameter cum width including the handle, 11.25 cm. Uranium 0.14% wt. Value $35-60.

Right, another deco lamp but this time the uranium has been cased with clear glass which makes it difficult to estimate the uranium content. I have therefore quoted the geiger reading when presented to the burner hole. The burner is worn and probably the original, the control wheel bears the words, "Flak's English Make. 3/4 in". Diameter cum width including handle, 11.25 cm. Uranium 2 cps. Value $35-60.

Photo 370, when I first saw this I thought it might be a piece of Fenton. I can confirm that it is not. The burner could be original but if it is then there is an anomaly. On the wick control wheel are the words, "English Made 3/4 in wick". On the base of the glass are the figures 6374 with a crossed 7. Clearly that part did not come from Britain. The habit of marking with "British Made" came about after the USA 1891 requirement and remained prevalent into post WW2 days so that does not help us with dating. The wear on the brass burner mount is considerable so I am going to date it *about* 1910 but I could be wrong. Uranium 0.17% wt. Value $60-90.

Chapter 41
Candlesticks

I have already shown a number of attributed candlesticks and I now show a few that are not. For some reason I find the uranium colors well suited for this purpose.

Photo 373, two candlesticks of deco vintage which clearly come from equivalent moulds. The left one is in an opaque green, 11.5 cm high, density 2.37 g/cc, uranium 0.37% wt. Value $5-15.
The right one is in clear green which changes to a pale cranberry at the base. Only the green contains uranium and I suspect the press mould was loaded with two separate gathers. The division between the two colors shows well under uv light. Height 11.5 cm, density 2.47 g/cc, uranium 0.12% wt respectively. Value $5-15.

Photo 371, two press molded candlesticks. Left, the density says it was probably not made on Tyneside. Height 18.5 cm, density 2.61 g/cc, uranium 0.31% wt. *About* 1895. Value $20-35.
Right, a fine illustration of a press molded piece of green uranium glass. Unfortunately I'm not sure who made it. However the density is more in line with what would be expected from Percival Vickers, Molineaux Webb, or one of the other Lancashire Glass houses but I have not been able to find it illustrated. Height 21.5 cm, density 2.92 g/cc, uranium 0.31% wt. Date *about* 1880. Value $30-45.

Photo 372, not a salt with a hole! It is a candle drip, designed to catch the wax running down the side of the candle. This one has been press molded. Diameter 8.5 cm, density 2.65 g/cc, uranium 0.31% wt. Date *about* 1890. Value $15-20.

Photo 374, Left, the top has been cut and there is no pontil mark. Height 6 cm, density 2.43 g/cc, uranium 0.28% wt. *Probably* Continental, *about* 1930. Value $15-20.
Right, This possesses the attributes of an early ninetieth century piece, the folded foot, broken pontil and iridised surface. I think it is another of those 1930's old look alikes. It resembles a style of candlestick made by Whitefriars in the 1930's but it is not close enough for an attribution. Height 7.5 cm, density 2.49 g/cc, uranium 0.62% wt. Value $15-20.

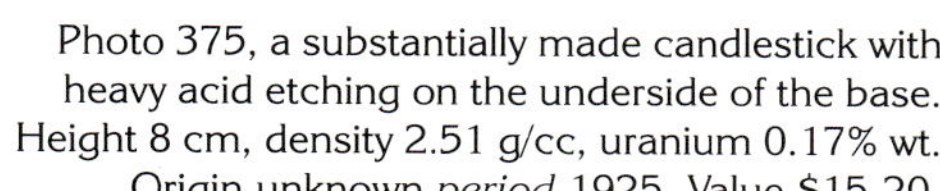

Photo 375, a substantially made candlestick with heavy acid etching on the underside of the base. Height 8 cm, density 2.51 g/cc, uranium 0.17% wt. Origin unknown *period* 1925. Value $15-20.

Photo 376, three examples of press molded 1930's candlesticks. They are probably all Continental and may well have come from Czechoslovakia. I don't think they are British but I could be wrong. Left is styled around the "Three Graces" . Jobling did make a piece on that theme but this is not Jobling. The other two have probably escaped from dressing table sets which were popular at that time.
Left, height 23.5 cm, density 2.49 g/cc, uranium 0.14% wt. Value $20-30.
Center, height 22 cm, density 2.47 g/cc, uranium 0.17% wt.. Value $20-30.
Right, height 11 cm, density 2.41 g/cc, uranium 0.12% wt. Value $15-20.

Chapter 42
Lampshades

These are a selection of lampshades that I have not been able to attribute. Those intended for use with electric light have a small hole while those for use with gas or oil have a much wider opening at the top. As already mentioned paraffin lamps came in the late 1850s. Gas lamps, were in use at the beginning of the nineteenth century but following the development of the incandescent mantle in the late 1870s and '80s they often had a down hanging shade. These required a small rim for the hanging screws to pick up on. The predecessor of the electric light we know today was a carbon filament lamp invented by an American engineer named Starr in 1841. However it was not until Edison and Swan, separately developed their light bulbs that they came into more general use in the 1880s . They held sway for a couple of decades before being superseded by the tungsten bulb around 1910. The tungsten bulb, operating at a much higher temperature is likely to have required a wider shade than the cooler carbon filament bulb. Electricity was expensive and only the wealthier would have had electricity at that time. By the 1930s it was common in all new houses although a lot of the older ones retained their gas lighting, in some cases until well after the end of WW2.

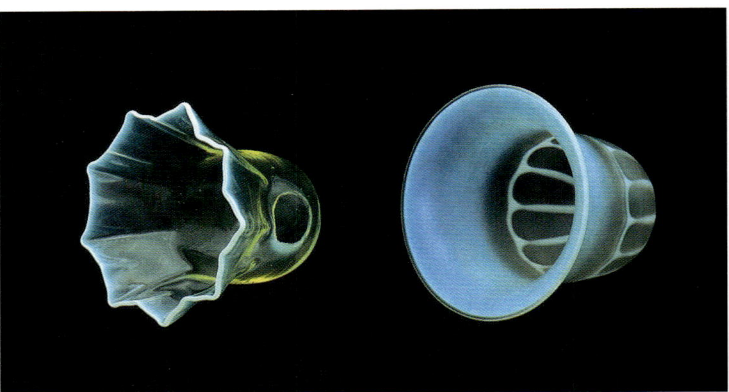

Photo 378, an electric lamp shade very much in the style of Whitefriars products of the 1890's. This could be one of theirs but there is no supporting evidence. I think this was probably intended for a carbon filament bulb and I am going to date it *about* 1900. Diameter 12 cm, density 3.03 g/cc, uranium 0.9% wt. Value $45-60.
Right, diameter 12.5 cm, density 3.13 g/cc, uranium 0.09% wt. This electric light shade could have come from Whitefriars or Stourbridge. Date *about* 1920. Value $45-60.

Photo 377, Left, an interesting piece of glass which is the product of a blow mould and hand finishing. Diameter 14.5 cm, density 2.38 g/cc, uranium 0.25% wt. Date *about* 1915. Value $45-60. Right, a shade for an electric lamp. Diameter 16 cm, density 2.98 g/cc, uranium 0.26% wt. Date *about* 1910. Value $45-60.

Photo 379, a quaint little shade but what was it for?. The top opening of 3 1/2 cm is too large for an ordinary electric light fitting and too small for a gas or oil lamp. The rim suggests that it would have been clamped in position and I wonder if it is part of a chandelier with small upward facing bulbs. Height 10 cm, density 3.18 g/cc, uranium 0.23% wt. Again with reservations I'd say 1920's. Value $30-45.

Photo 380, Gas lamp shade from the 1930/40 era. Diameter 13.75 cm, density 2.48 g/cc, uranium 0.31% wt. Value $30-45.

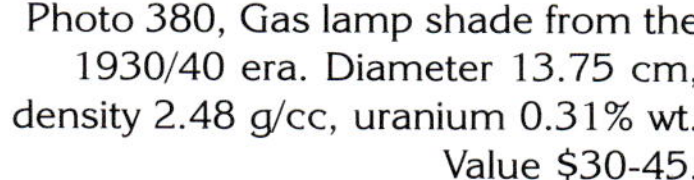

Photo 381, Left, an electric lamp shade which I can't date. The decoration is on a yellow ivory which does not skimp on uranium. Diameter 16.5 cm, density 2.42 g/cc, uranium 0.74% wt. Value $35-60.
Right, a Deco shade for electric light made from two layers of glass. The outer is a translucent green over an opaque white. Diameter 13.75 cm, density 2.46 g/cc, uranium 0.19% wt. Value $20-45.

Chapter 43
Plates, Dishes, Compotes, and Tazzas

Just as I wonder what folk would have thought had they known their drinking vessels were radioactive, so I wonder the same about their eating out of radioactive dishes and off radioactive plates. Uranium was used extensively for such items and I include here some of the non attributable to add to what I have already shown.

Photo 382, I would not be surprised if this plate had come from the factory of George Davidson as the density suggests it may. However this is not enough even for a tentative attribution. Diameter 18 cm, density 2.57 g/cc, uranium 0.25% wt, date *about* 1910. Value $15-20.

Photo 383, there is some suggestion that this may be American but I have no evidence. Diameter 11.5 cm, density 2.97 g/cc, uranium 0.28% wt. Date *about* 1870. Value $20-30.

Photo 384, the pattern is molded and the underside satinised. Diameter 16 cm, density 2.64 g/cc, uranium 0.56% wt. It is probably coincidence that it has the same uranium as Photo 386. Date *about* 1915. Value $30-60.

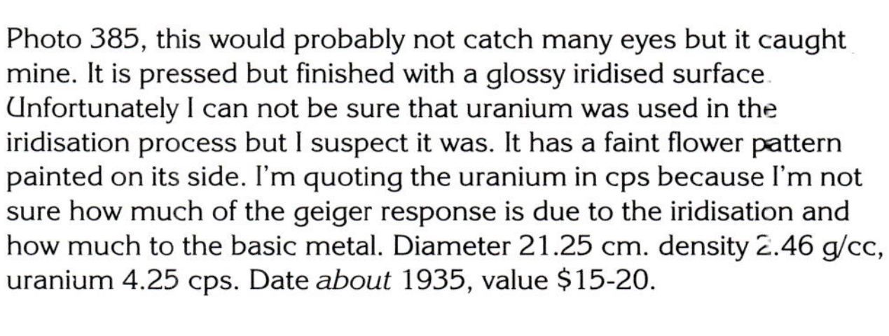

Photo 385, this would probably not catch many eyes but it caught mine. It is pressed but finished with a glossy iridised surface. Unfortunately I can not be sure that uranium was used in the iridisation process but I suspect it was. It has a faint flower pattern painted on its side. I'm quoting the uranium in cps because I'm not sure how much of the geiger response is due to the iridisation and how much to the basic metal. Diameter 21.25 cm. density 2.46 g/cc, uranium 4.25 cps. Date *about* 1935, value $15-20.

Photo 386, I would not have included this but for its size. It is the largest uranium plate I have ever seen. What purpose it served I do not know. Press molded with satin finish. Unfortunately the size prevented a density measurement being made. Diameter 33.25 cm, uranium 0.56% wt. I'm going to guess at *about* 1910. Value $20-35.

Photo 387, pressed patterned dish. I also have a plate of the same design. Although bought at different places their densities and uranium concentration are near identical. Diameter 22 cm, density 2.48 g/cc, uranium 0.08% wt. Date *about* 1935, value $15-20.

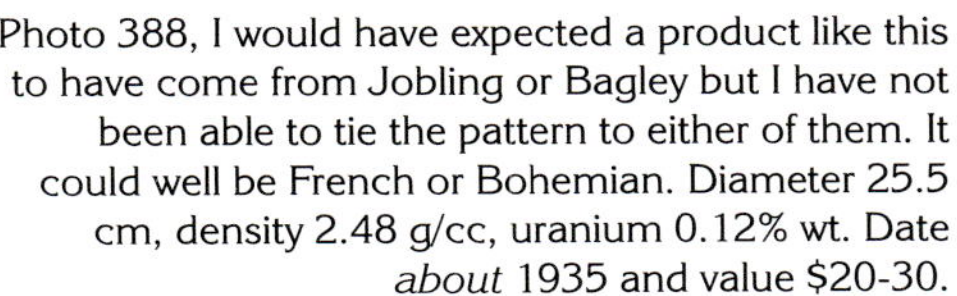

Photo 388, I would have expected a product like this to have come from Jobling or Bagley but I have not been able to tie the pattern to either of them. It could well be French or Bohemian. Diameter 25.5 cm, density 2.48 g/cc, uranium 0.12% wt. Date *about* 1935 and value $20-30.

Photo 389, another of those items where hunch tells me it is from the U S A but I have no evidence to support it. The grape vine pattern must be one of the most common but this has been made from a complex mould. Diameter 17.5 cm, density 2.45 g/cc, uranium 0.09% wt. *About* 1880. Value $20-35.

Photo 390, looks Bohemian and it would be tempting to think of it as "Annagrun", again I doubt it. While the metal shows considerable wear, the gilt work is good condition. Diameter 16.5 cm, density 2.48 g/cc, uranium 0.56% wt. Date *about* 1870. Value $45-70.

Photo 391, the foot and stem have been press molded in one and probably the top plate as well although it shows no such marks. The underside has a heavily etched pattern. Origin unknown. Diameter 14 cm, density 2.52 g/cc, uranium 0.16% wt. Date *about* 1930. Value $5-20.

Photo 392, this delicate tazza has a distinct Continental look about it. The milky effect near but not on the edge is fascinating. Had it been achieved by re-heating at a glory hole then the edge would have changed. Diameter 22.5 cm, density 2.73 g/cc, uranium 0.37% wt. I have difficulty in dating this piece, I think it is post WW2. Value $45-70.

Chapter 44
Scent and Toilet Water Bottles

These are highly collectable and therefore tend to be expensive items. A fair sprinkling of them was also made using uranium colored glass. The following photographs show a small but typical collection.

Photo 393 this unfortunate piece of Bohemian glass ware has lost its stopper and suffered a few small chips. But as I have said before, just because it has had a hard life that is no reason to shun it. The cutting is intricate and it has been hand polished. It has to be earlier rather than later and I wonder if it is an example of genuine "Annagelb." Unfortunately there is no way of knowing, the density and uranium are very close to Photo 400. Height 10.75 cm, density 2.44 g/cc, uranium 0.47% wt. Date *about* 1860, value (in good condition with its original stopper), $115-175.

Photo 394, this little chappie has a perfect ground pontil dimple on its base and started its life in a three piece mould. The stopper is hollow and the facets are cut. Overall height 13.25 cm, density 3.29 g/cc, uranium 0.26% wt. The heavy lead content says it could have come from an English glass house and I would date it *about* 1860. Unfortunately this specimen is damaged but in good condition I would value it at $110-145.

Photo 395, Left, the rubber squeeze bulb is missing from this spray. The glass is cut in a broken diamond pattern. The base is ground and polished. The spray device on the top is not brass but a plated alloy. No doubt this will help a more knowledgeable person that myself to suggest a date. Overall height as shown, 13.5 cm, density approximately 2.5 g/cc, uranium 0.62% wt. The similarity of density and uranium concentration between this and the bottle on the right hand side, may be more than coincidence. Value, as it is, $30-45.
Right, the slightly oval shape tells me that this was made without the use of a mould. The pattern, neck and stopper are cut and polished. The base is also ground and polished. Height 8.25 cm, density 2.5 g/cc, uranium 0.62% wt. It could have been made almost anywhere and as for date that is tricky as well. The fact that it is not molded at all and is not acid polished makes me think it is earlier rather than later so, with reservations, I say *about* 1870. Value $30-60.

Photo 396, Left, the marks of the three piece mould from which this was made are apparent. It has a ground pontil so was held on a punty while the neck was finished. Height 10 cm, density 2.5 g/cc, uranium 0.42% wt. Date *period* 1900. Value $35-50.
Right, one of a pair. The flats and ridges are cut rather than molded. The gold work is showing wear. *Probably* Bohemian. Not being an authority on scent bottles I have some difficulty in dating so I'll say *period* 1890. Height 6.75 cm, density 2.51 g/cc, uranium 1% wt. Value, (each), $30-45.

Photo 397, molded toilet water bottle with diamond pattern. Height 15.5 cm, density 2.43 g/cc, uranium 0.16% wt. Date period 1910. Value $15-30.

Photo 398, another spray bottle without its squeeze bulb. I suspect that in the pre-neoprene days the rubber would perish. This is very much in Deco style and will date *about* 1930. Diameter 9.5 cm, density approximately 2.4 g/cc, uranium 0.06% wt. Value, as it is, $15-20.

Chapter 45
A Miscellany of Items

Photo 399, this is a fine example of a Victorian luster. The uranium is only in the green trumpet. There is a small white snake wrapping itself around the stem of the trumpet. The domed foot is hollow and ground at its rim. It is only of modest size as lusters go but that makes it more attractive. The illustration is one of a pair. Height 24.5 cm, density of droppers 2.44 g/cc, density of trumpet 2.4 g/cc, uranium 0.43% wt. *Probably* Continental *about* 1900. Value of matching pair, $600-725.

Having slotted most pieces into groups according to their common purpose, inevitably there are a few which are without like companions and, so that they do not feel deprived, I include them under this inglorious heading.

Photo 400, when I bought this finger bowl the dealer assured me that a reputable auction house had identified it as "Annagelb". I think they must have been using the term generically rather than implying it was the original product of Josef Riedel. Bohemian it could well be, the density is what would be expected but I have not been able to find any link to the great man of uranium glass. Diameter 13 cm, density 2.48 g/cc, uranium 0.37% wt. There is little to go on for dating so I'll say *period* 1860. Value $45-70.

Photo 401, a molded finger bowl with a ground off pontil. The pattern is very similar to an illustration in the Whitefriars catalogue of 1855 but examination of the surviving records of that glass house does not indicate a green with this mix. Dating and attribution is again difficult but I think if I say *period* 1880 I will not be too far out. Diameter 13 cm, density 2.59 g/cc, uranium 0.37% wt. Value $35-60.

Photo 402, it looks like a simple bottle but I wonder if it were used as a carafe. It has been blow molded with 8 ribs and has the broken pontil mark. The ring round the neck was added separately. The top has not been ground to take a stopper. To have used uranium glass for an ordinary bottle would have been unnecessarily costly. Height 29.5 cm, density 3.21 g/cc, uranium 0.31% wt. Another item I find difficult to date but considering the style and density I would say probably about 1860. Value $30-45.

Photo 404, this is probably too small to be a piano insulator, I rather think it may have been intended to do the same job on a piece of furniture. It is far too thick and heavy to be table ware. Diameter 9.75 cm, density 3.36 g/cc, uranium 0.31% wt. The density suggest it contains about 35% lead which is high by all but the Midlands standards. Again I wonder why make such expensive glass for such a mundane object. There is a partial explanation. In the early days of pressed glass in England, the Midlands were to the forefront and they used full leaded mixes. Is this an early piece I wonder? Value $15-20.

Photo 405, because of the brass top ring and handle it was not possible to measure the density of this preserve jar. The glass is a milky opaline and the decoration probably hand painted. *Best guess* is French *about* 1915. Diameter 8.5 cm, uranium 0.25% wt, value $35-60.

Photo 403, the uranium in this little bowl is in the outer layer which is about 2.5 mm thick. The puzzle is how was it made? The inner layer is over a centimetre thick and contains virtually all the air bubbles, the top is a much darker brown that the lower part which is almost clear. It must surely have involved several gathers of glass, marvering and indenting between layers, then the final uranium glass layer before press molding. After that it would have been heavily polished, probably in acid, and the base ground flat. What a lot of effort for something so mundane. I will admit the more I look at it the more it grows on me. 10 cm square, density 2.46 g/cc which is an underestimate because there has not been any correction for the trapped air. Uranium 0.17% wt. I'm unsure on the date but would hazard *about* 1960. Value $15-20.

Photo 406, although they look like salts I suspect they were peppers. Both have hall marked silver tops and the marks are difficult to read through years of polishing! Left, best interpretation is that it is London between 1860 & 1875. Height 9 cm, density 2.54 g/cc, uranium 0.3% wt. Value $45-70.
Right, the marking indicate London between 1856 & 1875, the most likely interpretation of the date mark being 1869. The English hall marking of the silver does not necessarily mean that the glass came from England but the odds are that it probably did. Height 8 cm, density 2.49 g/cc, uranium 0.56% wt. Value $45-70.

Photo 407, today we think of a salt dispenser as either a hand held grinding mill or a cylindrical container with a single hole outlet on the top. This has not always been the case. At one time it was not uncommon for each diner to have an individual salt, then again the salt might be in a small single open dish. This practice has given way to the glass, pottery, plastic or stainless steel communal dispenser we see to-day. Like everything else I have come across, if it were made of glass, sooner or later someone would have used uranium to color it. In many cases I ask why? The salt container is seldom a thing of beauty out to trap the Victorian twilight! I have been able to attribute a number of those in my collection, this is one I have not It is one of two with identical pattern but which came from different moulds as they differ slightly in size. I think this is an earlier design and the density indicates it is a lead or barium melt. My guess is that it probably came from the Manchester area but I have not found it illustrated. Still there is very little in the way of catalogues and record books from those glasshouses. Size 8.5 x 6 cm, density 2.97 g/cc, uranium 0.28% wt. Date *about* 1880. Value $15-20.

Photo 408, Left, I don't really know what purpose this little chappie was intended to fulfil. Its too large for a salt, too wide for a cigarette holder, too shallow for a posy vase. It has a thick solid base with a ground pontil. I include it because its milky green color is unusual. Height 7 cm, density 2.43 g/cc, uranium 0.19% wt. Dating is difficult so let's say *period* 1910. Value $15-20.
Right, this small vessel was probably intended as a tooth pick holder. It is well molded and free from age induced defects. It could have come from anywhere but my feeling is that it was from Tyneside *about* 1900. Height 7.75 cm, density 2.53 g/cc, uranium 0.25% wt. Value $15-20.

Photo 409, To most folk this lopsided piece will not be a thing of beauty but to me it is. It must have a history to tell. It has been press molded, the base ground flat. The metal is heavily crizzled with both internal fine cracking and surface degradation. It shows all the signs of having had a long and hard life. As it cannot speak I can only speculate. Originally press moulders used leaded metal then they found a cheaper alternative with little or no lead. My hunch is that this is an in-between produced by some unknown glass house experimenting with cheaper metals, *about* 1860. Height 7 cm, density 2.57 g/cc, uranium 0.37% wt. Value $15-30.

Photo 410, a small translucent jade trinket or powder bowl. The base is ground flat as is the lid joint. The gold work is probably by transfer. I place it *about* 1900 and *probably* made on the Continent. Diameter 7.5 cm, density 2.41 g/cc, uranium 0.62% wt. Value $20-30.

Photo 411, these powder bowls *almost certainly* came from the same source but I have not found out where. They were also bought at widely different times and places. Both have been blow molded and have ground tops under the lids. The main differences is in color. Left to right, diameters 13.25 & 11.5 cm, densities 2.48 g/cc and 2.5 g/cc, uranium 0.37% wt and 0.31% wt respectively. Value each $20-45. Date *about* 1930.

Chapter 46
Jewelry

Few, if any, glass collectors show much interest in jewelry, which is not surprising because the glass versions of diamonds and precious stones are imitations. Nevertheless, when I discovered beads and imitation stones made from uranium glass, I added a few to the collection. Dating such items extremely difficult, because the pieces may well have been restrung, remounted, or even mixed. Dating criteria used on the other glass items, such as pontil marks, polishing techniques, etc, do not apply to this group. As brooches, necklaces, pendants, and earrings are worn next, or close to, the skin, a health hazard may be associated with the use of uranium glass jewelry. The items I have examined do not appear to have the high uranium concentrations that would cause concern.

Photo 412, two necklaces made from opaque green glass beads. Outer density 2.62 g/cc, uranium about 0.4% wt. Value $5-15. Inner, density 3.03g/cc, uranium about 0.68% wt. Value $5-15.

Photo 413, two necklaces one in yellow the other a light amber. Outer, restrung beads, density 2.95 g/cc, uranium about 0.4% wt. Value $5-20. Inner, beads made from an unusually high lead amber glass. Density 3.49 g/cc, uranium about 0.6% wt. Value $5-20.

Photo 414, the pendant stone is hand cut and polished, the claw attachment broken and the chain so tarnished I do not know what it is. Diameter 1.75 cm, density 3.3 g/cc. The geometry is too small to be able to equate the geiger reading to uranium concentration but the geiger shows 2 cps. Value $15-20. The necklace has nine amber glass stones mounted on a brass colored chain. Density could not be measured and the uranium is only indicative, the geiger reading 3 cps. Value $15-20.

Photo 415, Left, Diameter 3.75 cm, density has not been measured because of the amount of metal in the brooch, geiger reading 4 cps, indicating something like 0.25% wt uranium, value $5-15. Right, the stones are probably only iridised with uranium, diameter of broach 3.75 cm, density not determined, geiger counter reading 2.5 cps. Value $15-30.

Photo 416, I do admit that I find the color of these beads attractive. They are strung on nylon which is unlikely to be original. I bought these, together with matching ear rings, a decade ago at the Covent Garden market. When the lady vendor saw the geiger click away she at first thought I was some Government official about to arrest her for handling radioactive material and started by protesting her ignorance! Density 2.39 g/cc, uranium about 0.9% wt. Value $15-20.

Photo 417, density 2.4 g/cc, uranium about 0.3% wt. Value $15-20.

Photo 418, outer necklace, the uranium is only in the opaque larger beads. Density not measured, uranium 2 cps. Value $15-20. Inner necklace, sharp faced conical shaped beads, (goodness knows how they were made), density 3.58 g/cc uranium about 0.4% wt. This is the most dense piece of uranium glass I have so far found and equates to a lead content of over 40%. Value $20-30.

Photo 419, Only the beads contain uranium. The spacers are not glass and probably made of bone. Again I have to ask, why use uranium, especially in white! The density was not measured because of the non-glass spacers, uranium about 0.14% wt. Value $15-30.

Chapter 47
Pottery

Uranium was also used in pottery glazes. I have not researched these. Perhaps one day someone will and maybe write a book about it. For me it is another story in which I do not wish to become involved. When I consider the geiger readings from the two examples in Photo 420, I can only hope the glaze was not used on hot water bottles!

Photo 420, Not glass, but pottery glazed with uranium. The vase just bears the inscription "CANDY", the geiger reads 70 cps. The candlestick is marked "C. H. BRANNAM Ltd BARNSTAPLE. Made in England". The geiger reads 90 cps, which is about twice the highest reading I have found on glass.

Bibliography and References

Angus-Butterworth, L M, *British Table and Ornamental Glass*. Leonard Hill Books Ltd., London 1956.

Arnold Ken, *Australian Glass, 1900 - 1950, Valuation Guide*. Crown Castleton Publishers, Australia. ISBN 0 9587953 6 3.

Baker J and Crowe K, *A Collector's Guide to Jobling 1930s Decorative Glass*, Tyne & Wear County Council Museums, 1985. ISBN 0 905974 25 5

Brill Robert H, Fleischer Robert L, Burford Price P, Walker Robert M, *The Fission Track Dating of Man-Made Glasses: Preliminary Results*. Journal of Glass Studies, Vol. VI 1964.

Cable M, and Smedley, J W, *William Vernon Harcourt: Pioneer Glass Scientist and Founder of the British Association*, Glass Technology, Vol. 33, No. 3, June 1992.

Caley Earle R, *Analyses of Ancient Glasses 1790-1957. A Comprehensive and Critical Survey*, The Corning Glass Museum, corning Glass Center, Corning, New York, 1962.

Cottle Simon, *Sowerby Gateshead Glass*, Tyne and Wear Museums Service, July 1986, ISBN 0 905974 27 1

Dearden C P , Ex-Technical Director, Bagley & Co, Knottingly, Yorkshire.

Dodsworth Roger, *British Glass Between the Wars*, Dudley Metropolitan Borough Council. ISBN 0 900911 220.

Dodsworth Roger, *The Royal Brierley Collection of English Glass*, Sotheby's, London 1998.

Elville, E M, *English Table Glass*, London Country Life Ltd.

Evans W, Ross C, Werner A, *Whitefriars Glass, James Powell & Sons of London*, Museum of London, 1995. ISBN 0 904818 56X

Eveson S R, *Reflections, Sixty Years with the Crystal Glass Industry*, Glass Technology, Vol. 31, 1990.

Fleischer R L and Price P B, *Uranium Contents of Ancient Man-Made Glass*, General Electric Research Laboratory Report No 64-RL-3634M, March 1964, Schenectady, New York.

Fleischer R L and Price P B, *Uranium Contents of Ancient Man-Made Glass*, General Electric Research Laboratory Report, Reprint 8479, Schenectady, New York.

Freestone Dr Ian, *Romans & Uranium Glass - a Red Herring Question?* Letter to Nuclear Europe Worldscan, p 45, 1-2, 1998

Gilbert C S, *An Historical Survey of the County of Cornwall*, Plymouth, 1817.

Glass Association *Registration Numbers 1908 - 1945*, February 1996. Broadfield House Glass Museum, Dudley, England.

Glickman Jay L, *Yellow-Green Vaseline. A Guide to the Magic Glass*, Antique Publications, Marietta, Ohio, 1991. ISBN #0-915410-76-1.

Graziano J H, and Blum C, *Lead Exposure from Lead Crystal*, pp 141 -142, Lancet 337, 1991.

Greenwood N N, and Earnshaw A, *Chemistry of the Elements*, Butterworth, ISBN 075628324.

Gunther R T, *A Mural Glass Mosaic from the Imperial Roman Villa Near Naples*, Archaeologia, pp 99-105, Vol. 63, 1912.

Hajamach, Charles R, *British Glass 1800-1914*, Antique Collectors Club. ISBN 1-85149-141-4.

Heacock William, *Fenton Glass, The First Twenty-five Years*. O-Val Advertising Corp., Marietta, Ohio, 1978.

Heacock William, *Fenton Glass, The Second Twenty-five Years*. O-Val Advertising Corp., Marietta, Ohio, 1980.

Heacock William, *Fenton Glass, The Third Twenty-five Years*. O-Val Advertising Corp., Marietta, Ohio, 1989, ISBN 0-915410-36-2.

Jackson Lesley, *Whitefriars Glass, The Art of James Powell & Sons*, Richard Dennis, 1996. ISBN 0 903685.

James A J L Frank, *The Military Context of Chemistry; The Case of Michael Faraday*, Bull. Hist. Chem. 11 (1991).

Klein Dan, Lloyd Ward, *The History of Glass*, Macdonald & Co. (publishers) Ltd., 1989. ISBN 0-7481-0246-9.

Landa Edward R and Councell Terry B, *Leaching of Uranium from Glass and Ceramic Foodware and Decorative Items*, Health Physics, pp 343-347, Vol. 63, No. 3, 1992.

Lattimore Colin R, *English 19th Century Press-Molded Glass*, Barrie & Jenkins. ISBN 0-214-20598-3.

Lesser Richard, *Bref apercu de l'histoire non-nucleaire de l'element uranium*. pp 453-454, No 6, Novembre-Decembre, Revue Generale Nucleaire 1989.

Manley Cyril *Decorative Victorian Glass*, Ward Lock Ltd., London. ISBN 0-7063-6644-1.

McDonald David, Former Director of Johnson Matthey, unpublished research into the history of the Cock family. Courtesy of Johnson Matthey & Co. Ltd.

McDonald David *Percival Norton Johnson, The Biography of a Pioneer Metallurgist*. Johnson Matthey & Co. Ltd., 1951.

McKearin, George and Helen, *American Glass*, Crown Publications, New York.

Molineaux Webb Trade Catalogue. *Trade Catalogues, b*elieved to be Molineaux Webb and without doubt about 1851 or later, in possession of Manchester City Art Galleries, Manchester, England.

Morey George, *The properties of Glass,* Second Edition, Reinhold Publishing Corp. New York.

Murray Dr Sheilagh, *The Peacock and the Lions,* Oriel Press. ISBN 0 85362 1951.

Partington Prof. J R. *General and Inorganic Chemistry*, 2nd Edition, Macmillian, 1951.

Pellatt Apsley. *Curiosities of Glass Making*. Original Publication David Bogue, London 1849. Reprinted 1968 by Ceramic Book Company, Newport, Mon. England. (the reference quoted applies to the reprint).

Pollock-Hill S, Managing Director, Nazeing Glass Works Ltd., Broxbourne, Herts. EN10 6SU, England.

Pullin Anne Geffken, *Trademarks and trade Names from the Seventeenth to the Twentieth Century*, Wallace-Homestead book Company, Pennsylvania. ISBN 0-87069-462-6

Revi Albert Christian, *Nineteenth Century Glass*. Schiffer Publishing Ltd., ISBN 0-916838-43-9

Reynolds Eric, *The Glass of John Walsh Walsh, 1850 - 195*1. Richard Dennis, England., TA19 OLE. ISBN 0 903685 744.

Sheets Prof. Ralph and Thompson CC, *Thorium in Collectible Glassware*, Chemistry Department, Southwest Missouri State University.

Slack Raymond, *English Pressed Glass, 1830-1900,* Barrie & Jenkins, ISBN 0-7126-1871-6

Snow Dr P J D, *Letter to Editor*, p8, No. 41 Spring 1996 Glass Cone, (Journal of Glass Association, UK).

Taylor J R, Senior Technical Manager, Cookson Minerals Ltd., Stoke-on-Trent. Personal Communication, May 1990.

Thompson Jenny, *The Identification of English Pressed Glass,1842-1908*. Published by Mrs. Jenny Thompson. ISBN 0-9515491-0-3 and Supplement ISBN 0-9515491-1-1

Timberlake, Geof., Researching Nazeing Glass, Unpublished Lecture to Glass Association, 29/10/99.

Tooley Dr Fay, *Handbook of Glass Manufacture, 3rd Edition, Vol. II*. Ashlee Publishing Co. New York.

UKAEA United Kingdom Atomic Energy Authority, Windscale Report PG Report 403 (W). Unclassified 1962.

Weyl Woldemar A, *Colored Glass*, Society of Glass Technology, Sheffield. Reprinted by Dawson's of Pall Mall, London 1959.

Whitefriars Stock Book 1836, Museum of London, Whitefriars Folio 2 ref. 2.

Whitefriars Recipe Book 1832, Museum of London, Archive 3118/10

Wilkson R, *The Hallmarks of Antique Glass*, Richard Madley Ltd., London 1968

Wills Geoffrey. *Antique Glass for Pleasure and Investment*, John Gifford Ltd., London ISBN 70710222-7

Woodward H W. *Art, Feat, and Mystery. The Story of Thomas Webb & Sons*, Mark & Moody Ltd., Stourbridge ISBN 0-9506439-04

Yates Barbara. *The Glassware of Percival Vickers & Co. Ltd., Jersey Street, Manchester, 1844-1914*. pp 29-40, Vol. 2, Journal of the Glass Association, 1987. ISBN 0 9510736 13. ISSN 0951-3108.

Index